THE BATTLE OF
HASTINGS
1066

M. K. LAWSON

The
History
Press

Cover illustration: The Bayeux Tapestry, 11th century. By special permission of the City of Bayeux.

This edition first published 2007

Reprinted in 2016 by
The History Press
The Mill, Brimscombe Port,
Stroud, Gloucestershire, GL5 2QG
www.thehistorypress.co.uk

© M.K. Lawson, 2002, 2003, 2007

British Library Cataloguing in Publication Data.
A catalogue record for this book is available from the British Library.

ISBN 978 0 7524 4177 1

Typesetting and origination by Tempus Publishing Limited
Printed in India by Replika Press Pvt. Ltd.

For Rosamund, Blant, Irene

and Lillian

But to live outside the law, you must be honest;

I know you always say that you agree.

Bob Dylan, *Absolutely Sweet Marie*

CONTENTS

ABBREVIATIONS

Full details of these works will be found in the Select Bibliography.

AC	Baudri of Bourgeuil, *Adelae Comitissae*, ed. Hilbert.
ANS	*Anglo-Norman Studies.*
ASC	*Anglo-Saxon Chronicle*, ed. Plummer.
Asser	Asser, *Life of Alfred*, ed. Stevenson.
Barlow	Barlow, *Edward the Confessor.*
Bernstein	Bernstein, *The Mystery of the Bayeux Tapestry.*
BM	*The Battle of Maldon*, ed. Scragg.
BR	*Brevis Relatio*, ed. van Houts.
BT	*The Bayeux Tapestry*, ed. Wilson.
B&W	Brooks and Walker, 'The Authority and Interpretation of the Bayeux Tapestry'.
Carmen	*Carmen de Hastingae Proelio*, ed. Barlow.
DeVries	DeVries, *The Norwegian Invasion of England in 1066.*
DB	Domesday Book.
EE	*Encomium Emmae*, ed. Campbell.
EHD1	*English Historical Documents Volume 1*, ed. Whitelock.
EHD2	*English Historical Documents Volume 2*, ed. Douglas and Greenaway.
EHR	*English Historical Review.*
ESRO	East Sussex Record Office.

FNC	Freeman, *The History of the Norman Conquest*.
GG	William of Poitiers, *Gesta Guillelmi*, ed. Davis and Chibnall.
GND	William of Jumièges, *Gesta Normannorum Ducum*, ed. van Houts.
GP	William of Malmesbury, *De Gestis Pontificum*, ed. Hamilton.
GR	William of Malmesbury, *De Gestis Regum Anglorum*, ed. Mynors, Thomson and Winterbottom.
HA	Henry of Huntingdon, *Historia Anglorum*, ed. Greenway.
HÆ	Orderic Vitalis, *Historia Æcclesiastica*, ed. Chibnall.
HH	Henry of Huntingdon.
JW	John of Worcester, *Chronicle*, ed. Darlington and McGurk.
LKE	*The Life of King Edward*, ed. Barlow.
M&M	*Carmen de Hastingae Proelio*, ed. Morton and Muntz.
OS	Ordnance Survey.
OV	Orderic Vitalis.
RR	Wace, *Roman de Rou*, ed. Holden. All line numbers are those of Book III, unless otherwise stated.
Survey	English Heritage, *An Earthwork Survey and Investigation of the Parkland at Battle Abbey, East Sussex*.
TNE	*The Normans in Europe*, ed. van Houts.
TRHS	*Transactions of the Royal Historical Society*.
WJ	William of Jumièges.
WM	William of Malmesbury.
WP	William of Poitiers.
Writs	*Anglo-Saxon Writs*, ed. Harmer.

NOTE ON THE IMAGES OF THE BAYEUX TAPESTRY

The reproductions of the Bayeux Tapestry to be found in the picture sections are, unless otherwise stated, selections from the hand-coloured engravings associated with Victor Sansonetti and published in France in 1838. At the back of the book (pp.272-84) is a full set of the engravings published by Antoine Lancelot in the *Mémoires* of the Académie Royale des Inscriptions et Belles-Lettres for 1729 and 1733. See also the Appendix.

FOREWORD

I have incurred a number of debts in the preparation of this book. Two friends of long standing, Sue Reedie and Dr John Hudson, read much of it in draft, the former suggesting valuable amendments and taking me to task for excluding the possibility that the designer of the Bayeux Tapestry was a woman, the latter offering much-valued encouragement and a number of acute corrections. Many of the illustrations have been reproduced from volumes in the possession of the London Library in St James's Square, and the professionalism and care of their staff, and of those of the History Faculty Library in Oxford and the East Sussex Record Office in Lewes, have been greatly appreciated. Two successive librarians of St Paul's School, Gillian Drew and Alexandra Aslett, went to considerable trouble acquiring books and articles through inter-library loan, while my colleagues Richard Barker, Chris Fry, William Lines and David May have shown cheerful good humour in easing my encounters with computers and scanners, and Penny Holmes and Ian Tiley have given valuable assistance on digital imaging. Specialist advice on the geography of the battlefield is owed to Paul Littlewood, who has walked over it with me, as have my friend

Peter Sammut and my head of department Mike Howat; I am also especially grateful to Mike for never giving my academic work anything less than his unreserved support. John Davie has eked out my Latin, Marie-José Gransard my Old French, and Jennifer Attia and Jenifer Ball my modern French. This is a St Paul's volume in another and particularly important way too: between 1987 and 1995 boys in the Medieval History GCSE sets visited Battle every year as part of their coursework on eleventh-century warfare. They (for the most part) charged enthusiastically up the hill when ordered (in some cases recalling this joyfully years later, long after their teacher's carefully considered words of wisdom had been forgotten), frequently asked questions to which he had no answers, and not infrequently produced work which would have been worthy of publication; without them, it is certain that the following pages would never have been written.

My debt to Dr George Garnett is scarcely less. As the GCSE battlefield visits were coming to an end, he pressed me to address the students of the Norman Conquest Special Subject in Oxford, thereby obliging an initially reluctant speaker to get hitherto ill-assorted thoughts into a degree of order. It was this that brought me to earlier work on the subject, and especially to that of the great historians of the second half of the nineteenth century. To open Professor Freeman's remarkable *The History of the Norman Conquest of England*, or follow the bitter controversy after his death between his opponent J.H. Round and his champions T.A. Archer and Kate Norgate, is not only to read some of the most detailed work ever published on the battle, but also to be forcefully reminded of the qualities of scholars whose works are today read mainly by specialists. When this book was within two months of going to press my understanding of the present state of the Bayeux Tapestry was transformed by Dr David Hill's address to the Manchester Conference on Harold II and the Bayeux Tapestry. Since then I have profited greatly from the assistance of Dr Hill and John McSween, and especially from their kindness in allowing me to publish one of their photographs of the drawings of the Tapestry made by Antoine Benoît in 1729. Finally, it gives me pleasure to record my debt to Professor James Campbell, the value of whose friendship can be appreciated only by those who have enjoyed it, and whose generous hospitality never failed during the years in which the material discussed in these pages was being researched and analysed.

Chessington, Surrey
June, 2002

INTRODUCTION

On Saturday 14 October 1066 one of the most famous of all military conflicts took place upon and around the ridge in Sussex now occupied in part by the town named after it: Battle. Fighting is said to have lasted almost all day and into the evening; by its end, the last Anglo-Saxon king, Harold II, lay dead, while the remnants of his defeated army fled into the forest to their rear. The victor, Duke William of Normandy, was to face sporadic and sometimes serious resistance for the next five years, but never again did the English face him upon a major field of battle, and there thus flowed directly from his triumph the long-term historical consequences with which students of the Norman Conquest are so familiar: the replacement not only of an English king by a French one, but of the native aristocracy by his followers; the rejuvenation of the English church by foreign ecclesiastics led by Archbishop Lanfranc of Canterbury, an Italian by birth; the slow decline under William and his successors of the powerful systems of government developed by the late Anglo-Saxon state; the end of the close political links with Scandinavia which had characterised the pre-Conquest period, and that reorientation of

England towards France which meant that for almost the next half millennium, until Queen Mary lost Calais in 1558, English monarchs had possessions across the Channel and policies often designed to retain or expand them.

Yet its considerable impact on subsequent centuries is far from being the only reason why the battle of Hastings has been a much-visited subject, and why 1066 is still one of the most well-known dates in English history. It also has undeniable popular appeal – King Harold being struck in the eye by an arrow ranks alongside King Alfred's (supposed) burning of the cakes as one of the better-known episodes of the Anglo-Saxon period – and the steady stream of visitors to the part of the battlefield under the guardian-ship of English Heritage, and the popularity of reconstructions of the fight involving hundreds of warriors equipped with replica weapons and armour, suggest that public interest in it has seldom been greater. That interest is also stimulated by one of the most remarkable artefacts to have survived from the entire Middle Ages, the Bayeux Tapestry, which shows both the battle and (as has long been thought) Harold and the arrow. The Tapestry has much valu-able evidence to offer, and it is not the only broadly contemporary source of which this is true. Indeed, Hastings is generally so well supplied with sources that more is known about it than any other engagement fought in this country not only before 1066 but for centuries thereafter. Not least among them is the battlefield itself, much of it still open ground, and at least part of it arguably identi-fiable with a location shown in the Tapestry.

All this would seem to render it easy to write the history of what happened there, and writers and historians have not been slow to do so, for both popular and academic audiences. Unfortunately, the very natural desire of the audience to know, and of the informer to inform, has often led to descriptions of the conflict wearing an appearance of certainty which the nature of the primary sources actually does little to warrant. Battles are confusing affairs, not least for those involved in them, and even were there testimony from a number of eye-witnesses it would probaby be difficult to write a coherent and convincing account of fighting which lasted over eight hours and involved thousands and perhaps tens of thousands of men on each side. In fact, there is not a single eye-witness to be had, and the primary sources that do exist, relatively plentiful as they are, all suffer from significant limitations which need to be clearly understood before use can be made of them.

What emerges from this process, as this book will attempt to demonstrate, is not that there is nothing that can be known about the battle of Hastings, but that there are many important things that cannot, and never will be, known. Thus, seekers after easy hard facts – how many men there were on each side, for example, and where they were positioned at different points during the day – will not find them in the pages that follow. What they will find is the relevant evidence laid before them, along with often complex discussions of sources and issues, many of which are to a degree incapable of resolution. The battle may have ended the Anglo-Saxon period, but for the historian it shares one of the latter's crucial features – that the difficulties of dealing with the evidence mean that one often ends up not with clear answers so much as a range of possibilities, not one picture made up from the jigsaw, but a series of possible pictures, all with resemblances to each other, and all with significant numbers of pieces missing. It is one of the central theses of this book that since the late nineteenth century, which saw the formative work of the scholars J.H. Round, Wilhelm Spatz, Sir James Ramsay and F.H. Baring, too many writers have followed their lead in unjustifiably narrowing the range of possible interpretations of this crucial battle, and that it may in some respects have been a more fascinating conflict than it has often been given credit for, both in terms of the numbers involved and the ways in which the fighting was conducted.

If it is true that Hastings has at times attracted a great deal of attention, it is also true that there has been little real debate about it since the days of the men named above. Indeed, the flurry of interest in the Conquest occasioned by the 900th anniversary in 1966 has been followed by the appearance of important new editions of a number of the major primary sources, and almost all are now available in reliable translations.[1] There has also been a great deal of valuable secondary work upon the events of 1066 generally, and there is certainly no sign of any diminution of interest in the Bayeux Tapestry, although there is an urgent need for a proper critical edition of it, based upon rigorous examination of its fabric. However, in the last thirty years surprisingly little has been written about the battle itself,[2] with re-enactors tending to show more interest in the details of the fighting than historians. It may be that this is because the latter, on the whole, have come to the conclusion that there is little more to be said. If so, it is the purpose of this book to suggest that they have been mistaken.

[1] The *Brevis Relatio*, the *Carmen de Hastingae Proelio*, and the works of Henry of Huntingdon, John of Worcester, Orderic Vitalis, Wace, William of Jumièges, William of Malmesbury and William of Poitiers.

[2] Since 1970 there has been R. Allen Brown's article 'The Battle of Hastings' of 1978, and Jim Bradbury's book of the same title from 1998. *The Battle of Hastings*, ed. Morillo (1996) is a collection of reprints of earlier articles and translations of primary sources, including the editor's own short but valuable essay from 1990.

I

THE PRELUDE

In 1948, less than a decade after England had faced the prospect of an invasion even more terrible and destructive than that of 1066, Hope Muntz published her fine historical novel *The Golden Warrior: the story of Harold and William*. Dedicated to Winston Churchill, 'In Remembrance of 1940', its prologue imagined Duke William of Normandy passing through Dover during his visit to England in 1051:

> When the Duke landed, the townsmen saw a host march through their streets. They beheld Counts and Barons, Bishops like Princes, and mailed Knights, riding as though to battle. The sound of marching filled the town. Trumpets and clarions rang. The captains shouted commands and the ranks wheeled and turned as one man at their bidding. The men of Dover said: 'If this is peace, how does he fare in war?'

In a story that develops with all the dreadful inevitability of *Macbeth*, both Muntz and her readers knew that one day the men of Dover, and of all England, would discover the answer to this

question, and that it would be delivered by one of the most determined, ruthless and successful warriors of the Middle Ages, on one
of its most celebrated battlefields.

The Conqueror, aged about twenty-three in 1051, was related to
his host, King Edward the Confessor, for his great-aunt Emma had
married two earlier rulers of the English, Æthelred II (often
known today as the Unready) and then in 1017 the Danish Cnut,
who had conquered the country the previous year. By Æthelred
she had borne two sons, Edward and Alfred, who lived in exile in
Normandy after their mother's second marriage; by Cnut there
was a son, Harthacnut, and a daughter, Gunnhild, eventual wife of
the future emperor Henry III of Germany. There is a story that
Emma only consented to a union with Cnut after securing his
agreement that any male offspring of hers should inherit the
crown in preference to his sons (Swegen and Harold Harefoot) by
another consort,[1] and in the years after Harthacnut's birth she
must have become totally committed to his cause. In Normandy,
however, Edward and Alfred were not forgotten by her relatives;
Cnut's original desire to marry a woman some years his senior
may well have had a great deal to do with fear of Norman support
for them, and he later tried to strengthen his position even further
by uniting his sister Estrith with William's father, Duke Robert.
Unfortunately, Robert eventually repudiated Estrith, and by 1033
was recognising Edward as king of England and preparing a naval
expedition to establish him on the throne.[2] However, this sailed
and came to nothing, and Robert died two years later while
returning from a pilgrimage to Jerusalem.

Cnut also died in 1035, and the succession dispute which fol-
lowed between his sons Harold Harefoot (ruled 1037–40) and
Harthacnut (ruled 1040–2) was complicated by the arrival in
England of both Emma's sons by Æthelred. Edward raided the

[1] *EE*, pp.32–3; this work, the *Encomium Emmae*, was written for Emma probably in St Omer,
Flanders, *c.*1041. Swegen and Harold were the sons of Ælfgifu of Northampton, whose connection with Cnut continued after his marriage to Emma; see Lawson, *Cnut*, pp.131–2.
[2] Ibid., pp.109–12, and especially Keynes, 'The Æthelings in Normandy'.

south coast with forty ships, fought a battle at Southampton and then returned to Normandy laden with booty, but appreciating that he needed more soldiers.[3] Alfred's fate was less happy. He landed in Kent, and in attempting to reach his mother fell into the hands of an Englishman who had waxed great under Cnut, Earl Godwin of Wessex. Godwin brought him to King Harold and he was eventually blinded, dying as a result of the knife used to blind him entering his brain.[4] There is no evidence of popular support at this time for either Alfred or his brother, and the possibility of Edward ever ascending the English throne must have seemed remote; yet by 1041 King Harold, whose elder brother Swegen had predeceased him, was dead and his half-brother King Harthacnut in uncertain health.[5] The latter's mother, Queen Emma, may have feared the extinguishing of her influence should he die, and her long-neglected son by her first husband was accordingly summoned from Normandy to be sworn in as king. The following year Harthacnut had a seizure while drinking at a marriage feast, lingered speechless for some time, and expired on 8 June.[6]

In 1042, all three of Cnut's sons and their father having died young, King Edward thus found himself in a position which it must long have seemed impossible he would ever occupy, and for which he was ill-prepared. In exile for most of his adult life, he was scarcely acquainted with the great figures of the time, the earls Godwin of Wessex, Leofric of Mercia and Siward of Northumbria, or with the political system in which they operated. Godwin, in particular, seems to have enjoyed considerable influence over him. By 1066 the income from lands held by the

[3] GND, ii. 104–7; GG (drawing on GND), pp.2–3. On the Gesta Normannorum Ducum of William of Jumièges, see below, pp.93–5; on the Gesta Guillelmi of William of Poitiers, see below, pp.95–105.
[4] Alfred died on 5 February 1036 or possibly 1037; see ASC, C and D texts, i. 158–60; EE, pp.40–7; GND, ii. 106–7; GG, (elaborating on GND), pp.4–5; LKE, pp.32–3. The Life of King Edward was written in England by a Flemish cleric for Edward the Confessor's queen, Edith, between 1065 and 1067 (ed. Barlow, pp.xxix–xxxiii, xliv–lix); on the Anglo-Saxon Chronicle, see below, pp.58–60.
[5] GG, pp.6–7.
[6] ASC, C and D texts, i. 162–3. The D text is often in this period a conflation of manuscripts closely related to C and E, and therefore not at such points an independent witness.

different members of the Godwin family, if added together, rivalled that from the king's estates.[7] More to the point, in 1045 Edward married Godwin's daughter Edith, probably unwillingly, as subsequent events suggest. This move was presumably designed to perpetuate the influence of the family into future generations through the birth of a royal heir who would be partly of Godwin blood; if so, it failed. The years slipped past, and by 1050 it may have been obvious that Edward, then in his mid-forties,[8] would have no son. By now the king was finding the Godwin influence burdensome. On 29 October, Archbishop Eadsige of Canterbury, once a priest of Cnut's household, died. A relative of Godwin was a member of the monastic community which served Canterbury cathedral and was clearly the candidate favoured by the earl to fill the vacancy in the richest and most powerful bishopric in the country.[9] The king had other ideas. Following his accession, he had been joined from across the English Channel by a number of men to whom he had given offices and lands;[10] some of them were, if the *Anglo-Saxon Chronicle* is anything to go by, highly unpopular with the English. Nevertheless, Edward in 1051 chose as his new archbishop Robert of Jumièges, bishop of London since 1046, and a Norman.

Nor was this all. It was necessary for Robert, like all late Anglo-Saxon archbishops, to go to Rome for his pallium – an ecclesiastical vestment received from the pope, without which he was not a recognised holder of the see of Canterbury. During the journey he passed through Normandy, and it may have been at this time

---

[7] This is an issue which has attracted much attention in recent years, assisted by the statistics provided by Domesday Book; see now Grassi, 'The Lands and Revenues of Edward the Confessor', who concludes that in terms of landed revenue the predominance of the Godwins compared with the rest of the nobility was unmistakable and 'dangerously close' to that of the king himself; however, if crown income from other sources is added 'Edward's paramountcy is clear'.

[8] He may have been born in 1005, Barlow, p.29.

[9] *LKE*, pp.30–1.

[10] See Lewis, 'The French in England before the Norman Conquest', who stresses that Norman influence dated back to Emma's marriage to Æthelred II, and that the French presence in England before 1066 was neither confined to Edward's court favourites nor 'exclusively or distinctively' (125) Norman.

that, according to the contemporary Norman historian William of Jumièges, he took with him an offer that Duke William should be Edward's heir.[11] Even though they had every reason to be biased on the issue, and say some things which are difficult to believe,[12] much of what followed becomes intelligible if this and other statements by William of Jumièges and his fellow Norman writer William of Poitiers, and by the probably contemporary French *Carmen de Hastingae Proelio* (*Song of the Battle of Hastings*)[13] are accepted, and modern scholars have been convinced for the most part that Edward did give some kind of undertaking to the duke at about this date.[14] The same year (1051) he was visited by his brother-in-law, Count Eustace of Boulogne. The reason for Eustace's journey is unknown, but is not unlikely to have been his awareness of the promise, and a desire to press his own claim to the throne as the second husband of Edward's (dead) sister, Godgifu. However, as things turned out, whatever he said to the king was to prove less significant than events on his return journey: as he and his men passed through Dover they became

[11] *GND*, ii. 158–9, which gives no date. WP, *GG*, pp.20–1, says that Edward sent a son and grandson of Godwin (mentioned again, pp.68–9) to Normandy as hostages via Robert in confirmation of the promise, and with the consent of the English magnates; but this may have been in 1052, see below, p.25. The consent of the English is also mentioned by the *Carmen*, ll. 292, 738.

[12] Below, p.97.

[13] On the provenance of the *Carmen*, probably by Bishop Guy of Amiens, see below, pp.90–2.

[14] But not M&M, pp.65–8, who accepted no pledge made by Edward to William later than 1041, or more recently Garnett, 'Conquered England, 1066–1215', pp.62–8, who thinks that any promise by Edward seems 'highly unlikely'. Freeman (*FNC*, ii. 296–303, iii. 217–9, 684) rejected all the details in the French sources, while accepting that Edward gave an undertaking during William's visit in 1051; for a similarly grudging provisional acceptance ('even if Edward did nominate William as his heir in 1051'), see Barlow, pp.106–9. Others have accepted the promise with less reservation: Douglas, 'Edward the Confessor, Duke William of Normandy', 534–9; Oleson, 'Edward the Confessor's Promise', 223; Stenton, *Anglo-Saxon England*, p.561; Brown, *The Normans and the Norman Conquest*, pp.121–4; John, 'Edward the Confessor and the Norman Succession', 250–1; Bates, *William the Conqueror*, p.59; van Houts, introduction to *GND*, i. xlvii. The latter also points out (i. xlvi) that WJ would have been in contact with Archbishop Robert, as after his exile from England in 1052 Robert returned to Jumièges and died there in 1055. Garnett argues that Norman sources written after 1066 'retrospectively imposed upon England in 1051' a designation ceremony of the type frequently practised by the dukes of Normandy in establishing their heirs. Yet as Edward had spent much of his adult life there it would hardly be surprising if he decided to adopt the same practice, and of course he had himself been designated king by Harthacnut in 1041. The article by Douglas is seminal here.

involved in a brawl with the inhabitants in which deaths were sustained by both sides; as a result, the king ordered Earl Godwin to harry the town, which lay in his earldom. This must have put Godwin in a serious dilemma, as Edward may well have intended – should he do as he had been told and thus lose credibility with his own constituents, or should he defy the king's express command? Perhaps angered by what had happened both over the archbishopric and the inheritance to the throne, he chose the latter course, and as late Anglo-Saxon kings did not take kindly to disobedience, he and his sons also began to raise an army. When this became known, Edward called upon the earls Leofric of Mercia and Siward of Northumbria to do the same, and the stage looked set for civil war. At the height of the crisis, however, the nerve of Godwin's men seems to have failed, and his support fell away. The result was exile for him and all his sons, while the king consigned Queen Edith to a nunnery.[15] It was now, according to the D text of the *Anglo-Saxon Chronicle*, that William of Normandy visited England, presumably to thank King Edward for the offer of the throne and to accept it.[16]

The following year there was a dramatic reversal of fortune.[17] Perhaps, as Hope Muntz speculated, the sight of William and his men, together with the knowledge of Edward's promise, had not filled the English with joy. At any rate, when Godwin and his sons returned from exile, by force, their support seems to have been stronger than the previous year; once again civil war was imminent, but avoided by negotiation, the upshot of which was that the

---

[15] The main sources for the events of 1051 are the *ASC* D and E texts, i. 171–7; and *LKE*, pp.30–7. The latter attributes the crisis to friction between Godwin and Archbishop Robert which culminated in Robert raising the matter of Godwin's involvement in the death of Alfred (above, p.21) and asserting that he was now preparing the destruction of the king himself.

[16] Douglas, 'Edward the Confessor, Duke William of Normandy,' 527–34, suggested that this is a late and unreliable addition to D, and thought the duke too preoccupied with continental affairs to have made such a visit in 1051 (similarly, Douglas, *William the Conqueror*, pp.58–60, 169); Bates, *William the Conqueror*, p.34, thinks it 'possible' but 'intrinsically unlikely'. I agree with Douglas that the omission of the visit from the Norman sources is distinctly odd, but also with Hooper, 'Edgar the Ætheling', 201, n.18, that 'it seems inconceivable that D's account of the visit is fictional'; similarly, Oleson, 'Edward the Confessor's Promise', 221–2. On D, see further, below, pp.59–60.

[17] On 1052, see the *ASC* C, D and E texts, i. 177–83.

Godwins were fully reinstated in their lands and offices, while the queen emerged from imprisonment in the nunnery to take her place once more beside the king; some of his Norman followers, including Archbishop Robert, fled. This must have been a humiliating result for Edward, but it is possible that part of a face-saving deal struck for the return of his enemies was that they would accept William as heir to the throne, and that Archbishop Stigand of Canterbury (Robert's replacement) and the earls Godwin, Leofric and Siward swore an oath to this effect, as William of Poitiers claims; it may have also been at this point that two members of the Godwin family – Hakon, the earl's grandson by his eldest and deceased son Swegen, and his youngest son Wulfnoth – were sent to Normandy as hostages.[18] It is not known, of course, that either oaths or hostages were seen by the senior members of the Godwin family as placing significant limitations on their future behaviour.

Shortly after this, in 1053, Godwin himself died, and was replaced as earl of Wessex by his eldest surviving son, Harold. The following year the first moves were made to secure the return from exile in Hungary of the son of Edward the Confessor's half-brother Edmund Ironside, Edward the Exile, who had left England at the beginning of Cnut's reign, and was the only surviving male member of the royal house (as far as we know) apart from the Confessor himself. It is almost certain that his return was connected with the question of the succession, and very unlikely that it took place without the king's permission, but we cannot say who took the initiative in arranging it. Perhaps Harold, the rest of the Godwin family and

---

[18] GG, pp.18–21, 68–9, 120–1. This was the position of Oleson, 'Edward the Confessor's Promise', 223–4. WP implies that the oath was sworn and the hostages sent in 1051, but a degree of confusion on this might be understandable; Barlow, p.108, thinks that he fabricated the list of oath-takers to provide circumstantial detail, and it is certainly possible that he knew the *Carmen* and was elaborating on its statement (ll. 292–4) that Edward had made the promise to William with the assent of the people and by the counsel of his nobles; for a discussion of the hostages and their identity, see Barlow, pp.301–6. The authority for them being sent to Normandy after the Godwins' return is the post-Conquest writer Eadmer, *Historia Novorum*, ed. Rule, pp.5–6, who says that Edward was suspicious of Godwin and would not make peace unless he first received hostages as security.

others hoped that the king might be persuaded to change his mind about the duke[19] and he was prepared to consider doing so, or Edward, determined to prevent the accession of one of Godwin's sons, was providing himself with a second option should something go wrong with his first choice.[20] However, whatever hopes the return of the Exile may have raised were to come to nothing, as he died shortly after arriving in England in 1057, and before he was able to see the king. He left a son, Edgar, aged about five,[21] who was to survive all the great men of this history; it is not likely that Edward ever considered making him his heir,[22] although it need not follow that he was completely without support.

The next move on the succession issue was made when Earl Harold went to Normandy, probably in 1064 or 1065.[23] The French writers are quite clear that the purpose of this visit was to confirm the promise of the throne to the duke. The *Carmen de Hastingae Proelio* alludes to the making of a pact of friendship between Harold and William, to Harold's oaths and subsequent perjuries, and to the fact that Edward sent via his envoy a ring and a sword; this is a plausible detail, as these were two of the objects with which English kings were invested when they were crowned.[24] William of Jumièges says that Edward sent Harold, the greatest of his earls, to swear fealty to William about the crown and to confirm it with oaths. On the way Harold landed in Ponthieu (a small county which lay on the coast between Normandy and Flanders to the north), where he was

---

[19] Oleson, 'Edward the Confessor's Promise', 225–6, saw the initiative for Edward's return as entirely Harold's.

[20] This was Brown's suggestion, *The Normans and the Norman Conquest*, pp.126–7; WM, *GR*, i. 416–7, reports that Edward sent for the Exile because he saw Godwin's sons growing more powerful. His return is described by *ASC* D and E, i. 187–8. See also, Körner, *The Battle of Hastings*, pp.196–209; Barlow, pp.215–8.

[21] Ibid., p.218.

[22] But see van Houts, 'The Norman Conquest through European Eyes', 845–6. JW, ii. 582–3, says that he had decided that the Exile should be his heir, but on JW's prejudices, see below, pp.60–4.

[23] The date is not certain, see *FNC*, iii. 227, 243–4, 694–6, in favour of 1064; Keats-Rohan, 'William I and the Breton Contingent', 164–5, thinks that there is 'no doubt' that this is correct, and I use it henceforth; John, 'Edward the Confessor and the Norman Succession', 259–60, argued for late 1065.

[24] *Carmen*, ll. 233, 239, 295–300.

captured and imprisoned by Count Guy, until William's pressure secured his release. He then stayed in Normandy for some time, swore fealty about the kingdom with many oaths, and was finally sent back to the king with many gifts.[25] William of Poitiers elaborates on this: according to him, Edward wished to prepare for death by confirming his pledge with an oath and sent Harold, whose power would be able to check the customary perfidy of the English should it prove necessary; William secured his release after he fell into the hands of Count Guy, and he swore fealty to the duke at a council held at Bonneville, promising to be the vicar of William in Edward's court, and to do his best to ensure that England passed into William's hand after Edward's death; in the meantime, he would fortify the *castrum* of Dover for William's soldiers, and fortify, garrison and provision other *castra* chosen by the duke. Before the oath was sworn, but after Harold was received as his host's vassal, he was confirmed in his lands and powers; he seems also to have agreed to marry one of William's daughters.[26] Then, knowing his guest to be eager for renown, the duke furnished the Englishmen with weapons and the best of horses, and took them on campaign in Brittany. After their return, he kept them with him a little longer before sending Harold home loaded with gifts and accompanied by his nephew, previously one of the two hostages held in Normandy.[27] A very similar impression is given by the Bayeux Tapestry (see illus. 1-3), in so far as can be judged from scenes intended for an audience familiar with the story, and hence provided with only a sparse accompanying text. Edward fairly clearly directs Harold to go to Normandy, he encounters Guy, is delivered by William, and goes on campaign in Brittany; then, in a scene which contemporaries would have recognised as indicating that he had accepted the duke as his lord, he is shown being given arms by William, before swearing the oath and returning to England. There are differences of detail here – the oath is sworn at

[25] *GND*, ii. 160–1.
[26] *GG*, pp.68–71, 156–7 (on the marriage); there is a shorter version in William's alleged speech before the battle of Hastings, pp.120–1.
[27] Ibid., 70–1, 76–7.

Bayeux rather than Bonneville, and after the Breton campaign rather than before it – but the Tapestry, as one would expect of a source produced for a Norman viewpoint,[28] seems to confirm the case presented by the two Norman chroniclers and the *Carmen*.[29] Is it true?

The most detailed treatment of Harold's oath, as of many other events of this period, remains that of Edward Augustus Freeman (illus. 22), whose remarkable six volume *The History of the Norman Conquest of England*, a fraction of the published output of a scholar possessed of a range which allowed him to apply for the Camden Professorship of Ancient History in Oxford in 1861 and its Chichele Professorship of Modern History in 1862, is seldom consulted without profit almost a century and a half after it was first published. Even so, Freeman's initial work was done during the 1860s, at a time of strong anti-French feeling, in an England which knew much of Napoleon, French tyranny and the battle of Waterloo, but in which the *entente cordiale* still lay in the future; there had been a recent invasion scare, and he always referred to the contemporary French ruler Napoleon III as the 'tyrant'.[30] It must be reflective of this, and of the powerful nationalism of the Victorian period generally, that he was less than sympathetic to Edward's promise of the throne to William and associated events, and concerned to give the French sources no more credence than was absolutely necessary. Accordingly, in his discussion of the oath[31] he admitted that 'there was some groundwork for the Norman story', and that Harold 'made some engagement or other' (finally concluding that the 'oath was primarily an oath to marry William's daughter… accompanied by an act of homage'), but refused to pledge himself 'to the accuracy of a single detail', and rejected the French explanation of the reason for Harold's visit to

[28] But see below, p. 30, n. 37.
[29] See also OV, *HÆ*, ii. 134–7, who places the oath at Rouen, possibly as a result of misunderstanding WP.
[30] On Freeman, see *The Dictionary of National Biography. Supplement*, pp. 672–6; Bryce, 'Edward Augustus Freeman'; and Stephens, *The Life and Letters*. He was eventually appointed Regius Professor of Modern History in Oxford, in succession to Stubbs, in 1884, and died in 1892.
[31] *FNC*, iii. 215–53, 667–96.

the duke as 'absolutely fabulous'.[32] One of his final comments, that he had been discussing 'one of the most perplexing questions in all history', was to find something of an echo many years later in Sir Frank Stenton's assertion, near the end of probably the most widely read of all modern general histories of the Anglo-Saxons, that 'about the reason for Harold's journey' no 'convincing answer has ever been given'.[33] However, Stenton arrived at this conclusion as the result of a discussion in which he considered the evidence of the Bayeux Tapestry, but ignored the explicit statements of the *Carmen*, William of Jumièges and William of Poitiers about the genesis of that journey.

The reluctance of English scholars to accept that Edward required Harold to guarantee William's succession in Normandy did not end with Stenton,[34] and it is unlikely that there will ever be a consensus of opinion about the matter. Still, the weight of the primary evidence does not favour the doubters, even if it is impossible to be sure that they are mistaken. Against the quite clear statements of the French sources about Edward's intentions, both in 1051 and prior to Harold's journey, the broadly contemporary English writers, including all three surviving texts of the *Anglo-Saxon Chronicle*, can only oppose an ominous silence, apart from an obscure reference in *The Life of King Edward* to the earl being 'rather too generous with oaths, alas!', which may or may not be an allusion to the one sworn in Normandy.[35] Not until the post-Conquest Canterbury monk Eadmer (writing over forty years

[32] Ibid., 243, 218, 693, 243, 219.

[33] Ibid., 696; Stenton, *Anglo-Saxon England*, p. 578.

[34] See Barlow, pp. 220–9, who, however, accepts the possibility that WP's story 'is basically true'; Gibbs-Smith, *The Bayeux Tapestry*, pp. 10–11; Bates, *William the Conqueror*, pp. 60–1; Bradbury, *The Battle of Hastings*, pp. 63–72; Higham, *The Death of Anglo-Saxon England*, pp. 152–62. Bradbury and Higham (and B&W, 11) argue that as the Bayeux Tapestry shows a subservient-looking Harold greeting the king on his return to England this indicates that something had gone wrong with his mission; but it could equally mean that he had simply carried out Edward's orders (Bernstein, plate xxviii, is surely correct in saying that whether 'Harold's posture is meant to be reverential or apologetic is unclear'); M&M, pp. 68–72, judged the oath simply one of 'friendship and loyalty', without discussing how Harold came to be with William. DeVries, pp. 149–54, reviews recent opinion.

[35] *citius ad sacramenta nimis, proh dolor, prodigus*; LKE, pp. 80–1.

later) do we actually get an English account of Harold's visit, in which he went (against King Edward's advice) to secure the return of the Godwin hostages, was driven by a storm to Ponthieu, released from captivity on the duke's orders, informed by William of Edward's promise, and encouraged by him to swear the oath in return for the release of his nephew; Harold, perceiving that there was danger whatever way he turned, agreed.[36] That tales of this type circulated in England after, and perhaps before, 1066 is not to be wondered at, for the oath is likely to have been better known than the truth of the circumstances in which it was taken; even so, they smack of special pleading.[37] It does not seem inherently likely, for example, that Harold would have willingly put himself into the power of a great rival in order to secure the return of two hostages who had already been in Normandy for twelve years, and one of whom he was quite prepared to abandon to his fate when he broke the oath not long afterwards. Even so, this by no means exhausts the later reports. The early twelfth-century Anglo-Norman writer Orderic Vitalis says that when Harold returned to England he lied to Edward by alleging that the duke had given him his daughter in marriage and resigned his claim to the kingdom to his new son-in-law; the sick king was amazed, but fell in with his wishes.[38] William of Malmesbury, who knew both the Norman version of events and that of Eadmer, tells an even wilder story (which he says he thought

[36] Eadmer, *Historia Novorum*, ed. Rule, pp.6–8. Eadmer has the duke date the promise to when Edward and he were both young in Normandy; in fact, the king was more than twenty years William's senior. He also adds some familiar details, for example Harold's agreement to marry William's daughter. Barlow, *The Godwins*, p.76, is convinced by Eadmer's claim that Harold took the oath against his will and 'could surely have argued in any tribunal that promises extorted under duress were invalid'.

[37] The Bayeux Tapestry can be read in a way not incompatible with Eadmer, as Freeman noted, *FNC*, iii. 676–7. Bernstein, pp.115–7, argues that it was deliberately made ambiguous enough to suit both the Norman and the English accounts (similarly, B&W, 10–11). The Norman version of events has been accepted by Douglas, 'Edward the Confessor, Duke William of Normandy', 540–5, and *William the Conqueror*, pp.175–7; Oleson, 'Edward the Confessor's Promise', 227; Brown, *The Normans and the Norman Conquest*, pp.127–32; John, 'Edward the Confessor and the Norman Succession', 260–2; van Houts, introduction to *GND*, i. xlvii (but she has since changed her mind, compare *TNE*, p.104).

[38] *HÆ*, ii. 136–7. Chibnall (n. 1) regarded this as an embroidery 'drawn from popular tradition or possibly saga'; on OV, see below, pp.110–1.

plausible enough) to the effect that Harold went on a fishing expedition in the Channel, was blown to Ponthieu and imprisoned by Count Guy, and persuaded William to release him by pretending that he had been sent to confirm the promise of the throne.[39] It is certainly not impossible that he went to the continent of his own free will for diplomatic purposes which cannot now be recovered,[40] but there is not a scrap of evidence to support this view. On the evidence we do have the balance is in favour of the story told by the French being basically true: that he swore the oath, quite simply, because King Edward had sent him to do so.

Inaccurate as some of the details in the Norman accounts may be, they did not err in describing Harold as the most powerful magnate in England at the time the visit was made; indeed, the power of the Godwin family generally was by that time considerable. Not only had Harold succeeded his father as earl of Wessex in 1053, but two years later his brother Tostig received the earldom of Northumbria after the death of Siward. It was perhaps in 1057 that their sibling Gyrth was given East Anglia, to which was later added Oxfordshire, while the fifth of Godwin's sons, Leofwine, at some point received control of an earldom including at least Middlesex and Hertfordshire.[41] Such success is unlikely to have been achieved without friction between the Godwins and other leading families. It is no accident that the earls Leofric of Mercia and Siward of Northumbria supported the king in the crisis of 1051, and that Leofric at least was rewarded for doing so, his son Ælfgar receiving Harold's earldom of East Anglia,[42] but being obliged to relinquish it upon the latter's return the following year. He recovered it when Harold was promoted to Wessex in 1053, but was outlawed in 1055, perhaps because he had overstepped the

---

[39] *GR*, i. 416–9; on WM's strong pro-English bias, see below, p.68; HH, *HA*, pp.380–1, says that Harold was crossing to Flanders when he was driven ashore in Ponthieu.

[40] This was Körner's position, *The Battle of Hastings*, pp.109–21, anticipated in *The Bayeux Tapestry*, ed. Stenton, p.15; see also the ingenious suggestions of Higham, *The Death of Anglo-Saxon England*, pp.160–2.

[41] On Gyrth and Leofwine, *Writs*, pp.562, 567.

[42] *ASC* E, i. 177; see further Barlow, pp.114–5.

mark in laying claim to the Northumbrian earldom given to Tostig.[43] However, he allied with the Welsh king Gruffydd, defeated local English levies near Hereford and was reinstated; in 1058, the year after he had succeeded to the earldom of Mercia upon his father's death, the same process was repeated, Ælfgar's expulsion being followed by restoration with the help of Gruffydd.[44] A period of calm seems (these years are not well documented) to have followed; it did not last.

In 1065 Tostig's earldom of Northumbria rose against him. All the thegns of Yorkshire and Northumberland declared him an outlaw, killed every one of his retainers they could find, seized all the weapons and treasure in York, sent for Morcar, son of Earl Ælfgar, and chose him as their earl; they then marched south, along with the men of Nottinghamshire, Derbyshire and Lincolnshire, until they reached Northampton, where they were joined by Morcar's brother Edwin, who had received the earldom of Mercia upon their father's death.[45] Negotiations followed, and the king accepted what had happened; Tostig, his wife Judith and 'all those who wanted what he wanted' went into exile in Flanders with Judith's half-brother Count Baldwin V. Of course, these events would seem to have weakened the Godwins' position considerably. Both Mercia and Northumbria were now in the hands of brothers almost certainly unsympathetic to them, and it was probably obvious that Tostig would eventually attempt a return by force, as the whole family had done in 1052. However, it may be that Harold was not entirely sorry to see the departure of a powerful and ambitious brother who might have contested his own claim to the throne when the time came, and *The Life of King Edward* claims that Tostig accused him of inciting the rebellion.[46] If this was Harold's game he acted none too soon, for on 5 January 1066[47] the king at last died.

---

[43] As suggested, ibid., p.193; *ASC* C, D and E, i. 184–6.
[44] *ASC* D, i. 188; on Ælfgar, see *Writs*, pp.546–7; JW, ii. 584–5, says that he also had the assistance of the fleet which came from Norway in this year and joined him unexpectedly (below, p.38).
[45] The date of this is not known, but was in 1062 or later.
[46] *ASC* C, D and E, i. 190–5; *LKE*, pp.74–83.

On his deathbed, he finally seems to have changed his mind about the succession, although how far he was fully aware of, or responsible for, what he was doing might, of course, be doubted.[48] The C and D texts of the *Anglo-Saxon Chronicle* (which are here one source rather than two)[49] say that he 'entrusted' the kingdom to Harold, and *The Life of King Edward* that he commended it to Harold's protection.[50] If these statements stood alone we might be tempted to think that the earl was intended to act as regent until William's arrival, and the same impression could be derived from Baudri of Bourgeuil's statement of *c.*1100 that during his final illness Edward dispatched legates to Normandy confirming his promise to William in writing and that the Normans sent to deliver the duke's acceptance found him dead on arrival.[51] However, the *Chronicle* E text says baldly that Edward granted Harold the throne,[52] and this was fully admitted by the Normans. The Bayeux Tapestry (illus. 4) shows one of the men who offers Harold the crown pointing to the scene of King Edward speaking to his *fideles* on his deathbed, thus apparently indicating the warrant for what was happening, and William of Poitiers mentions the bequest to Harold twice.[53]

By 1066, if not by the time of his visit to Normandy, Harold had probably decided that he would take the throne whatever Edward's wishes, and he was crowned on 6 January, the day of the latter's funeral. He had, of course, broken his oath to William and must have known that he would have to fight to maintain his position, but as a foreign invasion would take time to organise the haste of the coronation is

---

[47] The date given by *ASC* C, D and E, but *LKE*, pp.124–5, says 4 January; see Barlow, pp.250, 253, who suggests that Edward died on the night of 4/5 January.

[48] See ibid., pp.249–53, who thinks it 'extremely doubtful' whether Edward was 'by modern standards... of sound testamentary capacity'.

[49] Above, p.21, n.6; below, p.60.

[50] *ASC* C and D, i. 194–5; *LKE*, pp.122–3.

[51] *AC*, ll. 271–8. As the legates are said to have sworn that the kingdom was William's this may be a confused version of Harold's visit of 1064; on Baudri, see below, pp.103–7.

[52] *ASC* E, i. 197.

[53] A point made by B&W, 21, and Bernstein, pp.117–21; note, however, Cowdrey's suggestion ('Towards an Intepretation of the Bayeux Tapestry', 101–2, 107–8) that the scene means that Edward intended to keep to his earlier intention of making William king and that Harold then falsely took the crown for himself; *GG*, pp.118–9, 140–1.

likely to have stemmed from a fear of opposition in England which was to prove well-founded. The C and D texts of the *Anglo-Saxon Chronicle* say that at Easter (16 April) 1066 Harold travelled from York to Westminster. On what he had been doing in Northumbria they (and the E text) are no more forthcoming than on his oath in Normandy, and it is left to William of Malmesbury's twelfth-century *Life* of Bishop Wulfstan II of Worcester to fill the deficit. According to this, Harold had travelled north because the Northumbrians refused to accept him as king, and together with Wulfstan he succeeded in overcoming their reluctance to be associated with southern softness.[54] It is also probable that they feared the restoration of the new king's brother Tostig as their earl, and that Harold gave guarantees about this. How far their current earl Morcar and his brother Edwin of Mercia were involved in these events is not known,[55] but it is known that Harold at some point married their sister Edith, and the period following his coronation may have been that point.[56]

His return south was quickly followed by one of the most famous events of this famous year – the appearance of Halley's Comet, every night of the week following Monday 24 April.[57] The Bayeux Tapestry (illus. 5-6) shows men marvelling at the star as the king sits uncomfortably on his throne and spectral ships appear in the border below, while William of Poitiers says that it was a prophecy of Harold's destruction.[58] These sources all had the benefit of hindsight, but such signs in the heavens were in the Middle Ages often

[54] WM, *Vita Wulfstani*, ed. Darlington, pp.22–3; this follows closely a life written in Old English by the Worcester monk Coleman at some date between 1095 and 1113 and now lost.

[55] Freeman guessed that they were, *FNC*, iii. 59–60.

[56] JW, ii. 604–5; OV, *HÆ*, ii. 138–9, 216–7; see *FNC*, iii. 625–7, iv. 755–6. As Edith, who had previously been the wife of King Gruffydd of Wales (d.1063), may have had two sons by Harold the marriage could have been before 1066, unless, as Freeman thought, they were twins born posthumously. However, a marriage alliance between Harold and her brothers could also be fitted plausibly into the negotiations which culminated in Tostig's expulsion in 1065, or the alliance could have been formed earlier still as part of an understanding that Harold would be the next king. I am grateful to Stephen Baxter for this last point, and for drawing Harold's sons by Edith to my attention.

[57] *ASC*, C and D, i. 194–5. It was also widely reported on the continent, van Houts, 'The Norman Conquest through European Eyes', *passim*. The omission of any mention of it in the generally pro-Godwinist (below, p.60) E text of the *Chronicle* may be no coincidence.

[58] *GG*, pp.142–3.

regarded as portents of great events, and the comet is likely to have been seen by many in England as a sign of God's wrath about Harold's broken oath and a very ill omen for the future. But this did not stop the king doing what he could to safeguard his position against his enemies, including his own brother.

That brother, as events were to show, had been completely alienated from Harold by the events of 1065, and while in Flanders he may have been in touch with Duke William, whose wife Matilda, daughter of Count Baldwin V, was like his own spouse a member of the Flemish comital family. Orderic Vitalis claims that Tostig actually visited Normandy and offered William assistance in his invasion, before sailing for England.[59] Whatever the truth of this, not long after the comet's appearance Tostig landed on the Isle of Wight 'with as big a force as he could gather' and was given money and supplies there. He then harried along the south coast until he came to Sandwich in Kent. However, Harold was at the same time gathering 'greater naval and land forces than any king in this land had ever gathered before' to meet an expedition by William, and when Tostig learnt that they would soon arrive in Sandwich he took sailors from there and went north with sixty ships to Lindsey, whence he was expelled by Edwin and Morcar. He then proceeded with twelve vessels (the reduction in the size of his force presumably being indicative of loss and desertion) to Scotland for a rendezvous with King Harald Hardrada of Norway.[60]

Only the E text of the *Chronicle* states that Harold 'went out against William with a naval force', and there is some reason to think that this refers to rather more than the simple deployment of a fleet mentioned by the C and D texts. Domesday Book for Essex lists an *Ailricus* who 'went away to a naval battle (*abiit in navale proelium*) against King William' and fell ill on his return.[61] Far away, in the

---

[59] OV, *HÆ*, ii. 140–3, along with the statement (142–5) that Tostig also visited King Harald in Norway. In his earlier additions to WJ's *GND* (ii. 162–3, see below, p. 110), Orderic claimed simply that William sent Tostig against England.

[60] *ASC* C, D and E, i. 194–7.

[61] DB, ii. 14b; see *FNC*, iii. 338, 716–7; *Writs*, p. 302.

monastery of Nieder-Alteich on the Danube, an annalist writing in 1075 reported that, in the summer after the appearance of Halley's Comet, Aquitanians fought the English in a naval battle, and having defeated them subjected them to their rule; men who had taken part in the campaign had said that 12,000 died on the side of the victors, along with an incomprehensible number of the vanquished.[62] That there was a fight at sea is made more plausible by the writer having spoken to participants in the war.[63] Perhaps Harold raided the Norman coast at some time during the summer of 1066, while he lay on the Isle of Wight awaiting the duke's arrival; or perhaps there was a bigger and much more significant conflict which has disappeared from the sources almost completely.

All the summer and part of the autumn Harold waited, with land forces stationed everywhere along the coast, but William did not attempt a landing. By 8 September the English provisions had run out and the men were allowed to go home, while the fleet returned to London. As it did so, King Harald of Norway sailed into the Tyne with 300 ships, along with Tostig, who had become his man. From there they proceeded into the Humber and advanced upon York. The presence of Tostig virtually guaranteed that this force would be opposed by his enemies Edwin and Morcar. On Wednesday 20 September they met the Norwegians in battle on the Ouse to the south of York,[64] and were defeated. The C text of the *Chronicle*, the only contemporary source to give any detail about the first of the three battles fought in England within twenty-five days, says that the English made great slaughter, but themselves had a great number slain, drowned or put to flight, and that the Norwegians remained in possession of the field.[65] There

---

[62] Van Houts, 'The Norman Conquest through European Eyes', 841–2. On Aquitanians in 1066, see below, pp. 173–4.

[63] Dr van Houts speculates that they may have been English.

[64] Not until the *Historia Regum* attributed to the twelfth-century chronicler Symeon of Durham (ed. Arnold, ii. 180) are we told that the site was Fulford; *FNC*, iii. 350, n. 1. HH (*HA*, pp. 386–7) says that it was still pointed out on the south side of York, in a way which suggests that he may have seen it.

[65] *ASC*, C, i. 196. The chronicler Marianus Scotus, writing in Mainz not long afterwards, says that Harald killed more than 1,000 laymen and 100 priests in battle, van Houts, 'The Norman Conquest through European Eyes', 839.

are more detailed accounts in Icelandic sagas from the early thirteenth century of which the most famous is Snorri Sturluson's *King Harald's Saga*, one of the components which make up his *Heimskringla (The Orb of the World)*.[66] This may preserve authentic traditions on a fight of which tales must have been told and re-told in the north for many decades, but few historians would place much trust in its statements today, and it is enough to simply record how the ferocity of the Norwegian attack, led by Harald's great banner 'Land-Waster', is said to have carried all before it after initial English success, and how the corpses of those of the English who fled into a marsh were piled so high that the victors could cross it dry-shod; it is enough to record it, and to pass on.

Following his victory King Harald accepted hostages from the citizens of York and began negotiations with the Northumbrians intended to gain their cooperation in his attempt to secure the English crown.[67] That attempt was part of a long-standing order as far as the English were concerned. For more than two centuries Scandinavians had both raided their shores and endeavoured to conquer parts of their territory, or the whole. In 1013 King Swegen Forkbeard of Denmark had succeeded, as had his son Cnut in 1016. Even after the Confessor's accession in 1042 events in Scandinavia can seldom have been far from English minds. His half-brother Harthacnut had been put in charge of Denmark by Cnut and was not able to become king of England until five years after the death of his father because of the threat to his position from King Magnus of Norway.[68] In the early 1040s Magnus was still attempting to conquer Denmark, but was also seen as a threat to the English. A post-Conquest source claims that Edward's mother Emma was accused of inciting him to invade England,[69] and in 1045 Edward took a fleet to

---

[66] Trans. Magnusson and Pálsson, pp. 142–4. For a recent treatment, see DeVries, pp. 11–13, 255–9, who discusses the Scandinavian sources, and places considerable credence in them.

[67] *ASC*, C, i. 197. JW, ii. 602–3, says that each side gave 150 hostages to the other.

[68] Magnus' father St Olaf had been expelled from Norway by Cnut in 1028, and killed in 1030 at the battle of Stiklestad when attempting a return. Magnus established himself in Norway at about the time of Cnut's death, after expelling Cnut's son Swegen.

[69] See Barlow, p. 58, who thinks Emma's guilt, but not the charge, unlikely.

Sandwich because his arrival was thought imminent.[70] In 1047 he at last succeeded in taking Denmark from Cnut's nephew Swegen Estrithson (whose brother Beorn at the time held an English earldom), but died in October of the same year. This allowed Swegen to re-establish himself, while Norway was secured by Magnus' uncle, Harald Hardrada. Both sent embassies to Edward in 1048, and Edward refused Swegen's request for naval assistance of at least fifty ships.[71] It was fortunate for the English that the following years saw much fighting between them, for both were potentially dangerous. Swegen was later to claim that Edward had on two occasions (both in the 1040s) promised him the English throne,[72] although as he may have sent forces to assist Harold in 1066 this story need not have been current before 1069–70, when he made an unsuccessful attempt to deprive the Conqueror of his conquest. According to a Danish source from the middle of the twelfth century, Harthacnut and Magnus had agreed that the kingdom of the first to die would pass to the other.[73] As Harthacnut claimed England at the time, this (if true) would have given Magnus and his successor some sort of claim also. Certainly Norwegian forces crossed the North Sea well before 1066. In 1058 they joined with the men of Orkney, the Hebrides and Dublin in a raid on England led by Harald Hardrada's son Magnus; although the author of the D text of the *Chronicle* unfortunately found it too tedious to write an adequate account of what happened,[74] it was clearly a harbinger of things to come. Eight years later Swegen and Harald had made peace, and the latter was preparing for action upon Edward's death.

Harald, like William, did not sail until the autumn, and it is likely that both were hoping to profit by doing so. Surely there would

---

[70] *ASC* D, i. 165.

[71] *ASC* D, i. 167.

[72] Adam of Bremen, *Gesta*, pp. 135–6, 152; see Barlow, pp. 58, 93. Adam wrote in the 1070s, and had met Swegen Estrithson; if the Danish king was telling the truth it would facilitate the interpretation, contrary to that adopted here, that the Confessor had no fixed plan for William to succeed him, but tended to play candidates off against each other as circumstances made convenient, perhaps with a cruel and whimsical humour; for this view, see Barlow, 'Edward the Confessor and the Norman Conquest', 107, 110–1.

[73] *Chronicon Roskildense*, ed. Gertz, i. 22.

[74] *ASC* D, i. 188–9.

already have been serious fighting involving the other, which would leave them to face a weakened victor? Harald was clearly also hopeful that the Scandinavianised part of eastern England known as the Danelaw would be sympathetic to his cause, for it was only just over a century since a Norse king, the celebrated Eric Bloodaxe, had ruled in York. It seems that after the defeat of Edwin and Morcar the Northumbrians were prepared to accompany him on a campaign in the south, and Harald withdrew to Stamford Bridge (illus. 42), some seven miles to the east of York, and probably a good communications centre, as it lay at the junction of several Roman roads; once there, he awaited the hostages he had been promised from the whole of Yorkshire, and grew careless.

Meanwhile, King Harold of England had gathered an army and was marching north by day and night. On Sunday 24 September he reached Tadcaster, eight miles south-west of York, where he put his force in battle array; the following day they passed through York and came upon the Norwegians unawares beyond the bridge (i.e. on the east bank of the river Derwent). In hard fighting, which went on until late in the day, both Harald Hardrada and Tostig were killed, along with a countless number of their Norwegian and English followers. Harold eventually gave quarter to the survivors, but they were few. Twenty-four ships are said to have sufficed for the return to Norway of a force which had arrived in 300; if so, the slaughter had been very great.[75] The contemporary sources are as sparing of detail on the battle of Stamford Bridge as on that five days earlier. The C text of the *Anglo-Saxon Chronicle* comes to an end midway through its account, and it was left to a twelfth-century hand to add the story of how a single Norwegian held the bridge against the English until someone went underneath it and stabbed him from below. Other post-Conquest sources tell a little more: Orderic Vitalis reported that in his day a great heap of bones was still to be seen on the field; both Henry of Huntingdon and William of

[75] *ASC* C and D, i. 197–9. JW, ii. 602–5, says the Norwegians came in more than 500 'great ships' and returned in twenty.

Malmesbury knew of the lone Norwegian hero, and the latter says that Tostig's body was buried in York after it was recognised by a wart between the shoulder-blades; Snorri Sturluson claimed that in negotiations before the battle Hardrada was offered seven feet of English ground, or as much more as necessary, should he be taller than other men.[76] Like the vast majority of English battlefields that ground has yielded no evidence in modern times of the bloody events which took place there. The recent digging by archaeologists of three trenches prior to modern housing development produced nothing. However, attention has been drawn to an undated mass burial at Riccall Landing on the east bank of the Ouse, the area in which the Norwegians left their ships, from which the remains of thirty-nine individuals were excavated in the 1950s and six more in the 1980s; the total number of burials has been estimated at between 500 and 600, and some of the bones recovered bear marks evidently caused by edged weapons and arrows, although a few of the remains were those of women and children. Clearly, they may be burials from the period of the battles of Fulford and Stamford Bridge.[77] Yet the latter, while doubtless celebrated in popular legend for many of the hard years that followed, never had and never can have the historian it deserves. Acting with a determination and speed of which the most famous commanders would have been proud, Harold had gained one of the greatest victories of Old English arms; and the last.

Three days later, on 28 September, William landed at Pevensey in Sussex, and reached Hastings the following day.[78] The very fact that

---

[76] *HÆ*, ii. 168–9; *HA*, pp.386–9; *GR*, i. 420–1, 468–9; *King Harald's Saga*, trans. Magnusson and Pálsson, p.150. HH gives details (perhaps drawn from a poem in Anglo-Saxon) that are not totally consistent with the accounts in the *Anglo-Saxon Chronicle*, stating that fighting began at dawn, that the great English numbers had pushed the Norwegians beyond the river by midday and that the hero held the bridge until three in the afternoon. Snorri offers a detailed account of the battle which in some respects echoes events at Hastings, except that here it is the English who are said to have used cavalry. Most historians give it little credence, but see Glover, 'English Warfare in 1066', 5–7; and on the battle generally, *FNC*, iii. 363–74, 720–8; Brooks, *The Battle of Stamford Bridge*; DeVries, pp.262–96.
[77] On evidence from English and Welsh battlefields generally, see the list which forms Appendix F of *Blood Red Roses*, ed. Fiorato, pp.211–39; on the 1950s finds at Riccall Landing, Wenham, 'Seven Archæological Discoveries in Yorkshire', 301–7.
[78] On the chronology of William's crossing of the Channel, see further, below, pp.189–90.

he was able to mount an attempt on the English throne at all in 1066 is remarkable when one looks at his career up to this point. Born the illegitimate son of Duke Robert of Normandy (and often called by contemporaries William the Bastard), he had been recognised as his father's heir when Robert went on pilgrimage to the Holy Land in 1035, and became duke following his death on the return journey. The ensuing years must have played a major part in shaping the future Conqueror's personality.[79] A period of great instability, characterised by extensive feuding among the magnates, followed the death of Archbishop Robert of Rouen, a brother of Duke Richard II, in 1037, and ten years later William's position was seriously threatened when there was a revolt which sought to replace him with his cousin Count Guy of Brionne, the legitimate son of one of Richard II's daughters. Fortunately for the young duke, he was not only recognised by the French king Henry I, but Henry came to his assistance in 1047, intervening with an army which played a major role in defeating the rebels at Val-ès-Dunes, south-east of Caen. Even then, William's position was far from secure. It took another three years for Count Guy to be banished from Normandy, and William also began to have difficulties with Geoffrey Martel (The Hammer), count of Anjou, whose ambitions now extended to the conquest of the county of Maine, which lay between Anjou and Normandy, and which he occupied in 1051. The following year he was reconciled with his former enemy King Henry and both then turned against William, who was again facing a serious rebellion within Normandy. In February 1054 a French army invading eastern Normandy was defeated by Robert, count of Eu, at the battle of Mortemer, and this forced the withdrawal of other troops led by the king. He and William were briefly reconciled, but 1057 saw a further royal invasion of the duchy along with Geoffrey Martel. William caught them as they were crossing the river Dives near Varaville and apparently succeeded in inflicting heavy losses on

[79] What follows is drawn from Douglas, *William the Conqueror*, pp.31–80, 173–9; Bates, *William the Conqueror*, pp.25–43; ibid., pp.90–8, provides a valuable summary of what is known about William's character.

those who had been unable to cross before the tide came in.[80] Hostilities with Henry continued, but deliverance was at hand. On 4 August 1060 the king died, leaving France to his young son Philip, who was under the guardianship of William's father-in-law, Count Baldwin V of Flanders. Only just over three months later, Geoffrey Martel died too, and a resultant succession dispute guaranteed that Anjou would not trouble William again for some time.

William's marriage to Baldwin's daughter Matilda had taken place c.1050,[81] and its legitimacy was eventually recognised by the church, which had originally opposed it for reasons which are not known. Useful as his connection with Baldwin was, however, it was the twin fatalities of 1060 which brought about a dramatic improvement in his position. By the end of 1063 he had made the most of his opportunities by conquering the county of Maine, and he next turned his attention to Brittany, encouraging some of the Bretons to rebel against Count Conan II, and leading a campaign there, accompanied by his guest Earl Harold.[82] Bretons were to accompany him to England in 1066, and William was fortunate that by then he could leave Normandy without undue concern about its safety while he was away. Had Edward the Confessor died before 1060 it seems almost impossible that he would have been able to back his claim to the English throne by the use of force. In 1066 he was ready and able, and in more ways than one. The struggles of his youth had produced a man with the charisma necessary in all medieval rulers, and also the required streaks of determination, ruthlessness and brutality. William could be a cruel man, as those who opposed him often found out to their cost, but in triumphing over adversity he had shown to contemporaries that any undertaking in which he became involved stood a good chance of success. It was this which drew to his banner men from beyond the confines of Normandy,[83] men confident of their leader's ability to deliver the

[80] GND, ii. 152–3. See further, below, p.179.
[81] GG, p.32, n.6.
[82] See Keats-Rohan, 'William I and the Breton Contingent', 162–6.
[83] Below, pp.173–6.

rewards of victory, and fortified by the knowledge that God was on their side.

The French vanguard at Hastings carried into battle a banner sent to William by Pope Alexander II. It is mentioned by William of Poitiers, who says that the duke sought the pope's approval, and received the standard with his blessing, so that he might attack his enemy with greater confidence.[84] It has been suggested that this author and other Norman writers may have based much of their material on William's claim to the English throne on an account produced for the pope's benefit;[85] otherwise, little is known about how the banner was acquired, although Orderic Vitalis names Gilbert, archdeacon of Lisieux, as the envoy entrusted with the mission to Rome, and describes it as 'the standard of St Peter the Apostle',[86] which may well be how the French soldiers were encouraged to regard it: those who fought with the help of the greatest of the saints would not expect to fight in vain, and in breaking an oath sworn on holy relics Harold must have known that he would be vulnerable to action of this kind. A letter written to William in April 1080 by Pope Gregory VII, who as the archdeacon Hildebrand had been actively involved in the negotiations of 1066, suggests that some had hesitated before sanctioning the spilling of blood,[87] but there is no evidence that any English embassy contested the duke's claims. Eventually, he would return like for like: among the pope's share of the spoils from the battle of Hastings was Harold's banner of the Fighting Man, upon which the image of a *homo armatus* was worked in the purest gold.[88] The idea that God might support those fighting in a righteous cause was not new in the West: in the late eighth century Charlemagne had sought the intercession of St Peter in his campaigns against the pagan

---

[84] *GG*, pp.104–5. Morton, 'Pope Alexander II and the Norman Conquest', argued against any papal approval of William's expedition, and suggested (378–80) that WP, 'an indefatigable but inept liar' and 'unsuccessful sycophant', has antedated a (supposed) banner bestowed on him in 1070.

[85] Van Houts, introduction to *GND*, i. xlvii.

[86] *HÆ*, ii. 142–3.

[87] Translated *EHD2*, No. 99; *The Norman Conquest*, ed. Brown, p.165. Freeman gives the Latin text, *FNC*, iii. 319, n.2.

[88] *GG*, pp.152–3.

Saxons, and William may have been well aware that in 1043 Pope Benedict IX had bestowed upon the emperor Henry III a *vexillum ex beati Petri parte* prior to a campaign against the Hungarians;[89] thirty years after Hastings the papacy would launch in God's name the greatest of all the military expeditions of the eleventh century – that now known as the First Crusade. In the meantime, the duke had been given what contemporaries, many of whom needed no convincing that heaven might intervene in human affairs in the most decisive way, would have regarded as one of his most powerful weapons. The months before his forces sailed for England may also have seen diplomatic negotiations other than those with the pope. William of Poitiers says that the duke made a pact with Henry IV, the king of Germany, according to which the Germans would come to his assistance if asked, and that envoys of Swegen Estrithson of Denmark promised loyalty, although he was, as it turned out, to prove the friend of the duke's enemies.[90]

Freeman guessed that it was on Sunday 1 October that Harold heard of William's landing on the south coast, but little is known of his actions and whereabouts between the battles of Stamford Bridge and Hastings.[91] The E text of the *Anglo-Saxon Chronicle* says that he fought the latter before all his army had assembled,[92] while William of Malmesbury reports that many deserted him on the march south because he had refused to share the booty from his victory, which he told Edwin and Morcar to take to London; hence, he had with him his '*stipendiarios et mercennarios milites*' (professional soldiers) but '*paucos... ex prouintialibus*' (few shire levies).[93] Orderic Vitalis suggests that it was in London that Harold was told

---

[89] Cowdrey, 'Anglo-Norman Laudes', 60; for other gifts of papal banners before 1066, see Morton, 'Pope Alexander II', 365.

[90] GG, pp. 104–7. WP calls Henry *Romanorum imperator*, but he was not crowned emperor until 1084; on the assistance allegedly sent by Swegen to the English in 1066, see below, p. 100.

[91] FNC, iii. 733; see also the detailed discussion in Douglas, *William the Conqueror*, pp. 396–400.

[92] ASC E, i. 198.

[93] GR, i. 422–3, 468–9. Gaimar, *L'Estoire des Engleis*, ed. Bell, ll. 5245–8, says the booty was handed over to Archbishop Ealdred of York, while one of the scholia added to Adam of Bremen's *Gesta*, p. 196, notes that Hardrada's mass of gold eventually came into the possession of William; on WM's evidence, see further, below, pp. 69–70.

of the Normans' arrival, and says that he spent six days summoning the English to war and gathering an innumerable multitude. He also tells the tale, which need not be completely without foundation, of how Harold's mother, Gytha, tried to persuade him not to fight, and was supported by his brother Gyrth, who brought up the problem of the oath to William, and offered to lead the English army himself. This Harold is said to have angrily rejected.[94] Certainly, he can have wasted no time in moving into Sussex; both William of Jumièges and William of Poitiers say that he hastened his advance to take William by surprise,[95] and given the success of such tactics against Harald Hardrada this seems by no means unlikely. Harold may well have been confident, and perhaps over-confident, but it is probable that he considered the forces at his disposal adequate for the task ahead.[96]

His adversary had not moved from the bridgehead he had established on the south coast, with fortifications at Pevensey and Hastings. The latter was a town with a mint, and may have had both effective ramparts and a garrison;[97] it was presumably occupied by the Normans, but of this no source tells. William had everything to gain by allowing the English to come to him, and in the fact that he did so we can probably discern his experience as a commander. Staying where he was enabled him to protect his fleet – William of Poitiers may err in claiming that there were 700 enemy vessels now in the Channel,[98] but the safety of his ships must have been one of William's prime concerns – and to ensure that the English would be as tired by their travels as his own men were refreshed by their relative inactivity. How long he would have been able to maintain

---

[94] *HÆ*, ii. 170–3. Dr Chibnall comments (171, n.4) that this 'reads like a popular romance'. Orderic had earlier added the same information to WJ's *GND*, ii. 166–9. WM, *GR*, i. 450–3, places a very similar story, here involving Gyrth but not Gytha, before Hastings. Other sources, HH for example (*HA*, pp.388–9), claim that Harold was in York when he heard of William's landing.

[95] *GND*, ii. 166–7; *GG*, pp.124–5; similarly, *Carmen*, ll. 281–2. As WP knew *GND* and perhaps the *Carmen* he need not be an independent witness.

[96] On the size of the English army, see further, below, pp.154–61.

[97] As my pupil Jonathan Hall has pointed out. Hastings was one of the forts of the Burghal Hidage (below, pp.131–2) and one of the Cinque Ports.

[98] *GG*, pp.124–5; the *Carmen*, l. 319, gives 500; OV, *HÆ*, ii. 172–3, only seventy.

himself in the area he had occupied had he been left to his own devices is a question that cannot be answered, but Harold may have felt the adoption of such a strategy too dangerous, and William was perhaps confident that he would do so. His ravaging of English territory may also have provoked Harold into action. Thus, by Friday 13 October the English must have been somewhere near the ridge which would one day be crowned by Battle Abbey, for William of Jumièges says that they rode through the night and appeared on the battlefield early the following morning.[99] The duke is likely to have already been in the vicinity,[100] after advancing from the coast when he heard of the English approach. He is said to have ordered his army to stand by during the night in case of an attack;[101] there was little danger that he would be taken by surprise, and Harold probably erred in hoping otherwise. At around 9 o'clock on the morning of Saturday 14 October, the French moved forward; their vanguard bore the papal banner, and it was later told that they began a song of Roland, so that the great hero's martial example might encourage those about to fight.[102]

[99] GND, ii. 166–7.
[100] On this, see below, pp. 196–7.
[101] GND, ii. 168–9; the Carmen, l. 285, notes his watchfulness.
[102] GR, i. 454–5.

2

THE SOURCES: PART ONE

Few things are more difficult to describe than the events of the battlefield. To say nothing of that lack of coolness which is essential to accurate observation, an individual spectator commonly sees only a small portion of the engagement, and is apt to overrate the incidents occurring in the fore-ground of his view, while those which take place in the distance are but slightly noticed. Acts comparatively insignificant thus become magnified, while those of far greater importance are occasionally either much distorted, or altogether overlooked. Allowances must also be made for party prejudices, and for the flowers of rhetoric almost inseparable from such descriptions. Now if even contemporary accounts of modern battles are found to differ *inter sese* in some essential particulars, it must be a matter of great difficulty to frame an intelligible history of the sanguinary conflicts of ancient times from the materials furnished us by partial and often incompetent chroniclers and written from oral traditions at periods considerably subsequent to the transactions themselves.[1]

---

[1] Lower, 'On the Battle of Hastings', 15.

It would be difficult to improve upon these words, addressed by the Sussex historian Mark Antony Lower to an assembly at Battle Abbey on 23 July 1852, as a brief analysis of the difficulties involved in elucidating events at the same location on 14 October 1066. More is known about Hastings than any battle fought in the West since the end of the Roman empire, and any event in English history prior to 1066 and for another century thereafter, until the murder of Thomas Becket by four of King Henry II's followers in Canterbury in 1170 produced a number of contemporary accounts, several based on eye-witness testimony, and one the work of a bystander who almost had an arm severed in the struggle. There is no eye-witness on Hastings (and as Lower said, it would not be an end of our problems if there were), but secondary writers such as William of Jumièges, William of Poitiers, the author of the *Carmen de Hastingae Proelio*, and Orderic Vitalis may well have spoken to combatants, and some of them were working before King William's death in 1087; the same period probably also saw the production of the Bayeux Tapestry, whose designer had access to details not included in other contemporary sources. However, all this might tend to paint a picture which is considerably rosier than the reality, for even contemporaneity is no guarantee that medieval evidence will be easy to use. In theory, source criticism seems a straightforward business: one identifies the author's background, his motive for writing and the likely origin of his information, then his statements are compared with others to establish his general reliability, and a rough rule-of-thumb worked out for assessing his plausibility on matters with which he alone deals. Unfortunately, such methods often break down in practice, partly because of our imperfect knowledge and understanding of the world in which the sources were produced. Thus, it can be difficult establishing exactly why a particular piece was written and discovering very much about the author concerned, even if his identity is known; it may be equally difficult cross-checking his statements when other information on his subject is either non-existent or inadequate, and even when statements can be checked it tends to be characteristic of medieval authors, and probably of the transmission of historical knowledge generally, that a source which is wildly inaccurate on one point is not necessarily so on others. In general, while there is enough evidence on the murder of Becket to establish the main outline of what happened, this is not true with Hastings, in any case a much more complex event, which is served by insufficient material of proven reliability. Even so, nobody who seeks a proper understanding of the battle, and of what can and cannot be known about it, is able to avoid critical analysis of this material, and the intractable problems which sometimes result. That is why this chapter and the one which follows are the crux of this book.

By no means the least of our witnesses is the battlefield itself (illus. 39). Important because it can to an extent be cross-referenced with the documentary evidence, and because any discussion of the deployment of the two armies needs to bear it in mind, it can also suggest much about the strength of Harold's position and why the battle seems to have been so hard fought. Shortly after the conflict, and probably in 1067,[2] Norman bishops drew up a list of the penances to be served by surviving French soldiers; this was subsequently confirmed by a papal legate, Bishop Ermenfrid of Sion, and included the provision that:

> Whoever does not know the number of those he struck or killed shall, at the discretion of his bishop, do penance for one day a week for the rest of his life, or, if he is able, make amends either by building a church or by giving perpetual alms to one.[3]

King William may well have considered himself within the category of those who knew not the number of those they had slain, and as a man of conventional piety doubtless believed that God had, through the papal banner, given him the victory that the righteousness of his cause demanded. Thus it was probably early in his reign

---

[2] On the date, I follow Cowdrey, 'Anglo–Norman Laudes', 59, n.68; also *Councils & Synods I*, ed. Whitelock *et al.*, ii. 582. 1070 is an alternative.

[3] *Penitential articles issued after the Battle of Hastings*, c. 1. I have quoted the translation in *The Norman Conquest*, ed. Brown, p.156.

that he decided, as an act of expiation and thanksgiving,[4] to build Battle Abbey upon the site of his triumph, although the church was not consecrated until early in 1094.[5] The twelfth-century historian William of Malmesbury says that the altar (illus. 24-5) was positioned where Harold's body had been found, while the author of the Battle Abbey chronicle reports that it occupied the spot where his standard had been seen to fall.[6] There is little difficulty in believing that these places were one and the same, or that William did issue instructions to this effect. The abbey chronicle also tells how the monks, who came from the French abbey of Marmoutier on the Loire, told the king that the site was unsuitable for buildings, being on a waterless hilltop. They were quite right, but he nevertheless insisted that this was where the abbey should be,[7] and as a result those erecting structures over the following centuries often had to make substantial alterations to the original ground level. Today, the slope to the south of the high altar (illus. 23) 'bears little relation to the much steeper one up which the Norman cavalry would have had to charge', while further west the outer courtyard was extended and levelled after the Dissolution by building up the hillside to the south.[8] The foundation of the abbey, at a time when relics of the battle, and perhaps not least the grave-pits, must still have marked the field, is more than adequate proof that the fight did take place in what has traditionally been recognised as its location.[9]

[4] The *Brevis Relatio*, p.33, written in Battle 1114x20, says that William had the abbey built in memory of his victory and for the absolution of the sins of all those killed there. Searle, *Lordship and Community*, p.21, suggests a date for the foundation no earlier than 1071 and perhaps in the mid-1070s.

[5] *ASC* E, i. 229. This source also refers (i. 219) to the abbey's foundation, 'on the very spot where God granted him the conquest of England', in its obituary of the Conqueror.

[6] *GP*, p.207; *Chronicle of Battle Abbey*, ed. Searle, pp.44-5. The latter was probably written in the last third of the twelfth century (p.8). I do not fully share Bradbury's scepticism (*The Battle of Hastings*, pp.172-3) of its account. His statement that 'the altar story does not emerge until a century after the event' takes no account of WM and is incorrect. In his *GR*, i. 492-3, WM reported that the principal church at Battle was situated where Harold's body was said to have been found among the heaps of corpses. *BR*, p.32, says that a Norman soldier told the duke before the fighting began that he thought he could see Harold's standard on the crest of the ridge.

[7] *Chronicle of Battle Abbey*, ed. Searle, pp.42-5.

[8] Hare, 'The buildings of Battle Abbey', 80-2.

[9] It would be unnecessary to stress this but for the recent suggestion (Bradbury, *The Battle of Hastings*, pp.168-78) that the battle was fought on Caldbec Hill, a short distance to the north.

Harold drew up his men on and perhaps to the south of a slightly curved ridge which, allowing for the curve, is roughly 1¼ kilometres (just under a mile) long, and from which the ground falls away on all sides, except at one point to the north, where there is a connecting neck of land which is now the site of Battle High Street. The slope to the south was steepest near the point at which he placed his standard, and this spot occupied the crest of the ridge at a height above mean sea level of about 85 metres. From here the ground runs away both to the east and the south-west, in the latter case dropping about 15 metres over the approximate 250 metres to the western end of the abbey terrace, but then only one metre more over the roughly 500 metres to the point at the westernmost extremity of the ridge where the modern 2½-inch Ordnance Survey map places a height marker of 69 metres.[10] To the north of this is woodland sometimes known as Long Plantation,[11] and west of it, as stated, the ridge comes to an end, dropping quite steeply at points into a drainage channel which contains a small stream bordered on the east by Saxon Wood (called Sacristy Copse on the Battle tithe map of 1859, illus. 38). Due west of the marker the ground falls 24 metres in about 200 metres (an average of just over 1 in 8),[12] while to the south of it there is a fall of 29 metres in about 250 metres (an average of between 1 in 8 and 1 in 9). The visitor to the field who now walks due east from the area of the marker through a patch of vegetation will come after slightly less than 500 metres to the north-eastern edge of Horselodge Plantation (named Mountain Plantation on the tithe map) at a height of between 50 and 60 metres.[13] This

---

[10] OS Explorer Sheet 124, *Hastings & Bexhill*. The measurements quoted are all taken from this map. For the flat top of the western part of the ridge, see illus. 52 and 59.

[11] It is so named on the OS 6-inch map, Sheet TQ 71NW, revised in 1974 and published in 1976, and on earlier maps in the 6-inch series. Some OS maps give no name.

[12] See further on the western end of the ridge, below, pp. 147-9, and illus. 43 and 56.

[13] I follow OS Explorer Sheet 124 in referring to the vegetation on the south-western face of the ridge by this name, but earlier maps are both more specific and more revealing on its genesis. The tithe map shows three plantations in this area, one centred on the hillock and named Mountain Plantation, another slightly further west which is not named, and a roughly circular one north-west of the latter and denoted Devil's Plantation; the OS 6-inch map of 1931 (see pp. 54-5) is similar, but gives only the name Horselodge, which was evidently originally that of the central plantation of the three. Their absence, with Long Plantation, from the estate survey of 1811 (ESRO, BAT 4435) may well mean that all were created between that date and 1859. However, the gorse on the hillock (see below) is likely to be natural.

covers some of a small but noticeable ridge which is part of the general fall of the ground to the south-west, and which at its highest (north-eastern) point forms a distinct hillock. In the south-eastern corner of the plantation are two small ponds, and to the rear of the hillock a rather larger one;[14] another pond, almost as big as the latter, forms to the west of it after a period of extended rainfall (illus. 29, 37).[15] Possibly the result of open-cast iron working[16] at some unknown date, the two larger ponds, if they existed in 1066, may have played some sort of role in the battle.[17]

Due north of the large ponds the slope rises 10 metres in about 125 metres before reaching the 70-metre contour line just south of the western end of the abbey terrace (illus. 27). Due south of the hillock there is a very steep gradient (down which English Heritage has provided a flight of steps) leading to extensive low ground at a height of around 45 to 40 metres. The amount of moisture which enters this area from the clay (see below) of the western part of the battlefield is considerable, and today much of it debouches into New Pond (illus. 30-2), constructed in 1815, and then eventually flows down to Powdermill Lake and south to the coast. Before New Pond was built the land to the west of it would have been subject to more flooding than is now the case, and a map of 1724 (illus. 33) shows that a distinct area of marsh lay due south of the western edge of the main ridge, in ground now occupied by the easternmost part of Warren Wood, gradually becoming much larger as it extended downstream to the vicinity of Powdermill. These areas are likely to be distinctly boggy even today, and there were not in 1724 apparently

---

[14] All three are shown on the 2½-inch map.

[15] This second pond appears on the modern 25-inch OS map, but not on most other OS sheets. After a period of dryness, it reappeared in the very wet autumn of 2000, but had disappeared by August 2001.

[16] The ironstone in the clay has been known to turn rainwater red. This was mentioned by the twelfth-century chronicler William of Newburgh, who thought that it was blood, and in the nineteenth century by the Duchess of Cleveland; see Stevenson, 'Senlac and the Malfossé', 301. On the Horselodge Plantation ponds see further, below, p.56, n.20. There is also a pit which looks like the product of human activity, and which sometimes contains water, in the most southerly part of Long Plantation.

[17] Below, p.207, n.19.

as many trees in this vicinity as there are now.[18] To the east of New Pond the ground rises past the three Stew Ponds (illus. 70) which did exist in the early eighteenth century and which would have reduced the amount of water flowing west still further, and when one comes to the saddle which carries the road to Hastings (illus. 47-8) the slope to the north is much less severe than at the point where Harold was killed, rising about 10 in 175 metres. Due east of the saddle, in the area which now contains Battle railway station, the ground falls away again (illus. 60), and the slope to the north gradually disappears as the eastern part of the ridge falls away too, coming to an end more or less where Marley Lane, the road which runs out of Battle to the east, crosses the railway line (illus. 61). The road itself seems to be cut into the ridge, and this is particularly noticeable near the former Battle primary school, where the existence and depth of the cutting suggest that there may originally have been a gradient to the east so steep that wheeled vehicles could not readily negotiate it (illus. 63-4). South of this part of the ridge rises a stream which flows eastwards, but this drainage area, being situated on porous sandstone (see below) rather than impervious clay, does not carry the same volume of water as its bigger brother to the west.

There is considerable vegetation on parts of the ridge today, but no way of knowing the situation in 1066. Obviously, at least some of it was sufficiently open for fighting to take place, and most of the battle scenes in the Bayeux Tapestry show no trees. This is not negligible evidence, as the Tapestry is not shy about such features (almost fifty appear in it in all), and does depict trees both in the section where the French are attacking English troops on an eminence (illus. 46) thought by Freeman to be identifiable with the Horselodge Plantation hillock,[19] and in that where the English are being pursued at the end. Nor, of course, despite the relatively untouched nature of

[18] ESRO, BAT 4421 (7), one of a series of maps of the Battle Abbey estate drawn by Richard Budgen. Apart from the easternmost part of Warren Wood this stretch of boggy ground lies outside the land in the ownership of English Heritage.

[19] FNC, iii. 444, 490; his map of the field (opp. p.443, and below, p.139) shows it as 'The English Outpost'. See further, below, pp.138-9.

much of the field, can one be certain that its features are exactly the same today as they were 900 years ago. The crest of the ridge, as noted earlier, has undergone significant alterations, while a recent survey by English Heritage has revealed signs of ridge-and-furrow cultivation on parts of the battlefield, and that the ponds around

Horselodge Plantation were at some point dammed and provided with sluices, evidently so that the stream into which they drained to the south-west of the ridge could be put to industrial use further down its course; the construction of New Pond, easily assumed to be primarily ornamental in its purpose, may also have been connected

The battlefield according to the OS 6-inch map of 1931 (surveyed 1872/3, revised 1928). Sussex (East) Sheet LVII. Not to the original scale.

with the same desire to be able to hold water over the winter so that it could be released during a dry summer to feed the mill-ponds at Powdermill and elsewhere, thus facilitating continuous production of the gunpowder for which Battle was famous between the seventeenth and nineteenth centuries. Still, apart from the abbey the area to the east is the only one to have been built on, much of it today containing private houses erected relatively recently.[20]

Orderic Vitalis, writing in the early twelfth century, repeatedly refers to the site of the battle by the name of Senlac.[21] This was adopted by Freeman (although subsequent historians have preferred Domesday Book's 'battle of Hastings') on the not unreasonable grounds that as Hastings is some miles away 'a name for the spot is wanted', and because he knew that the term had survived in 'the local names for the south-eastern part of the town'.[22] His suggestion that Orderic 'cannot have invented the word', with the implication that it was of English origin, was scornfully rejected shortly after his death by J.H. Round, who announced that to 'anyone acquainted with "Old English" it must instantly occur that "Senlac" is an impossible English name'.[23] But with this Round overreached himself, and in 1913 his position was challenged by W.H. Stevenson, who showed that the name Sandlake 'may be found scores of times in deeds ranging from the twelfth century downwards' in the archives of Battle Abbey, and suggested that it did indeed partly derive not from the Old French *lac*

[20] The first edition of the OS 6-inch map, Sussex Sheet LVII (surveyed 1873–4), shows only the railway station, a gas works, some buildings on the Hastings road and the National School on Marley Lane. The 1931 map, Sussex (East) Sheet LVII N.E. (see p.54–5), hardly differs. The preliminary results of the English Heritage survey were announced to their staff at a meeting at Battle on 26 March 2002; I am grateful to Mark Bowden, Senior Investigator of the National Monuments Centre, for inviting me to attend it. On Battle gunpowder, see Blackman, 'The Story of the old gunpowder works'; there were five gunpowder mills on the stream, that at Powdermill being the largest, although one, at Farthing Mills, was not served by the tributary which rises on the battlefield; production ceased in 1874. Rather than being the result of iron extraction (see above, p.52), the surveyors raise the possibility that the Horselodge Plantation ponds, and other apparent quarries on the battlefield, were created by the extraction of sand and clay subsequent to the battle (*Survey*, pp.11, 14, 16).

[21] *HÆ*, ii. 172–3, 180–1, 185–6, 190–1, 266–7, 356–7.

[22] *FNC*, iii. 746. He was not the first to use Orderic's term, see Lappenberg, *A History of England under the Anglo-Saxon Kings*, ii. 301; Lingard, *The History of England*, i. 188.

[23] Round, anonymous article in the *Quarterly Review* of 1892, 11; repeated, *Feudal England*, p.339.

but from the Old English *lacu* – a stream or watercourse; the Old English *Sand-lace* he thus interpreted as meaning 'a sandy brook or a brook that brings down sand'.[24] His final conclusion, based on documents as late as the sixteenth century, was that the area of Sandlake, one of the divisions of the medieval town:

> marched with the abbey precincts from the south-east corner to a spot opposite the parish church on the north, and that some part... was south of the abbey. Even if the abbey-site was never within... Sandlake, these facts prove that the spot where Harold fell and where the high altar of the abbey was erected was within a few yards at most of the limits of... Sandlake.[25]

Yet whether Senlac must mean something as precise as 'sandy brook' is far from certain, for the names Upper Lake and Lower Lake are still in use in Battle for the road which runs to the north of the abbey and continues down the southern slope of the ridge towards Hastings, and as both are in positions too near its summit for them ever to have referred to any substantial body of running water (except in the event of torrential rain) the meaning of 'lake' here is probably that of a small channel or drain (deriving from *lacu* and surviving in dialect use into modern times).[26] Moreover, on the estate map of 1724 (illus. 34) Lower Lake is actually named 'Sanglake'.[27] Certainly the geology of the site (illus. 35) is no stranger to sand.[28] The western part of the ridge, and part of the northern face of its eastern part, consist of Wadhurst Clay, which

[24] Stevenson, 'Senlac and the Malfossé', espec. 293–6; similarly, Mawer and Stenton, *The Place-Names of Sussex*, ii. 499; Ekwall, *Concise Oxford Dictionary of English Place-Names*, p.412, gives *sand-lacu* as 'sandy brook'; Stevenson's *Sand-lace* is the dative form.

[25] Stevenson, 'Senlac and the Malfossé', 300; for an earlier commentary, see Lower, 'On the Battle of Hastings', 37–8.

[26] See *OED* under 'lake', 'leach' (both thought to be connected with the Old English verb *leccan*, to moisten) and 'letch'.

[27] ESRO, BAT 4421 (6), another map in the series drawn by Richard Budgen.

[28] The following description is drawn from the British Geological Survey 1:50,000 Series, Sheet 320/321, *Hastings & Dungeness*; see further Lake and Shephard-Thorn, *Geology of the country around Hastings and Dungeness*. I am also grateful to Paul Littlewood for comment on the ground.

further south and west is eventually replaced by Tunbridge Wells Sand. There is a small outcrop of this too at the point where the monastic buildings were erected, and a fault line divides this from the Ashdown Beds (also a sandstone) which form most of the eastern portion of the ridge. The road now known as Lower Lake cuts into this Ashdown sand (the surrounding ground surface being at points several feet higher) and it may be that there was once a sandy channel in this location from which the area known as Senlac, and eventually the battle, took their names.[29] Alternatively, if the name does denote a sandy brook this could refer to either of the streams which rise on each side of the saddle which carries the road to Hastings, the first (and more insubstantial) flowing east and the second west to New Pond and eventually Powdermill Lake, for the impervious Wadhurst Clay which contributes so much to the volume of the latter, and through which it runs, is at points very sandy in its nature (illus. 41, 44), and the thickets of gorse which today cover some of the area of Horselodge Plantation must be growing on a superficial capping of sand. It is unlikely, but not completely impossible, that both these derivations contain elements of truth, the district of Sandlake perhaps being named after a sandy channel, and the battle of Senlac after a sandy stream.

The documentary sources produced by the English are nothing like as extensive as those which issued from their conquerors. The most important are the two versions of the *Anglo-Saxon Chronicle* which deal with the battle, that is those denoted D and E by historians. The latter is the tersest of all the written evidence, and perhaps the most contemporary. E is a manuscript written in the abbey of Peterborough in the third decade of the twelfth century,[30] but one of the sources of which it made use was a chronicle produced in the monastery of St Augustine, Canterbury during the

---

[29] The road may not originally have run in this channel. A number of commentators have noted the way in which the present road skirts the abbey grounds and suggested that originally it took a more direct line over or very near the spot where Harold was killed; see, for example, Lemmon's map in *The Field of Hastings*. However, in this case the gradient to the south would have been very much steeper, and this suggests that the present line need not be far from that of the original.

[30] E is Bodleian Library, MS Laud Misc. 636; Ker, *Catalogue*, pp.424–6.

mid-eleventh century.[31] The St Augustine's monks knew a great deal about events in the south of England during the Confessor's reign and sometimes had strong views about them, for this part of E tends to be distinctly pro-Godwinist. The last entry clearly linked to St Augustine's is that for 1061, but the information on Harold's naval expedition against William in 1066, which could have been launched from Sandwich, hints that this predecessor of E was still in Canterbury in that year, as does its use of the word 'courageous' to describe his victory at Stamford Bridge. Its very simple record of the battle of Hastings, which confines itself to saying that he fought before all his army had come, and was killed along with his brothers Gyrth and Leofwine, also seems sympathetic.[32] Under 1065, E comments that the Northumbrians' ravaging of Northamptonshire left it and neighbouring shires the poorer for many years. This statement (which is also in D) is obviously not contemporary, but may have been added at a subsequent stage in the text's transmission. Nothing is certain, but E's account of the battle, such as it is, was perhaps written at a time very close to that of the event itself.

The *Chronicle* D text is more informative, even if its provenance is more difficult to establish. Providing the significant information that the English force was a large army (*mycelne here*), that it met at the hoary apple tree, and that William came upon it by surprise before it was properly ordered (*Wyllelm him com ongean on unwær ær his folc gefylced wære*), it, too, is sympathetic to Harold, who is said to have fought most resolutely with those who wished to follow him (a hint that some did not?), and to have been killed with his brothers Gyrth and Leofwine and many good men, after great slaughter on both sides. Rather later in the entry there appears an idea which was also taken up by others – that the misfortunes of the English were God's punishment of sin.[33] The date of the scribe responsible for

---

[31] As Charles Plummer established, *ASC*, ii. xlviii–l.

[32] Ibid., i. 198.

[33] Ibid., i. 199–200.

it is uncertain,[34] as is his location, although Worcester is a strong possibility. He cannot have been writing soon after the battle, as the entry for 1065 shares E's comment on the long-term effects of the ravaging of Northamptonshire by the Northumbrian rebels, but like E he may (or may not) have been copying older material on the battle itself. D uses texts of the C and E type frequently for this period, and continues to use E into the 1070s (D itself comes to an end in 1079). If our C did not break off before getting to Hastings, it might well have shown that D's account of the latter owed something to a manuscript of the C type, as it certainly does in the earlier part of its entry for 1066. If so, and as C itself is in this period a contemporary manuscript written in the monastery of Abingdon,[35] the authority of D's information might be somewhat strengthened. Of course, date of composition is only one factor to be taken into account when assessing a source's reliability; another is bias. Even so, D's comments on the battle are not obviously prejudiced, although the favour which this source seems to show Harold's family elsewhere – notably in its omission from its C text exemplar of the information that Godwin was involved in the opposition to Edward the Confessor's brother Alfred in 1036 – can perhaps be discerned within it.[36]

Not long after its composition, D, or a manuscript very like it, lay before John of Worcester, who compiled a Latin chronicle on the basis of various sources, including probably more than one manuscript of the *Anglo-Saxon Chronicle*,[37] in the first half of the

---

[34] D is British Library, MS. Cotton Tiberius B. iv; Ker, *Catalogue*, p.254, thought that at 1051 'the manuscript is perhaps a contemporary record', but Plummer (*ASC*, ii. lxxviii–ix) judged none of D 'probably from much before 1100', while Dumville, 'Some aspects of annalistic writing', 34, suggests limits of 1080x1130 for its compilation. Its most recent editor, G.P. Cubbin, claims Ealdred (bishop of Worcester *c.*1046–62, archbishop of York 1061–69) as 'the person responsible for the creation of D', and that 'D was compiled in the 1050s' (*Anglo-Saxon Chronicle... MS D*, p.lxxix). Plummer argued that the material on St Margaret of Scotland in 1067 is a late insertion, and that the entry as it now stands was not written until after her daughter's marriage to Henry I in 1100.

[35] British Library, MS. Cotton Tiberius B. i. Ker, *Catalogue*, p.252, commented that the 'entries for 1065, 1066... appear to be contemporary, or nearly contemporary, with the events described'. On Abingdon as the home of C, *ASC*, ii. xcii.

[36] A point made by Plummer, ibid., ii. lxxxii.

[37] See Plummer's remarks, ibid., ii. lxxxiii–vi.

twelfth century.[38] John was one of the famous quartet of Anglo-Norman historians which also included William of Malmesbury, Henry of Huntingdon and Orderic Vitalis, and which brought to the study of the past a professionalism hardly equalled in England since the days of the great Northumbrian scholar Bede (d.735), and not always equalled even by Bede himself. John assembled a wide range of sources, and sometimes draws the reader's attention to discrepancies between them (something Bede's historical works never do);[39] he also provided his readers with carefully researched lists of the bishops of all the English sees, and genealogies of the royal families of the different Anglo-Saxon kingdoms, while his additions to the eleventh-century entries in the *Anglo-Saxon Chronicle* are extensive and have usually to be taken seriously. Doubtless many things contributed to the golden age of English historical writing reflected by his works and those of his fellows, but one of them was an awareness of the changes brought about by the Norman Conquest and a desire to record the proud history of the Anglo-Saxons before it passed forever into oblivion. Among his sources was Eadmer's *Historia Novorum in Anglia* (*History of Recent Events in England*), in large part a biography of Archbishop Anselm of Canterbury originally completed just after his death in 1109, but with stories to tell about Harold's visit to Normandy[40] and the events of 1066. Eadmer does not describe the battle itself in detail, but confines himself to commenting that Harold fell in the line after heavy fighting had been joined, and that the French who were there still said (clearly implying that he had spoken to participants) that although fortunes had fluctuated there was such a slaughter and flight of the Normans that their victory could only be attributed to the power of God in punishing Harold's broken oath.[41] Eadmer, while a great friend of an Italian who had

[38] His most recent editors suggest terminal dates of 1095x1106–1140x1143, and that 'within these limits, the 1120s and the very early 1130s seem crucial', JW, ii. lxxxi.
[39] For this and what follows, see Campbell, 'Some Twelfth-Century Views of the Anglo-Saxon Past', pp.213–4.
[40] Above, pp.29–30.
[41] *Historia Novorum*, ed. Rule, pp.8–9.

become archbishop of Canterbury as a result of the Conquest, was nevertheless strongly pro-English in his sympathies,[42] and it is not difficult to detect a native bias in these statements. Nor was John of Worcester without his prejudices in the same kind of area, and they were prejudices which unfortunately, and despite his virtues in other respects, to an extent invalidate his comments on the same subject matter.[43] Thus, he takes considerably further the tendency of the D text of the *Chronicle* to offer reasons, if not excuses, for the English defeat. The report of William's landing at Pevensey adds that he was accompanied by an innumerable multitude of horsemen, slingers, archers and infantry, as he had brought with him strong forces from the whole of France. King Harold is then said to have moved his army to London in a great hurry and to have advanced into Sussex as quickly as he could, although half his forces had not yet assembled and he was well aware that the stronger men in all England had fallen in the two earlier battles. He fought before a third of his army was drawn up, on Saturday 22 October (an error for Saturday 14 October), but because his forces were arrayed in a narrow place many withdrew from the line, and very few of constant heart remained with him. Nevertheless, from the third hour (i.e. about 9 o'clock) until twilight he most stoutly resisted his enemies, and fought so strenuously that it was scarcely possible for the enemy to kill him, until, alas, at dusk, after many had fallen on both sides, he himself fell; the earls Gyrth and Leofwine, his brothers, were also among the dead, and the more noble of almost all England.[44]

Internal criticism alone might cast doubt on the plausibility of this account. For example, if Harold's forces were really so inadequate why did the battle last as long as it did? Yet when it is considered within the context of this author's remarks on the year as a whole it is not difficult to see what has happened. It must be indicative of the passions which the Conquest excited even fifty years later that John, who is said by Orderic Vitalis to have been

[42] See Williams, *The English and the Norman Conquest*, pp.165–8.
[43] See further, ibid., pp.168–9.
[44] JW, ii. 604–5.

English,[45] is (unlike his fellow historians) strongly in favour of King Harold. He is also the only near-contemporary source to assert that the latter was crowned by Archbishop Ealdred of York rather than Stigand of Canterbury, whose position as archbishop was not recognised by the papacy, and whom Norman sources identify as the bishop responsible in an attempt to further impugn Harold's legitimacy.[46] Both sides had a motive to lie, and in this case it is impossible to be sure which is telling the truth.[47] Ealdred had been bishop of Worcester before his promotion to York, and John may be using an authentic tradition. On the other hand, the enthusiasm which he subsequently shows for King Harold must give pause. Alleging him to have been the *subregulus* ('underking') before Edward's death, John continues by extolling the excellence of his rule: he destroyed unjust laws, was a patron of churches and monasteries, and was pious, humble and affable to all good men, while detesting criminals; these his subordinates were ordered to seize, as also to prepare for the defence of the country by land and sea.[48] There is nothing of this sort in the surviving texts of the *Anglo-Saxon Chronicle*, and one might doubt whether John had much warrant for it. His account of Hastings seems to be biased in the same direction. Here, the *Chronicle* E text's statement that Harold fought before all his army had come looks as though it has been elaborated into 'before half his army had come', while D's assertion that the English were attacked before they were properly arrayed becomes 'before a third of his army had been drawn up'. Similarly, D's statement that Harold fought alongside those who wished to follow him may hint that some did not, and John apparently works this up into many of the English withdrawing from the line because the space was too

---

[45] *HÆ*, ii. 186–7.

[46] WP, *GG*, pp.100–1. The Bayeux Tapestry (illus. 5) shows Stigand standing beside the newly crowned king, thus apparently making the same point. OV, *HÆ*, ii. 136–9, says that Stigand performed the coronation without the consent of other bishops; he also presents a much less rosy picture of Harold's reign than JW.

[47] For a full discussion, see *FNC*, iii. 612–18, who predictably came out in favour of the Worcester writer, and Chibnall's note, *HÆ*, ii. 138, n.1.

[48] JW, ii. 600–1.

narrow. Finally, and significantly, he omits altogether D's assertion that the English army was 'large'. It is not possible to dismiss all the details he supplies, because the restricted nature of the English deployment seems to be confirmed by other writers.[49] Nevertheless, one could be forgiven for doubting whether much of what he says has any great authority behind it.

The sympathy for the English shown by Eadmer and John is also to be found in the work of a greater writer, their contemporary William of Malmesbury, who visited Worcester and perhaps met John; certainly he used the latter's chronicle as one of his own sources. William apparently wrote his *Gesta Regum Anglorum* (*History of the Kings of the English*) as a result of a visit paid to Malmesbury by King Henry I's queen, Matilda, shortly before her death in 1118. As the granddaughter of Edward the Exile and great-granddaughter of King Edmund Ironside,[50] Matilda (whose English name had been Edith) was a member of the Old English royal family, and she asked William to write an account of her royal predecessors; he agreed, being unwilling that the deeds of such men should be forgotten.[51] The *Gesta Regum* he claims to be the first history of the English written in Latin since the days of Bede,[52] and both here and in his *Gesta Pontificum*, on the history of the English church, he used many of the techniques of a modern historian, cross-checking his sources and often drawing the reader's attention to results which were not satisfactory. He gives details, for example, of the murder of Edward the Confessor's brother Alfred which he claims to be well-known, but about which he expresses reservations because they are not in the *Anglo-Saxon Chronicle*. Similarly, he warns the reader that in his own day the English and the Normans still disputed the rights and wrongs

[49] Below, p.205-6, on the great density of the English line.

[50] She was the daughter of Edward the Exile's daughter Margaret and King Malcolm III of Scotland. Henry had married her in 1100, probably to bolster his support among the English. *ASC* E (i. 236) points out that she was of 'the rightful royal house of England'.

[51] *GR*, i. 6–9. This information is from a letter written to her daughter the empress Matilda; it survives in only one manuscript of the *Gesta Regum*.

[52] *GR*, i. 14–15.

of the quarrels between the Godwin family and King Edward's Norman supporters, and that the truth is therefore uncertain.[53] His history of the abbey of Glastonbury was researched there,[54] and he visited many cathedrals and monasteries in the course of his studies, examining their archives and listening to their oral traditions. The list of classical and medieval sources (including administrative documents) of which the *Gesta Regum* made use either at first or second hand is a remarkable one.[55] It is not therefore surprising that William of Malmesbury's comments on the battle of Hastings are part of a more general treatment of the events of 1066 and their significance, of a type considerably more ambitious than anything attempted by the sources discussed thus far.

He was of mixed descent, probably having a French father and an English mother, and he states explicitly what John of Worcester leaves implicit – that the battle was a fatal day for England ('our sweet country', as he calls it) because of the damage that was to come about as a result of the change of lords. He then embarks upon some general reflections on Old English history: the Anglo-Saxons had once been famous for their practice of Christianity, but in the years before the Conquest their attention to literature and religion had decayed, monks had ignored their Rule by wearing fine vestments, and the nobles had given themselves up to good living, eating until they were surfeited and drinking until they were sick. Indeed, entire days and nights had been spent in drinking, and the vices which result from drunkenness had followed. Thus it was that they engaged Duke William with more rashness than military science, dooming their country to slavery through a single, easy victory. The Normans, on the other hand, did not eat to excess; a race which could hardly live without war, their arrival in England had revived its religious life, so that churches appeared in every village

---

[53] *GR*, i. 336–7, 354–5. See further, Thomson, *William of Malmesbury*, esp. pp.1–38, 72–5; Gransden, *Historical Writing in England*, pp.166–85; Williams, *The English and the Norman Conquest*, pp.171–4.

[54] Campbell, 'Some Twelfth-Century Views', p.214, describes it as 'perhaps the most remarkable piece of historical research of its day'.

[55] See *GR*, ii. 458–68.

and monasteries in the towns, both built in a style previously unknown.[56]

These comments come after William of Malmesbury's account of the battle, and their apparent even-handedness is at first sight reflected in his treatment of it. He had heard that the English had spent the previous night drinking and singing while the Normans were confessing their sins and receiving communion, and Harold he regards as a usurper; yet his prowess as a warrior is admired, as is the band of Englishmen, few in number but brave in the extreme, who fought and died for their country.[57] It is thought that he used texts of the *Anglo-Saxon Chronicle* D and E type,[58] and he says much that evidently came from William of Poitiers' *Gesta Guillelmi*, but he also had information from other sources, some of them probably oral, which have not survived: only he, for example, tells how Harold refused to share the booty from the battle of Stamford Bridge and was accordingly accompanied to Hastings mainly by professional soldiers, and how the Conqueror fell as he came ashore at Pevensey, to be reassured by one of his men that he was holding England, and would be king.[59] Hence, his comments about the battle are both visibly linked to those of other writers, and also independent of them in ways that matter. He may have had the statements of William of Poitiers (and perhaps also the *Chronicle* D text) in mind when he says that he disagrees with those who assert that the English army was large, thus diminishing their courage and bringing dishonour on the Normans, whom they intend to praise; for it is hardly a commendation that they conquered a people impeded by their numbers.[60] He also states that the English used a dense formation covered by shields (the shield-wall) and that this was broken by a feigned retreat on the part of the Normans, who turned upon the disordered ranks of their enemy. Knowledge of the

[56] GR, i. 456–61.

[57] Ibid., i. 454–7.

[58] ASC, ii. lxxxvi–vii. In earlier passages of GR he refers to chronicles in Old English more than once.

[59] GR, i. 422–3, 450–1.

[60] Ibid., i. 422–3.

latter probably came from William of Poitiers, but this source says nothing of the protective shields, and mentions two feigned flights following upon one real one, which Duke William managed to halt. Even after this, according to him, the English fought on doggedly, while William of Malmesbury seems to have thought that their flight, once begun, continued; it was during this retreat that, having occupied a hillock, they threw back the Normans into the valley below, destroying them by hurling spears and rolling down stones; also, they were able to avoid a deep ditch, but killed so many of their enemies there that the bodies made the hollow level with the surrounding ground. Of the hillock, William of Poitiers says nothing whatever, while differences of detail make it improbable that the ditch story owes very much to a similar tale placed at the end of the battle in the *Gesta Guillelmi*.[61] Similarly, William of Malmesbury's account of the duke's military prowess, and of the three horses which were killed beneath him, is shared with the earlier writer, while he added the information that Harold fought so effectively that he could destroy horse and rider with a single blow (possibly a detail drawn from a *chanson de geste*), and that as none could come near him he was eventually killed from a distance by an arrow.[62]

In short, not only is this a more detailed and ambitious account than that of John of Worcester's chronicle, it also has to be taken much more seriously. Yet despite William's qualities as a historian it cannot be accepted at face value. Thus, while he may well have had sources which have not come down to us, they need not have been particularly reliable. The tale about Duke William's fall as he came ashore, for example, is very like one which the Roman historian Suetonius tells of Julius Caesar,[63] and may have been taken from a source which (like William of Poitiers)[64] sought to flatter the duke by making the obvious comparison. It has also been pointed out

---

[61] On ditches at Hastings, see further, below, pp.207, 219-21, 233-4; there may have been more than one incident involving them.

[62] The suggestion on the *chanson* I owe to Dr John Hudson.

[63] *GR*, ii. 230; Suetonius, *Divus Iulius*, c. lix.

[64] Below, pp.97-9.

that William of Malmesbury is sometimes more critical of his sources when dealing with the distant past than when speaking of more recent history; in particular, he gives more credence to miracle stories than one can be at all comfortable with.[65] This is a reminder that he was not free of the constraints imposed by his religious beliefs, and raises the possibility that his account of the Conquest may have been both influenced and to a degree distorted by his desire to see it as the judgement of God on a sinful people, the kind of judgement natural to any churchman, and one which he would in any case have come across repeatedly in his perusal of Bede's *Ecclesiastical History*; it is one which he also expressed in his life of Bishop Wulfstan II of Worcester, who is said to have prophesied to King Harold himself that disaster would befall the country if it did not mend its evil ways.[66] William of Malmesbury's views were probably also shaped by the fact that, while he pays lip-service to the Normans, his heart lay with their opponents. This is very clear once one turns to other material in the *Gesta Regum*. For example, it reports a portent which allegedly appeared on the border between Brittany and Normandy – two women, one of a happy and the other of a sad disposition, who were joined together at the waist so that what they ate went into a single digestive tract. Eventually one died, and the other had to drag her corpse around until nearly three years later she died too. Some speculated that they represented England and Normandy, the demands of the latter being supported (in William of Malmesbury's day) by the wealth of the former, until perhaps she would eventually succumb to the violence of her rulers; the conquest was, he says, a calamity, which had resulted in the extinction of the ancient nobility and the ravages of taxation.[67]

---

[65] Campbell, 'Some Twelfth-Century Views', pp.222–3.

[66] WM, *Vita Wulfstani*, p.23. The wearing of long hair by men is one of the evils mentioned, it being evident that those who chose to imitate women in their appearance would prove ineffective in defence of their country; however, the bishop carried with him a little knife with which he trimmed the offending locks whenever possible. WP (*GG*, pp.178–81) says that the long-haired Englishmen taken by William to Normandy in 1067 yielded nothing to the beauty of girls.

[67] *GR*, i. 384–7.

In the light of this, one is entitled to ask if his treatment of 1066 is quite as impartial as it appears. Had he really received information about Harold's prowess in the battle, for example, or did he insert it himself to balance the material on Duke William's martial exploits?[68] Is it significant that he tells how the duke punished a soldier who slashed at the English king's thigh as he lay on the ground, but omits William of Poitiers' statement that the face of the corpse was so badly damaged as to be unrecognisable, or that William of Poitiers says the Conqueror refused to hand the corpse over to Harold's mother in return for its weight in gold while in the *Gesta Regum* it is handed over without ransom after a large sum had been offered?[69] Similarly, might there be a degree of nationalist bias in his insistence that the English army was small but fought with great bravery? If so, he could have found justification in sources which might seem to lend the idea credence. His account of 1066 clearly owes something to a text of the *Anglo-Saxon Chronicle* similar to E, which of course says that the English fought before all their forces had come, and may also have given rise to William's rather surprising statement that Harold took no military precautions before he knew of the threat from Norway.[70] One could certainly deduce this from E (which says nothing about the preparations to meet the Normans on the south coast) if one ignores its statement about the naval expedition against Duke William;[71] it may even be that William of Malmesbury's copies of the *Chronicle* did not contain this sentence. Yet this will not quite do, for both the D text and John of Worcester do describe Harold's preparations, and William's familiarity with their material at this point is suggested by the fact that, like them, he calls Harald of Norway Fairhair rather than Hardrada.[72] He would not have concurred with the favour John shows to Harold,

[68] As Thomson and Winterbottom suggest, *GR*, ii. 235.

[69] *GR*, i. 456–7, 460–1; *GG*, pp. 140–1.

[70] *GR*, i. 446–7.

[71] Above, p. 35.

[72] *GR*, i. 422–3; *ASC* D, i. 199; JW, ii. 602–3. So do other twelfth-century sources, see Plummer's comments, *ASC*, ii. 256. WM's reference to those who thought the English disorganised by their numbers may well be an allusion to *ASC* D, see above, p. 59.

but may have been influenced by his efforts to diminish the size of the army which fought at Hastings.[73] It looks as though William of Malmesbury, like other historians, sometimes took from his sources no more than the material which suited his own interpretation – that the war was a minor one because it was God's purpose that the English would never again fight in defence of their freedom.[74]

Not long after he began work on the *Gesta Regum*, his contemporary Henry of Huntingdon turned to a similar task. Like William, Henry may have been the product of a mixed marriage, being the son of Nicholas, archdeacon of Huntingdon, and an unknown Englishwoman.[75] He says that he did the work at the command of Alexander, who became bishop of Lincoln in 1123, and the first version of his *Historia Anglorum* (*History of the English*) ended with 1129; there were also a number of subsequent versions, the sixth and final one taking events down to 1154.[76] Although a secular cleric rather than a monk, he shared with William of Malmesbury and others the idea that the Conquest was God's judgement upon a sinful people. Indeed, the whole of his history is one with a 'serious and an almost despairing moral purpose',[77] in which all five invasions of Britain – by Romans, Picts and Scots, Anglo-Saxons, Danes and Normans – are viewed in this way.[78] But it had other purposes too. One was to act as a readily intelligible handbook to English history, an end which its author sought to achieve by carrying out a thorough reordering of the accounts of the early Anglo-Saxon period which he found in Bede and the *Anglo-Saxon Chronicle*;[79] another, subsidiary perhaps, but still important, was to entertain. Written in fairly simple Latin, the ten books of roughly equal length could each have been read at a single sitting, and contained

[73] Above, pp.63–4.
[74] *GR*, i. 422–3.
[75] *HA*, pp.xxiv–vi. The Englishness of Henry's mother his most recent editor deduces from his familiarity with the English language and the theme of the *HA*; there is no direct evidence.
[76] *HA*, pp.lxvi–lxxvii.
[77] Campbell, 'Some Twelfth-Century Views', p.213.
[78] *HA*, p.lix. See also on HH, Partner, *Serious Entertainments*, pp.11–50; Williams, *The English and the Norman Conquest*, pp.176–80.
[79] Campbell, 'Some Twelfth-Century Views', pp.212–3.

plenty of incident. His descriptions of battles, in particular, were couched in a poetic style (he was a 'not inconsiderable poet') and sometimes enlivened by rhetorical speeches of his own composition; one of these he eventually put into the mouth of Duke William before Hastings.[80]

As Henry of Huntingdon saw the Conquest as the wages of sin, it is hardly surprising that his treatment of the Godwin family is very unsympathetic. He comments on the savagery of the behaviour of Harold and Tostig, and illustrates this with a story of how they quarrelled at Windsor in 1063, and of how Tostig then went to Hereford, where Harold had prepared a banquet for King Edward, killed and dismembered his brother's servants, and placed their heads, arms and legs into the vessels which contained the drink.[81] His account of the events of 1066 begins with the death of King Edward and Harold's usurpation of the throne, ignoring the *Chronicle* E text's notice[82] of his designation by Edward and subsequent election. Then he turns to the reasons why Duke William decided to invade and describes William FitzOsbern tricking the other Norman magnates into agreeing to participate, and the assembly of a very large fleet at St Valéry. From here Henry follows the *Anglo-Saxon Chronicle* with minor additions down to the defeat of Harald Hardrada (he gives the story of the lone Norwegian hero who defended the river crossing at Stamford Bridge) and then moves swiftly to Hastings, where he says Harold drew up his lines in open country (*in planis Hastinges*) and William deployed five companies of horsemen against him. In the third version of the *Historia*, written *c.*1140,[83] he prefaced his account of the battle with a speech by Duke William which was supposedly so successful in incensing his men that they charged the enemy before he had finished. As the opposing forces came together, one Taillefer juggled with swords before the English and killed one of their standard-

[80] *HA*, pp.lviii–lx.

[81] *HA*, pp.382–3.

[82] For his use of texts of the C and E type, see *ASC*, ii. lv–lviii; *HA*, xci–iii.

[83] On the date, see *HA*, pp.lxx–i, and n.61.

bearers as they stood stupefied, repeated the trick, and was then killed himself. Next, clouds of arrows filled the air, but the English could not be broken by the enemy because Harold had formed his men into a single very dense formation, like a castle. William then ordered a feigned retreat, but as his men retired they came to a cunningly hidden and large ditch where a great many of them fell. As the pursuit continued, however, the Normans broke through the English centre, and the latter too then suffered heavy casualties as they recrossed the ditch, where the greater part of them died. Then the duke ordered his archers to shoot into the air so that the enemy might be blinded, and this too caused heavy casualties. As twenty of his strongest horsemen took a mutual oath that they would capture the royal banner known as the 'Standard', and did so despite losses, Harold was hit in the eye by an arrow, and then killed along with his brothers Gyrth and Leofwine when a mass of enemy cavalry broke through. Thus the English were defeated.[84]

Several significant features of this story, for example the feigned retreat and the deaths in a ditch, appear elsewhere, and it is important that Henry of Huntingdon's account cannot in fact be shown to have borrowed anything directly from any other written source that has survived. The documentary sources upon which he drew were much less extensive than those of William of Malmesbury,[85] and included neither the histories of William of Jumièges and William of Poitiers, the Latin *Carmen*, nor (probably) the Bayeux Tapestry.[86] The *Carmen* certainly mentions the juggler Taillefer[87] (by the Latin name *Incisor-ferri*) and gives an account of his exploits neither identical nor very dissimilar to Henry's, but it is likely that both were drawing on the same story or stories, and Henry's ability to give the name in the vernacular, and his use of the French word 'Standard', may mean that his Latin account of the battle drew on a *chanson* in French verse.[88]

---

[84] *HA*, pp.384–95.

[85] Upon them, see *HA*, pp.lxxxv–cvii.

[86] On the Tapestry, see below, pp.75–85.

[87] *Carmen*, ll. 389–404.

[88] For this argument and other uses of 'standard', see Greenway's comments, *HA*, pp.cvi–vii. The word also appears in the rather earlier Battle Abbey *Brevis Relatio*, below, p.113.

Shortly before 1140 another secular clerk, Geoffrey Gaimar, applied himself to a rather different process by turning the *Anglo-Saxon Chronicle* into French verse for Constance, the wife of Ralph FitzGilbert, an Anglo-Norman landowner in Lincolnshire. Gaimar's *L'Estoire des Engleis* is the earliest surviving history written in French,[89] and a powerful reminder that churchmen were not the only people interested in the past; for others, too, it provided both instruction and entertainment. The desire to entertain was never far from the minds of writers like William of Malmesbury and Henry of Huntingdon, and the extent of their success is demonstrated by the considerable number of manuscripts of their works which has survived, and by the works themselves, for their authors were men of wide interests and knew how to tell a good story. William, for example, does not stop at recounting how a Malmesbury monk named Æthelmær prophesied that the appearance of Halley's Comet in 1066 portended the downfall of his country, but adds some startling information about the exploits of the prophet's youth: hoping to fly like Daedalus, whose story he took to be true, he had fixed wings to his hands and feet, jumped off a tower and flown for some distance, before crashing to the ground and being crippled for life; he always regretted not having fitted a tail to his backside.[90] The twelfth century was not only a great age of historical writing, it was also a great age of story. At the request of the same Bishop Alexander of Lincoln who interested himself in Henry of Huntingdon, the Oxford cleric Geoffrey of Monmouth wrote a work on the prophecies of Merlin which became popular throughout Europe, and followed it up with his immensely influential and almost entirely fictional *Historia Regum Britanniae* (*History of the Kings of Britain*), of which the chief hero was King Arthur. A treatment of the *Historia* in French verse was quickly produced by Wace, and this was in turn paraphrased into English verse by Layamon; and by the latter's

---

[89] Campbell, 'Some Twelfth-Century Views', p.211.
[90] *GR*, i. 412–5.

time Chrétien de Troyes had already written of Guinevere, Lancelot and Percival, and of the Round Table.

Gaimar, too, began by composing for Constance a version of Geoffrey of Monmouth in French verse (it has not survived), and to this he later added *L'Estoire des Engleis*. The dividing line between history and fiction in such works might at times seem almost non-existent, and Gaimar's desire to entertain is very obvious, for the later sections of his work in particular are full of romance, but this should not obscure the fact that such writers could derive from popular songs and stories material which contained authentic elements,[91] and that Gaimar had heard tales about the events of 1066 there is little need to doubt. By this point[92] his debt to the *Anglo-Saxon Chronicle*, at least in the copies which survive today, is not very extensive, and his accuracy not always dissimilar: early in the year, for example, he wrongly has Queen Edith dying at the same time as King Edward, and he has nothing at all to say about Harold's accession to the throne. However, he does give details on Tostig's harrying of England and his subsequent operations with Harald Hardrada which are not in any other source. They are said to have had 460 ships[93] and to have found themselves opposed by the men of seven shires under the earls Edwin and Morcar, whom they defeated after great slaughter on both sides. Stamford Bridge he names *Punt de la bataille* ('the bridge of battle') and says that nobody could count a half of those left on the field. Then the French landed at Hastings with 11,000 ships,[94] and when Harold heard of it he gave to Bishop Ealdred (i.e. Archbishop Ealdred of York) the booty taken from the Norwegians and then spent five days summoning an army in the south, although he could obtain few troops because of his earlier losses; still, accompanied by his brothers Gyrth and Leofwine and their men he advanced into Sussex. Gaimar has surprisingly

---

[91] On the probable authenticity of some elements of Gaimar's treatment of the early eleventh century, see Lawson, *Cnut*, pp.77–9. The same point is true of Wace's *Roman de Rou*, upon which see below, pp.114–20.

[92] What follows is *L'Estoire des Engleis*, ed. Bell, ll. 5129–338.

[93] *L'Estoire*, l. 5200; two of the four surviving manuscripts give 470.

[94] *L'Estoire*, ll. 5242–3; one manuscript reads 9,000.

little to say about Hastings itself.[95] The story of Taillefer occupies the bulk of the lines which he originally devoted to it, although his version differs from that of Henry of Huntingdon. Here, Taillefer juggled with a lance, throwing it into the air three times and catching it by the head before hurling it into the English lines on the fourth occasion and wounding a soldier; then he juggled thrice with his sword before approaching the enemy lines again, cutting off the hand of one of their men and striking at another; but now he found that it was in an evil hour that he had asked for the first blow, for the English killed both him and his horse. Battle was then joined and lasted until the evening, but eventually the English had the worst of it and Harold and his brothers fell. Gaimar later inserted a section on the exploits of Alan (Rufus) of Brittany into his comments on the battle and mentioned that the Conqueror rewarded him with the fair castle of Richmond (Yorkshire),[96] but it looks as though he thought events in Sussex, like the character of King Harold, of less interest to his audience than the fighting in the north which had preceded them.

Having surveyed the most important written sources produced in England by authors of native or semi-native origin within a century of the battle, it is now time to turn to the Bayeux Tapestry. Not in fact a tapestry at all, but a series of eight conjoined linen strips of various lengths (the first two being much more extensive than the rest) embroidered with wools of eight different colours, it is today about 68.38 metres long and of a height which varies between 45.7 and 53.6 cm.[97] It was once longer, as it breaks off at what is easily assumed to be the end of its depiction of the battle of Hastings, and even what remains was heavily restored in the nineteenth century and probably at earlier dates too. Certainly, it is easy to be unaware how much of the Tapestry's existing stitchwork is not original, and

---

[95] Gaimar's account of the battle is discussed by Eley and Bennett, 'The Battle of Hastings', 47–54, who think it 'anti-Norman' and 'an anglocentric epic of Harold'.

[96] *L'Estoire*, ll. 5309–26; see Bell's note on this section, p.267.

[97] *BT*, pp.10–11; *B&W*, 2, suggest that 1.35 to 3 metres have been lost from the eighth strip, which need not have been originally the final one. The Tapestry's length varies, of course, according to the amount of tension it is under.

an edition which addresses these problems is greatly to be desired; there was a time, for example, when it seems to have been the custom of those who displayed the work to visitors to allow them to remove small pieces as souvenirs, a number disappearing in this way and eventually having to be made good.[98] Thus, there are points where the accuracy of the restorations and the status of some of the accompanying inscriptions become matters of the greatest importance and it is necessary to turn to early drawings and to reproductions published in the eighteenth and early nineteenth centuries, although even they do not always represent the original state of affairs; in this respect the Tapestry is a much less straightforward source than is often assumed.[99] How much further it took the story of the conquest there is no way of knowing, but the common belief that it originally ended with William's coronation in December 1066 seems plausible enough. Although not recorded before 1476, most commentators accept that it was made for (or at least in the circle of) Bishop Odo of Bayeux, the Conqueror's half-brother, within about fifteen years of the battle (Odo was imprisoned by William, for reasons which are not known, in 1082) and that it was made in England and almost certainly in Kent, of which he had become earl.[100] Three of his tenants in the shire – Wadard, Vital and Turold – are shown and

[98] Dr David Hill, paper given to the Manchester Conference on Harold II and the Bayeux Tapestry, April 2002. I am grateful to David Hill and John McSween for allowing me to see a draft of their forthcoming *The Bayeux Tapestry*, and for much illuminating discussion.

[99] On this, the earliest drawings and the engravings published in 1729–30 and 1733, see the Appendix. Charles Stothard's hand-coloured version for the Society of Antiquaries was published in 1819, and hand-coloured engravings based on Victor Sansonetti's work, and limited to 100 copies, in 1838. B&W, 25, say that the pen and ink and watercolour drawing now in the possession of Mount Holyoke College in Massachusetts was made prior to nineteenth-century restoration, but Brown, *The Bayeux Tapestry*, p.155, simply dates it to that period and thinks it probably based on Stothard or Sansonetti; Hill and McSween have evidence that both it and Sansonetti derived from Stothard.

[100] On the Tapestry's provenance, see Wormald, 'Style and Design', pp.29–34; B&W, 8–18; Bernstein, pp.37–50 (with good reproductions of manuscript illuminations whose similarity to Tapestry scenes suggests a Canterbury origin). However, all acknowledge that manufacture in Normandy is a possibility, and the Norman case is argued by Grape, *The Bayeux Tapestry*, pp.44–65; for persuasive criticisms of his position, see Gameson, 'The Origin, Art, and Message of the Bayeux Tapestry', pp.162–74. Although I refer to the designer as male, this should not be taken to exclude the possibility that the work was done by a woman.

named within it,[101] in addition to the prominent role played by Odo himself, and this is strong evidence that its audience included the kind of men who had fought in the battle, almost certainly (because of the expense involved in acquiring the necessary equipment) in chain-mail and on horseback. It is thus hardly surprising that war is one of its prime concerns, or that Hastings occupies more than a quarter of its surviving length.[102] Another central theme is Harold's oath and its breaking (the work begins with his visit to Normandy), and this too would have been of great interest to men whose lives were to a large extent defined by the obligation of loyalty to their lord.[103] Some of the Tapestry's audience was also expected to be familar with fables of the type associated with Aesop.[104]

Like most pictorial sources, the Tapestry is much better at showing what things looked like than at recording events in any detail, and if it were the only material to have survived on the Conquest historians would be hard put to make much of it. Nevertheless, it does tell a story, accompanied by a sparse commentary in Latin, and that story begins with Harold's visit to the continent, his seizure by Count Guy of Ponthieu, release by William and arrival in the ducal palace. From there he joins the Normans on a campaign against the Bretons, on the way distinguishing himself by rescuing fellow soldiers from quicksand as they cross the river Couesnon; the expedition then proceeds to Dol, from which its quarry Count Conan flees, and then to Dinan, where he is obliged to surrender. After

---

[101] B&W, 8 and n.22. Wilson (*BT*, p.176) thinks Turold (see illus. 7) may be the dwarf holding the horses rather than one of the messengers sent by Duke William to Guy of Ponthieu in 1064, and is attracted by the idea that he 'is the artist of the Tapestry'; see also *EHD2*, p.257. The 'dwarf', however, may be an attempt at some kind of perspective.

[102] The extent to which war dominates the subject matter of the Tapestry is stressed by, among others, Gameson, 'The Origin', p.207.

[103] Dodwell, 'The Bayeux Tapestry and the French Secular Epic', pp.52–9, noted the prominence of themes of loyalty and disloyalty in the later French secular *chansons de geste*.

[104] The significance of these scenes, which appear in the borders and whose concern with deceit is probably linked to Harold's oath, has never been established with any precision; see, for example, Cowdrey, 'Towards an Interpretation of the Bayeux Tapestry', pp.99–100; Bernstein, pp.128–35; Gameson, 'The Origin', pp.159–60 and n.11; Lewis, *The Rhetoric of Power in the Bayeux Tapestry*, pp.59–73; Albu, *The Normans and their Histories*, pp.91–105.

this we are shown William bestowing arms upon Harold as an indication that he has become the duke's man, the taking of the oath and Harold's return to England and appearance before King Edward. There follows the king's burial and death (with a deathbed scene which suggests that Harold was there granted the throne),[105] his coronation and the appearance of Halley's Comet. At this point the scene shifts to Normandy, where William orders the building of ships; arms and provisions are carried down to them and they cross the Channel to Pevensey, the landing being followed by the plundering of the surrounding district for food, which Bishop Odo duly blesses as they sit at table. A castle is built at Hastings, the approach of Harold is announced, and the French cavalry are shown leaving for the battle; on both sides scouts report the arrival of the enemy, and after the duke has exhorted his men to prepare themselves (the only example of reported speech in the entire work)[106] a long line of horsemen, broken only by four archers, attacks the English shield-wall from left and right. At this point the battle (or to be more precise, the bodies of the dead) overflows into the lower border. The deaths of Harold's brothers Gyrth and Leofwine follow, French horses are in great difficulties near a watercourse, and fighting takes place around a hillock, the legend at this point informing us that *Hic ceciderunt simul Angli et Franci in prelio* ('Here the English and French fell at the same time in the battle'). It seems reasonable to assume that French losses were by this stage serious, as Bishop Odo comforts the boys and Duke William removes his helmet, apparently to show that he is still alive. From here, and for no obvious reason in terms of the outcome of the fighting so far depicted, the battle moves to its close; the lower border is now occupied by French archers, while further attacks by the horsemen result in the death of Harold and the flight of the remnants of his army; as he is killed, men in the lower border are already stripping the dead of their armour.

---

[105] Above, p.33.
[106] Bernstein, p.258.

A summary such as this does scant justice to the power, artistry and everlasting fascination of many of the Tapestry's scenes, but as a record of a battle which lasted many hours and involved thousands and perhaps tens of thousands of men on each side it is inevitably somewhat lacking. The limitations of the medium would have made it very difficult for it to give much indication of strategy, tactics and the reasons for the French victory, even if this had been the designer's purpose, which it almost certainly was not. Thus, it is hardly surprising that there is no sign of the French retreat and English pursuit which feature so prominently in some of the written sources.[107] What its patrons required was a decorative hanging which would justify the Conquest and show them in their hour of glory. It is fair to assume that they would have expected a degree of accuracy in terms of what soldiers looked like and the ways in which individuals fought, and there is little reason to suppose that they were disappointed in these respects.[108] It has been suggested that one of the Tapestry's 'most remarkable mistakes' is the depiction of the wearing of trousered mail by both sides when the French horsemen in fact used skirted mail, and that it is therefore 'a more dependable source for the armour and weapons of the English than of the Normans'.[109] This may be so, but it is not the area in which the work is at its most misleading. A more serious limitation, and one which arose inevitably from the nature and interests of the aristocratic audience for which it was made, is the impression that Hastings was won by French horsemen with the assistance of archers, most of whom are relegated to the lower border, where they do not impinge too

---

[107] But see below, p.223, n.63.

[108] See Mann, 'Arms and Armour', and his comment (p.57) that 'One has confidence in the accuracy of the military scenes by comparing the obvious naturalness of other scenes that are familiar to us today, such as those of hawking, hunting...'. Even so, the Tapestry cannot be trusted implicitly: it is likely to be inaccurate, for example, in suggesting (illus. 12) that French horses crossed the Channel in vessels of such shallow draught that they could simply step over the gunwale on landing; see Bachrach, 'On the Origins of William the Conqueror's Horse Transports', 506–9.

[109] B&W, 19–20. Peirce, 'Arms, Armour and Warfare in the Eleventh Century', 238, suggests that the Tapestry's apparent French mail leggings simply depict the way in which skirted mail clung to the legs and thighs. No surviving coat of mail of the eleventh or twelfth centuries is currently known, but Peirce estimates the likely weight as 11.4 kg (25 lb); see ibid., 237–40.

much on the stirring depictions of military prowess in the register above. Only near the beginning of the conflict is an exceptionally long line of cavalry broken up by the figures of the only archers to appear in the main register (illus. 17), and the individual wearing mail is also one of the only two armoured French infantrymen shown in the entire battle, the second being engaged in decapitating an unarmed Englishman shortly before the death of Harold.[110] That this cannot possibly be an accurate reflection of the composition of William's forces is confirmed by William of Poitiers, who speaks of the duke's men advancing in three lines, the first and third being missile troops and squadrons of horsemen, and the second being heavy infantry.[111] The role of such infantry in the battle may well have been a significant one, but it was ignored by the Tapestry designer in exactly the same way that he had earlier given the impression that cavalry had been important in the assault on Dinan during the campaign in Brittany (illus. 9); but few castles ever surrendered as a result of horsemen charging their walls (which is what the onlooker is encouraged to believe), as is tacitly acknowledged by the depiction of the two dismounted figures who are setting fire to the defences. Similarly, it may be unwise to assign too great a significance to scenes in the Tapestry's account of Hastings in which individual French horsemen are engaging armoured and isolated English infantrymen (illus. 19), for these may have been elements precisely tailored to the requirements of the piece's patrons;

[110] This is the figure used by Bernstein (pp. 166–78) to argue that the Tapestry designer incorporated the idea that the Norman conquest of England was comparable with the Babylonian conquest of the Judah of the Old Testament king Zedekiah, who like Harold violated an oath of fealty to his overlord and was eventually blinded (in Harold's case by an arrow); prior to his blinding, Zedekiah was obliged to witness the killing of his two sons, and Bernstein suggests that the figure being decapitated in the main register, and the one in the border below who has already had his head struck off, are an allusion to this. His thesis is weakened by the probability that the Tapestry did not originally show Harold as struck by an arrow (see the Appendix, below), but it is not impossible that its audience were even so expected to be familiar with this event, and it is worth noting the similar parallel drawn between the Conqueror and the biblical Jephthah (like the duke a bastard) in Fulcoius of Beauvais' poem *Jephthah* of *c*.1075; on *Jephthah*, see *TNE*, pp. 132–3, and van Houts, 'Latin poetry', 42. In counting the number of archers in the main register I have omitted the apparent horse archer in the much restored final scene.
[111] *GG*, pp. 126–7; see further below, pp. 212–5.

the accuracy of the depictions of cavalry charging the English shield-wall and what look like light infantry on the hillock (one of whom is being transfixed by a spear-thrust delivered by a trooper with his spear couched beneath his arm, see illus. 20) may well also be suspect, especially in the case of the latter, as an eminence covered in some kind of vegetation is not the most obvious ground for cavalry.

Yet even had their desire to see their own role in the battle celebrated to the exclusion of almost everybody else not imposed limitations on the Tapestry designer, the constraints of the medium in which he was working would probably have pushed him in a similar direction. If French armoured and unarmoured infantry had been depicted in any numbers, for example, it would have been difficult to distinguish them from English troops of the same type without making the battle scenes much more complex than they actually are. The same argument may also work in reverse. Only one English archer (illus. 18) is shown compared with his many French counterparts, but it would be dangerous to contend on these grounds alone that there were fewer English missile troops present, when the designer may have been simplifying life (as well as pandering to the social prejudices of his patrons) by omitting them. Still, arguments such as these emphasise only that his work must be used with great care, not that it has nothing to offer. Far from it. None of the written sources can equal it in giving a visual impression of what certain aspects of the fighting were like, for this was something with which they assumed their audience to be broadly familiar; none describe the wielding of the great English battle axe, much less give the sort of impression of its fearsome destructive power that can easily be derived from the embroidered image, or show the shield-wall (illus. 18) which the armies of the Anglo-Saxon state employed time out of mind, and this last time. In these senses the Tapestry brings us closer to what happened that day than any other source ever can. More prosaically, it is also important, as will become obvious when discussing the deployment of Harold's forces,[112] in showing fighting

---

[112] Below, pp. 149–54.

around the watercourse and the hillock, for no surviving source earlier than William of Malmesbury says anything of the latter, while it will eventually be necessary to consider whether the watercourse has any connection with the ditches and deaths therein of which so much has already been said, and has still to be said.

The Tapestry is a unique survival from the eleventh century, but was probably far from unique in its own day.[113] When it surfaces in the historical record during the fifteenth century it was being hung around the nave of Bayeux cathedral to celebrate the annual Feast of Relics, and as it locates Harold's oath (on relics) at Bayeux it can be argued that Odo commissioned it for his cathedral church. This may be so, but nor is it impossible, as has often been said, that it was originally intended for a secular dwelling in England, and found its way across the Channel at a later stage. Indeed, the prominence it gives to three of Odo's tenants in England rather points this way, for it is easier to see why a hanging exhibited in, say Canterbury, might have included them than to understand why a Bayeux audience should have had its attention drawn to these particular men rather than anybody else. Moreover, as a secular hanging it would fit into a known historical context. Depictions of famous events, in various media, already had a long history by the late eleventh century: sculptured reliefs from ancient Mesopotamia can be set beside Trajan's Column (an account of the Roman emperor Trajan's conquest of Dacia in the early second century AD) and the paintings of biblical and classical scenes, together with Charlemagne's conquest of the (continental) Saxons, which graced the walls of the Carolingian palace at Ingelheim; similarly, decorations in his palace at Magdeburg celebrated the German Henry the Fowler's victory over the Magyars in 934. Moreover, there is from the Anglo-Saxon period a great deal of documentation which witnesses the importance of textiles, some of them worked in gold and ornamented with jewels, and of great worth.[114]

[113] A point made by B&W, 26.

[114] See the immensely informative material in Dodwell, *Anglo-Saxon Art*, pp. 129–69, 174–87. The only surviving examples of Anglo-Saxon embroidery in gold and silk are those of *c*.800 now in Maaseik (Belgium) and the tenth-century ecclesiastical vestments found in the tomb of St Cuthbert in Durham cathedral; small but potent reminders of what has been lost.

Ironically, the sight of Harold's banner of the Fighting Man, woven in the purest gold, would have served to remind the French troops who faced it of the riches of the country they were attempting to conquer, and thus of the fruits of victory. The English made great use of decorative hangings both in churches and in their homes, as is revealed by Wills which survive from the tenth and eleventh centuries. At some point between 984 and 1016, for example, a lady named Wulfwaru bequeathed to the monastery of Bath 'a set of bed-clothing with tapestry and curtain', to her son Wulfmær 'a hall-tapestry', and to her second son Ælfwine 'a tapestry for a hall and tapestry for a chamber'.[115] The sources say much more about the existence of such works than of the decorations which they bore, but there is an important reference in the twelfth-century chronicle of the abbey of Ely (here probably based on documents of the late tenth century) to a piece which they received from the widow of Ealdorman Byrhtnoth, who was killed in battle against the Vikings at Maldon in 991. Just after his death, she gave them, in addition to a gold torque and various estates, a hanging which showed the deeds of her husband. If these deeds did not include feats of arms it would be very surprising, and it looks therefore as though the piece was similar to the Bayeux Tapestry and the decorations of the continental palaces at Ingelheim and Magdeburg in being intended to celebrate the achievements of its patron at the same time as it decorated his living quarters.[116]

[115] *EHD1*, No. 116; cited with other examples, Dodwell, *Anglo-Saxon Art*, p.132.

[116] *et cortinam gestis viri sui intextam atque depictam in memoriam probatis eius, Liber Eliensis,* ed. Blake, p.136; see Dodwell, *Anglo-Saxon Art*, pp.134–6, and the detailed and valuable treatment by Budny, 'The Byrhtnoth Tapestry or Embroidery', who discusses the various possibilities raised by the words *intextam atque depictam,* and questions whether the item had necessarily hung in Byrhtnoth's home. More complex explanations of the Bayeux Tapestry's purpose have sometimes been advanced: for example, Brown, 'The Bayeux Tapestry: Why Eustace, Odo and William?', argues that, at the time of his disgrace in 1082, Odo had it made for the Conqueror to remind him of past services; Lewis, *The Rhetoric of Power*, thinks he created it as a portable propaganda piece to justify his importance in England after 1066 and the introduction of Norman feudalism. Few possibilities can be discounted altogether, but such explanations seem to me to strain credibility. Lewis (p.11) is also one of several recent authors (notably, Brilliant, 'The Bayeux Tapestry: A Stripped Narrative for their Eyes and Ears') who believe that the scenes and Latin inscriptions were used as the basis of an oral performance by an interlocutor. They do not, however, cite other evidence of the use of European decorative wall-hangings in this way.

Another reference to what may have been 'a continuing tradition of heroic hangings in England', even if in a slightly different context, is to be found in the contemporary *Life of King Edward* when it describes a ship given to the Confessor by Earl Godwin which had a sail worked in gold and depicting the sea battles of noble kings.[117] It is almost certain that one reason for the survival of the Bayeux Tapestry is precisely the fact that it was not worked in gold, and therefore was much less likely to be destroyed in later times by those covetous of precious metal, and that its use of wool would have meant that it was regarded by many Anglo-Saxons not as 'a triumphal monument unequalled in the West since the fall of the Roman Empire', but on the contrary as 'quite ordinary'.[118] It is surely significant that when the poet Baudri of Bourgeuil imagined a hanging depicting the Conquest in the chamber of the Conqueror's daughter Adela he said that it was of golden, silver and silken thread, and embellished with gems and pearls, and that William of Poitiers stresses the skill of Englishwomen in the weaving of gold thread.[119] It may well be that Bishop Odo would have required something equally lavish in any commission of this type, and that the surviving Tapestry was in fact made for one of his followers who settled in Kent.[120] Moreover, if it was at the time a rather less remarkable work than it seems today, and produced in a world where textiles which showed heroic events were by no means uncommon, this raises the possibility that it was far from being the only such depiction of the Conquest to come into existence in the years following 1066. Given the resources of England's

---

[117] Dodwell, *Anglo-Saxon Art*, pp.136–7, citing *LKE*, pp.20–1.

[118] Bernstein, p.36; Dodwell, *Anglo-Saxon Art*, p.139.

[119] Baudri, *AC*, ll. 211–2, 229–30; WP, *GG*, pp.176–7; Dodwell, *Anglo-Saxon Art*, p.139. Tilliette, 'La chambre de la comtesse Adèle', 147–9, doubts whether Adela's rooms could possibly have been as lavishly furnished as Baudri imagined. The poet Serlo of Bayeux commented on the beautiful decoration of Odo's court, van Houts, 'Latin poetry', 45; on Baudri, see further below, pp.105–9.

[120] B&W, 18, claim that nothing 'suggests that Turold, Wadard and Vital were such important lords that they could commission so magnificent and vast a work', but this begs several questions, not least the fact that as the agency which actually produced the Tapestry is unknown (a workshop staffed by female slaves, perhaps?) there is no way of balancing its cost against the resources of men who may have profited greatly from the Conquest.

new French masters, and their probable pride in their exploits, it is not unreasonable to suggest that there may have been many such items. In any case, it would obviously be dangerous to make too much of apparent similarities between the version of events given by the one which happens to have survived and those of the written sources which happen to have survived. Duke William's use of missile troops and removal of his helmet at a critical juncture appear in two of the earliest French sources (the *Carmen de Hastingae Proelio* and William of Poitiers' *Gesta Guillelmi*), but they say nothing of fighting around the Tapestry's hillock and watercourse, although the Tapestry does share what may well be the same information with other, later writers. The Tapestry's designer may in fact have drawn on a wide range of sources, many of them probably oral, before going about his work. In dealing with the evidence which has actually come down to us it is sometimes too easy to forget the very much larger body of information which existed in the decades following the battle, was available to those who created the small corpus which has survived, and has since disappeared forever. Moreover, this is a point which is just as important in dealing with the French material as when considering that from England.

3

THE SOURCES: PART TWO

The sources which probably or certainly originated in France within twenty years of the battle are much more voluminous than those written in England, but also present considerably greater problems. The earliest may well be that known as the *Carmen de Hastingae Proelio* (*Song of the Battle of Hastings*), attributed to Guy, bishop of Amiens, who was a member of the ruling house of Ponthieu, being the brother of Count Hugh II and uncle of Guy I, and related to the French royal family and the counts of Boulogne.[1] Around 1125, Orderic Vitalis stated that Guy was the author of a poem in the style of Virgil and Statius which described the battle of Senlac, condemning Harold and praising William, and that by the spring of 1068, when he was the most eminent of the churchmen to visit England in the entourage of William's queen Matilda, it had already been composed.[2] Whether Orderic had himself seen the poem is not certain, and although William of Poitiers, too, may have been familar with it,[3] the *Carmen* seems to have been little known

---

[1] On what is known of Guy, see Barlow's comments, *Carmen*, pp.xlii–liii.
[2] *HÆ*, ii. 184–7, 214–5.
[3] Below, pp.102–4.

in general, and long remained so. Only in 1826 were two twelfth-century manuscripts (the second a copy of the first) discovered in the Royal Library in Brussels and identified as Guy's work, partly because of the content matter and partly in the belief that the *L.W. salutat* of the second line can be extended and translated as 'Guy (Wido) salutes Lanfranc' (Lanfranc was abbot of Duke William's monastery of St Stephen at Caen, and from 1070 archbishop of Canterbury).

If it is really Guy's poem, the *Carmen* is one of the most detailed contemporary sources available on the battle of Hastings. After a short prologue, it opens by comparing the Conqueror to Julius Caesar and recording how contrary winds hindered his crossing of the Channel. For a fortnight he waited at St Valéry, at the mouth of the river Somme, before setting sail and landing in England about 9 o'clock in the morning. Once there, he built a fortification to pro-tect his ships and his men ravaged the surrounding countryside. When Harold heard of this he was returning, laden with booty, from the defeat of his brother; he made a speech to his magnates and they agreed to fight the invaders, but first a monk was sent to the duke's camp to ask him to leave. During the resultant conversa-tion William referred to the earlier agreements he had made with Harold, including the oath, and offered him the lands his father had held if he agreed to be his vassal; then he sent an envoy to Harold who summarised the grounds upon which he claimed the English throne and urged him not to go back on his oaths. This was scorn-fully rejected, and as his ambassador returned with the news that 500 English ships had been dispatched to obstruct his passage home, the duke deployed his troops for battle, having frustrated by his watchfulness Harold's plan to attack him during the night.

In his front rank were archers and crossbowmen, and although he had intended placing cavalry behind the infantry the onset of the conflict forbade this. The English poured forth from the forest to their rear and in a dense formation and on foot, as was their cus-tom, occupied a nearby hill (*mons*) and valley (*vallis*) and land not cultivated because of its roughness. Harold planted his standard on the crest of the hill and strengthened his flanks with noble men, while William, who commanded a better regulated line (*moderantius agmen*), climbed the steep slope. His missile troops opened the battle with arrows and crossbow quarrels and the infantry (*galeati* – literally, 'helmeted men') crashed shields against shields. Meanwhile,[4] a juggler on horseback named Taillefer (*Incisor-ferri*) threw his sword into the air in front of the French lines, killed an Englishman who dashed forward to meet him, decapitated the corpse and displayed the head to his advancing comrades, who rejoiced that the first blow was theirs and called upon the Lord.[5] Then the archers and crossbowmen opened fire[6] and the French attacked the English left, the Normans the centre and the Bretons the right.[7] However, the English were in a very dense formation in which the bodies of the dead could not fall, and which could only be overcome by the military skill of William's men. The French[8] pretended to flee and were pursued by the English, whereupon the duke's left and right wings turned upon the pursuers, as did also those who had simulated flight. Many of the English – 10,000 is the number given – were killed at this stage of the battle, but the rest fought on, and used their superiority in numbers to force the Normans into a real flight. At this point Duke William took off his helmet and made a speech to his men stressing that the way to survive was not by running away but by conquering; they rallied, and their leader then killed Harold's brother Gyrth, who had unhorsed him with a spear cast, and many others, including the 'son of Helloc', who had brought down a second horse acquired from one of the duke's fellow soldiers by force. Count Eustace of Boulogne then gave him a third mount, and together they cleared the field of the English.

[4] Guy's account of the battle is not always very coherent, and although he describes the incident which follows after the beginning of the fighting he apparently thought that it preceded it.

[5] This may be a reference to the Norman battle-cry *Dex aïe*, 'May God help', as suggested by M&M, p.27, n.2.

[6] A repetition of the information given before the Taillefer story.

[7] This is the most probable meaning of ll. 413–14; but it is not impossible that Guy intended to indicate that the French were on the left and the Bretons on the right; see *Carmen*, p.lxxix, n.266, and below, p.209, n.26.

[8] Barlow, *Carmen*, p.27, n.4, suggests that Guy means by this the Normans in the centre.

The French were already seeking the spoils of war (i.e. stripping the dead) when Harold was seen on the crest of the ridge repelling all who assailed him, and William and Eustace, accompanied by Hugh, the noble heir of Ponthieu, and one Gilfard (known by his father's surname) attacked and slew him: the first speared his chest through his shield, the second decapitated him with his sword, the third spilt his entrails with a spear thrust and the fourth hewed off his thigh.[9] Upon the news of Harold's death all English resistance collapsed, and some fled while others asked for quarter, as evening was falling, in a place where the duke had killed 2,000 and innumerable other thousands. He spent the night on the battlefield while Hugh of Ponthieu pursued the fugitives, and the following day buried his dead while leaving the English strewn on the field as carrion; Harold's corpse he ordered to be interred on the seashore, having refused the request of the king's mother that it be handed over to her, if necessary in exchange for its weight in pure gold.[10] The author of the *Carmen* does not conclude his account with the end of the battle, but follows William to Dover, to London, and finally (in the surviving texts) to the coronation on Christmas Day.[11]

Yet was he really Bishop Guy of Amiens, and if so how reliable is his work? Ever since the discovery of the manuscript there have been doubts whether the poem is truly that which Orderic Vitalis attributes to Guy, and these found their fullest expression in an article published by R.H.C. Davis in 1979. Despite the fact that its

[9] There has been much discussion of this difficult passage, in which 'it is not easy to sort out the four individuals among a welter of epithets in an unpunctuated text'; see M&M, pp.116–20; Davis, 'The *Carmen de Hastingae Proelio*', pp.86–8; and Barlow's comments, *Carmen*, pp.xxxv, lxxxii–v. I follow Barlow, who thinks that the 'better-supported of the interpretations' makes the four: Duke William, Count Eustace, Hugh of Ponthieu (younger brother of Count Guy I and nephew of Guy of Amiens) and perhaps the French baron Robert son of Giffard, who witnesses charters in England after 1066; on the third and fourth, see the important work of van Houts, 'Latin poetry and the Anglo-Norman court', 54–5. An alternative quartet (favoured by Davis) omits the duke and comprises Count Eustace, the (in this interpretation, unnamed) noble heir of Ponthieu and the Norman barons Hugh II of Montfort-sur-Risle and Walter I Giffard, who both fought at Hastings according to WP, GG, pp.134–5.

[10] On this element of the *Carmen*, which seems to reflect knowledge of the *Iliad*, see below, p.104.

[11] Like the Bayeux Tapestry, they break off incomplete, but the coronation seems a likely ending, *Carmen*, p.xc.

author addresses King William in the present tense, thereby implying that he was still alive at the time of its composition, Davis
argued that it contains elements which are not acceptable in a text
supposedly written shortly after 1066, that it is actually 'a literary
exercise' composed 'in one of the schools of northern France or
southern Flanders' probably between *c*.1125 and 1140, and that 'as a
source for the history of the Norman Conquest it is simply ridiculous'.[12] Such views have not unnaturally tended to inhibit historians' use of the *Carmen*, but cannot be said to have carried the day.
Ten years after they appeared Dr van Houts surveyed the considerable body of surviving Latin poetry addressed to William I and his
children and commented that:

> If Professor Davis is right in his conclusion that the *Carmen* is a
> school product written fifty to seventy years after 1066 it would be
> the only surviving poem of the period to pretend to an authentic-
> ity which it did not possess. On the basis of my survey I find this
> extremely difficult, if not impossible, to accept.[13]

Beyond this, Davis cannot be said to have provided any really convincing reason for assigning the poem to the period he suggested,
and some of his argumentation seems flawed. He referred, for
example, to the description of the death of Harold as 'the most
improbable scene in the whole poem' and judged it, like the story
of Taillefer, to be 'legendary'.[14] The difficulty here is that not all
material which might look legendary can be assigned to a late date
on that basis alone. It is possible, as can be widely illustrated (one
need only think of some of the wild rumours which swept Britain

[12] Davis, 'The *Carmen de Hastingae Proelio*', espec. pp.98–9.

[13] Van Houts, 'Latin poetry', 53. By 'authenticity' van Houts means the poem's appearance of
contemporaneity in addressing William as still alive; if the *W* of *L. W. salutat* in the second line
does not refer to Guy (*Wido*) the text gives no reason to suppose that it must be the work
which Orderic attributed to Guy of Amiens.

[14] Davis, 'The *Carmen de Hastingae Proelio*', pp.86–8; Brown, 'The Battle of Hastings', 18,
thought that 'the whole improbable incident recorded by the *Carmen* goes far to condemn that
source itself'.

during the First World War) and as some commentators on the *Carmen* have stressed,[15] for inaccurate reports to circulate very soon after the event to which they relate, and the fact that the *Carmen* contains statements which can only be paralleled in (surviving) sources of the twelfth century does little to indicate that it must itself be of that date. The case for Guy's authorship of the poem has been restated in the recent edition by Professor Barlow,[16] and can be accepted in the absence of strong arguments to the contrary, even though it is not watertight, and the reasons why the piece was written are far from clear.[17] However, if it is true that Guy accompanied William's queen to England in 1068, his relations with the Conqueror's family were clearly close, and there is little difficulty in believing that reasons there were, even if they cannot now be identified.

As to his reliability, this cannot of course be taken for granted. Dr van Houts, who thinks that the *Carmen* was composed in 1067, has suggested that Guy obtained some of his information from his secular lord Ralph, count of Amiens, whom he met at the French royal court in the middle of 1067, and who had himself been present at the Conqueror's Easter court at Fécamp in April, where English hostages and the spoils of war had been on display, doubtless accompanied by a great deal of talk. Dr van Houts has also noted that Guy knew three of the four men who are said to have killed Harold – Eustace of Boulogne, Robert son of Gilfard and Hugh of Ponthieu (his own nephew) and that he met Robert in August 1067 when they both witnessed a French royal charter.[18] It is not surprising, of course, that he should assign a major role in the battle to his nephew Hugh, and given his likely sources of information that the only Norman he mentions by name is Duke William himself.[19] As a

---

[15] Engels, 'Once more: the *Carmen de Hastingae Proelio*', 9–10; and Chibnall's contribution to the discussion which followed this paper at Battle in 1979, 20; Orlandi, 'Some Afterthoughts on the *Carmen de Hastingae Proelio*', 117, n.2; Barlow, *Carmen*, p.xxxv.

[16] *Carmen*, pp.xxiv–xl; supported by David Bates' review, *EHR*, cxvi (2001), 173–4.

[17] *Carmen*, pp.xli–ii; van Houts, 'Latin poetry', 56, suggests that it was addressed to Lanfranc so that he could use his influence with the papacy on Guy's behalf.

[18] Van Houts, 'Latin poetry', 54–5. Presumably Guy also knew Duke William.

[19] This assumes that the third and fourth alleged slayers of Harold have been correctly identified in p.90, n.9 above.

poet producing a piece of entertainment he may well have felt free to write what we would regard as fiction,[20] and certainly his description of the crown which William had made for himself and of the coronation ceremony which followed have been regarded as 'obviously imaginary' and 'simply made... up'.[21] On the other hand, the insertion of fictional elements cannot be taken as indicating that he knew nothing about the battle at all,[22] and there is in any case adequate evidence to the contrary. Guy's description of the hill and valley occupied by the English army and of the roughness of the ground, as of the forest which lay to the rear, are near enough to the truth to suggest that they are not of his own invention, and so very probably is his description of the breaking of their line by a French retreat, unless one were to adopt the scarcely tenable position that all the later sources which mention this feature of the battle have taken it at one or more removes from his poem. Even all the elements of his account of the death of Harold cannot be rejected with complete confidence.[23] The *Carmen* may not have been written for modern historians,[24] but it is a detailed and almost contemporary source which probably owes something to eye-witness accounts, and despite all its attendant problems it cannot be ignored.

Whether or not the date of 1067 for the composition of the *Carmen* is accepted, it cannot be assigned to one later than Guy's death in 1074 or 1075. By then another surviving French account of the battle, that of the Norman monk William of Jumièges, was also in existence. William is thought to have written most of his *Gesta Normannorum Ducum* (*Deeds of the Norman Dukes*), which in its early books draws heavily on an earlier work by Dudo of St Quentin, in the 1050s, and to have subsequently added a section on the Conquest; as this ends with the Conqueror's operations late in 1069 it may have been completed early the following

---

[20] Engels, 'Once more', 9, comments that 'the margin for fiction is... much larger in poetry than in prose'.

[21] Barlow, in *Carmen*, pp.xxxvi–vii.

[22] Another point made by Engels, 'Once more', 10.

[23] Below, pp.225, 230-1.

[24] Van Houts, 'Latin poetry', 56.

year.[25] Despite the fact that King William, to whom the *Gesta* is dedicated, attended the consecration of the new church of St Mary at Jumièges in July 1067,[26] its concluding section is rather brief, and it is difficult to avoid the conclusion that William of Jumièges must have heard far more about the Hastings campaign (not improbably from eye-witnesses with events still fresh in their minds) than he chose to write down.

His work comments on the undertakings given to Duke William on the succession to the English throne by both King Edward and Earl Harold,[27] and lays stress on the latter's perfidy in breaking his oath. It then mentions Halley's Comet, the duke's assembly of a force of 3,000 vessels at St Valéry and the crossing to Pevensey, and the building of fortifications both there and at Hastings. Harold is said to have hastened to take him by surprise, gathered very large forces and ridden through the night, appearing on the battlefield at about dawn. However, William had adopted measures to deal with a night attack and his men had been standing to arms. Early in the morning he formed them into three divisions and advanced against the terrible enemy. Fighting began around the third hour and went on until nightfall. Harold fell pierced with wounds during the first onset and when the English heard of this they turned, as night was falling, and began to flee. The duke returned to the battlefield from the pursuit at about midnight, despoiled the enemy corpses (they say that many thousands of the English were killed) and buried his own dead the following morning, subsequently setting out for London, where he was eventually crowned.[28]

This seems a sober enough account of the battle, and the only real problem with it is the surprising statement that Harold was killed early in the day, for this not only contradicts a number of other sources but also appears internally inconsistent, as the English

---

[25] I follow here van Houts' dating, *GND*, i. xxxii–v; for WJ's sources, see xxxix–l, and for a recent discussion of *GND*, Albu, *The Normans in their Histories*, pp.51–81.

[26] *GND*, ii. 172–3.

[27] Above, pp.23, 26–7.

[28] *GND*, ii. 160–71. WJ's 'they say' (*referuntur*) looks like an allusion to his sources.

are said to have fled when they heard of his death, yet as they did so night was falling. Dr van Houts, the most recent editor of the *Gesta*, believes that William of Jumièges made a statement that is 'incontrovertibly false' because he 'was adding these chapters... before accurate reports were available',[29] but given the Conqueror's visit to Jumièges in 1067 this is not entirely convincing, and there is quite a lot to be said for Professor Gillingham's suggestion that a scribal error early in the transmission of the text produced a 'first attack' (*in primo militum congressu*) from an original 'final attack' (*in postremo militum congressu*), especially as the oldest surviving manuscript dates only from *c.*1100.[30] This would both bring this account into line with other sources on the time of Harold's death, and also make better sense in itself, as his fall late in the day would then explain why his men fled as night was approaching. Even so, it is no more than a possibility, for it should be noted that Orderic Vitalis, who followed the existing text of William of Jumièges on this matter, may well have had a manuscript much closer to the author's autograph than any now extant.[31]

The number of surviving manuscripts suggests that the *Gesta Normannorum Ducum* was a very popular work, and not long after it was written it was used by a scholar who provides the most detailed contemporary French account of the events of 1066, William of Poitiers. His *Gesta Guillelmi* (*The Deeds of William*) was known to both Orderic Vitalis and William of Malmesbury, but like the *Carmen* seems not to have become widely disseminated, and the text has come down only through a seventeenth-century printed edition taken from a manuscript incomplete at both beginning and end, and which has since disappeared. Orderic, who had a fuller copy and may have met its author,[32] says that it was dedicated to King William to gain his favour, and that William

---

[29] *GND*, i. liii–iv.

[30] Gillingham, 'William the Bastard at War', 146, n.36; *GND*, i. c–ci, on the manuscript; van Houts rejects this idea, *GND*, ii. 169, n.3.

[31] Below, p.110.

[32] As Chibnall suggests, *GG*, p.xvi.

of Poitiers had been a soldier before entering the church; a Norman by birth, he was called 'of Poitiers' because he had studied there, becoming famous for his learning and an archdeacon in the diocese of Lisieux when he returned home; he was also for a long time one of the king's chaplains, and attempted to describe the events which he had both seen and participated in, although he was prevented by adverse circumstances from continuing his work up to the king's death (in 1087).[33] Perhaps born *c.*1020, he may have studied in Poitiers around 1050 and obtained his archdeaconry in the 1070s; he seems also to have been one of the canons of the church at St Martin at Dover, having received his share of the prebends (formerly held in common) from Bishop Odo of Bayeux.[34] It is possible that he was too closely connected to Odo (of whom he speaks well), and that the latter's imprisonment by the Conqueror in 1082 had something to do with the 'adverse circumstances' which prevented the completion of his work.[35]

The *Gesta Guillelmi* as it exists today begins with the demise of King Cnut in 1035 and ends in 1067, but Orderic says that his version concluded with the death of Earl Edwin of Mercia (in 1071), and elements of the lost ending can be deduced from his use of it.[36] William of Poitiers was at work upon it in the 1070s, for the passage which refers to the Conqueror then being aged around forty-five[37] must date from about 1073, and he uses the present tense of Bishop Hugh of Lisieux, who died in July 1077.[38] However, he also refers to the dedication of the abbey of St Stephen at Caen which occurred in September 1077, and this raises the possibility of later revision,[39] as does Orderic's belief that he intended taking the work down to King William's death.

[33] *HÆ*, ii. 78–9, 258–61, 184–5.
[34] See Chibnall's comments, *GG*, pp.xv–vii.
[35] Davis, 'William of Poitiers', pp.120–3.
[36] Ibid., pp.129–30, guessed the contents of the lost parts of *GG*.
[37] *GG*, pp.16–7.
[38] *GG*, pp.92–5.
[39] *GG*, pp.84–5, and see Chibnall's n.3.

In saying that the *Gesta Guillelmi* was, like the *Gesta Normannorum Ducum*, dedicated to William to gain his favour Orderic is presumably referring to statements in its (lost) opening sections, and there is no difficulty in believing him to be correct; but it does not follow that William (who is not known to have been a patron of learning) in any sense commissioned it. Whether he did or not, of course, its author had every motive to flatter his subject, and other eleventh-century works of a similar type sound timely warnings of just how misleading such flattery might be. The *Encomium* written *c.*1041 for William's great-aunt Emma of Normandy, for example, makes much of her marriage to Cnut but fails to mention that she had previously been the wife of his enemy King Æthelred II; similarly, Helgaud of Fleury's biography of the French king Robert the Pious (d.1031) is less than open about its subject's marital affairs, and suppresses all mention of his first wife.[40] In these instances there are other sources of knowledge which reveal the extent of the distortion, but the student of William of Poitiers is not in such a fortunate position, for over many of his statements there is either inadequate control or no control at all. Even so, he says things that are difficult to believe. It was suggested in Chapter 1, for example, that the basic outlines of the story told by the *Gesta Guillelmi* and William of Jumièges about the undertakings given to Duke William on the English succession are probably correct, but it is not at all easy to credit the claim that fear of the duke's power played a significant role in establishing Edward the Confessor on the English throne,[41] given that at the time he was having difficulty in asserting his authority over Normandy. Similarly, the statement in connection with the duke's campaign against Maine in 1063 that the county had formerly been under Norman control has been described by his most recent editor as 'untrue'.[42]

There are also problems arising from the extent of William of Poitiers' classical education and the use to which he put it. He shared with two other scholars who wrote on Hastings, Guy of

---

[40] Campbell, 'England, France, Flanders and Germany in the Reign of Ethelred II', p.192.
[41] *GG*, pp.18–19. Davis, 'William of Poitiers', p.110, thought that WP was using an earlier source here.
[42] *GG*, pp.60–1, and n.3.

Amiens and Baudri of Bourgeuil (see below), the tendency of learned men of this period to place within a classical framework their panegyrics of great figures, who could then be lauded by the comparison of their deeds with those of the heroes of antiquity. As far as the Conqueror was concerned the minds of such writers turned naturally to Achilles and Aeneas (victors over Hector and Turnus respectively), and even more naturally to Julius Caesar, who had not only invaded Britain but also subsequently become involved in a conflict with Pompey which could readily be likened to that between William and Harold.[43] It is thus unsurprising that the *Gesta Guillelmi* should contain not only allusions to Virgil's *Aeneid*, Statius' *Thebaid* (on the struggle for the throne of ancient Thebes), the works of the historian Sallust and perhaps the *Ilias latina*, but also references to Suetonius' *Twelve Caesars*, Lucan's *Pharsalia* (on Caesar's defeat of Pompey at the battle of Pharsalus in 48 BC) and above all to Caesar's own *The Gallic War*. Nor was William of Poitiers' use of these works at all lacking in finesse. Professor Davis stressed that he:

> was a classical scholar and stylist of distinction, intent on producing a work of great literature... he was capable of imitating the style of quite a number of ancient authors, choosing for each of his themes the model which seemed most suitable, and often interrupting his narrative for a passage of pure rhetoric... He thought himself into the relevant style and used it boldly; in his comparison between the invasions of Julius Caesar and William the Conqueror, which naturally favours the latter, he moves about Caesar's *Gallic Wars* with the ease of a master, using its facts solely as they are relevant to his purpose.[44]

[43] In addition to the major works under discussion here, other more minor ones compare William with Caesar. These include an anonymous distich quoted by HH (pp.410–11) and the anonymous *Plus tibi fama*, attributed by van Houts to Godfrey of Rheims and dated by her to 1070; a distich by Bishop Hugh-Renard of Langres of *c*.1075 contains what she describes as 'an echo of the Caesar theme'; see van Houts, 'Latin poetry', 41–2.

[44] Davis, 'William of Poitiers', pp.101–2. GG, pp.189–90, lists WP's citations from classical and medieval sources. The *Ilias latina* is a Latin rendering of the *Iliad* in 1,070 lines believed to be from the time of the emperor Nero; it is not thought that the full text of the *Iliad* was available in western Europe in WP's time, but see below, p.104.

These features of his work bring with them some intractable difficulties. When he says, for example, that the Conqueror at one point concealed the loss of men who had been shipwrecked by burying them in secret, is he recounting something which actually happened, or being overcome by a desire to compare Duke William with Xerxes? Similarly, the banquet which he allegedly held at sea while waiting for the rest of his fleet to catch up with him is sufficiently reminiscent of feasts described in Virgil's *Aeneid* for one to doubt whether it ever took place,[45] while in the account of events just before the battle of Hastings we are told that French scouts reported the approach of the English and that the duke hastily ordered those who could be found in his camp to arm themselves, as many of his men were out foraging. The impression is given that the latter played no part in the battle, but they may have been introduced into the narrative at this point because William of Poitiers knew that foraging troops feature prominently in Caesar's account of his expeditions to Britain in *The Gallic War*: in 55 BC the Seventh Legion was attacked when foraging and had to be rescued by Caesar with troops assembled from his camp, and the following year three of his legions and all his cavalry were attacked while out foraging.[46]

The account of the battle itself[47] begins by telling how the duke took communion, hung round his neck the relics upon which Harold had sworn his oath, and did not regard putting his coat of mail on back to front as a bad omen. He then made a speech which William of Poitiers based on one contained in the works of Sallust, and led his men into battle behind the banner sent by the pope; in front were infantry equipped with bows and crossbows, behind them armoured infantry, and at the rear squadrons of horsemen, including the duke himself. Harold's army, of immense size and

---

[45] GG, pp.108–9, 112–3 (and see 112, n.2, citing *Aeneid*, i. 695–747; vii. 107–34; viii. 175–83). Both examples are given by Davis, 'William of Poitiers', p.103; see also Professor Foreville's discussion in her edition of GG, pp.xxxviii–xliii.

[46] GG, pp.124–5; Caesar, *The Gallic War*, iv. 32, v. 17, pp.220–3, 256–7. See further on the unconvincing nature of WP's account of the opening of the battle, below, p.196.

[47] For WP's account of the prelude to the conflict, see below, p.195.

strengthened by help sent from Denmark, assembled on a hill (*mons*) near the wood through which they had just passed; dismounting from their horses, they adopted a dense formation on foot. The duke, who was not dismayed by the roughness of the ground, climbed the steep slope and the battle opened with an exchange of missiles, the English throwing spears and projectiles of various kinds, murderous axes and stones tied to sticks. After this the French horsemen weighed in with their swords, but the fighting was evenly balanced and they gained no advantage, for their enemies were assisted by the advantage of the higher ground, their great and closely packed numbers, and their weapons, which easily penetrated shields and other defences (presumably a reference to the axes shown on the Bayeux Tapestry). At this point William's infantry, Breton horse and such auxiliaries as were on his left wing began to give way, along with almost all the rest of his line; there was a belief that their leader had himself fallen, and he countered this by removing his helmet, making a speech stressing that nothing was to be gained by flight and everything by victory, and charging once more into the fray at the head of his men. At this they rallied, surrounded and destroyed some thousands of the English who had followed them, and continued to attack the rest, who were little diminished in strength despite their losses.

Even now, they were so tightly packed that the dead could scarcely fall, but inroads were made by the weapons of the strongest soldiers (*fortissimorum militum ferro*),[48] and the attackers included men of Maine, Frenchmen,[49] Bretons, Aquitanians and above all Normans. William of Poitiers mentions by name the exploits of Robert, son of Roger of Beaumont, fighting with his men on the right wing in his first battle, but says that he does not intend to describe all the deeds of individuals, as even an eye-witness (which he, by implication, was not) could hardly have followed everything. He then moves to what appears the turning point of the battle: the

---

[48] On the translation of this phrase, see below, p.224, n.64.

[49] By *Francigenae* WP meant men from the area around Paris controlled directly by the French king.

Normans twice feigned flight, again surrounded and annihilated thousands of their English pursuers, and then renewed their assault on the rest, shooting arrows and striking the enemy, who were still so densely massed that the wounded could not withdraw. A list of ten notable leaders on the French side is followed by a passage extolling the military virtues of Duke William: he led from the front, and swiftly avenged the loss of the three horses killed under him; astonished at seeing him fight on foot, even soldiers who had been wounded took heart from the sight.

As the day declined the English realised that they could no longer stand against the Normans, for their losses had been heavy and included the king and his brothers. Accordingly, they turned to flight and were relentlessly pursued, until given renewed confidence by a broken rampart and maze of ditches (*praerupti ualli et frequentium fossarum*). Here they made a stand, and when William arrived on the scene he thought them English reinforcements; despite being advised to withdraw by Eustace of Boulogne, who was about to retire with fifty men, he charged the enemy and destroyed them, although it was here that some of the nobler Normans fell, their bravery brought to naught by the difficulty of the ground. Returning to the main battlefield, he surveyed the English dead. The king's two brothers were found very near him, but Harold himself, lacking all ornament (which presumably means that his corpse had been despoiled) could not be recognised by his face, but only by certain signs. He was carried into the French camp and eventually interred by William Malet on the seashore, the duke having refused his mother's offer of the body's weight in gold in exchange for it. William then, after burying his own dead and allowing those of the English who wished to do so to collect remains for interment, set out for Romney, where he punished those responsible for killing Frenchmen who had landed there by mistake, and then Dover.[50] The submission of Canterbury and eventually London followed, and his coronation. After its account

[50] GG, pp.126–45. Harold's mother, not named by WP, was Gytha, widow of Earl Godwin.

of the new king's triumphant return to Normandy in 1067 the *Gesta Guillelmi* devotes many lines to a detailed comparison of his successes against the English and Caesar's against the Britons, taking care to lay much stress on the superiority of the former.[51]

An immediate problem with this account is whether it is directly related to that of the *Carmen*, with which it has significant features in common: both describe an exchange of monkish envoys before the battle and the English, so numerous that their advance had turned rivers dry,[52] as densely massed on a *mons* near a wood when it began; in both the French missile troops led the way and opened the fighting, and there was a flight which the duke halted by taking off his helmet, making a speech in which he stressed that there was nothing to be gained by running away, and then turned to advantage by leading a counter-attack which resulted in heavy English losses; both say that William had horses killed beneath him and emphasise his personal prowess, and that as evening came on and they learnt of Harold's death the English became dispirited; in both accounts Harold's body was buried on the seashore after William had refused an offer of its weight in gold from his mother.[53] The direction of the borrowing obviously depends on whether the *Carmen* is really the poem composed by Guy of Amiens: if it is, William of Poitiers may have made use of it; if it is not, then the anonymous creator of Professor Davis' twelfth-century literary creation perhaps used William of Poitiers. But that direct and extensive borrowing there has been, few have doubted. Engels has spoken of 'a sort of dialogue between the *Carmen* and the *Gesta Guillelmi*, perceptible in what seem to be reactions of William of Poitiers to passages in the *Carmen*', and joined earlier commentators in stressing that the two have certain vocabulary in common: both say, for example, that the duke held a *hasta* ('spear') when he rallied his troops (the first use of the word in the *Gesta Guillelmi*, which has previously employed *lancea*), and that Harold was buried

[51] *GG*, pp.169–75.
[52] *GG*, p.126, n.5, notes the similarity with passages in Juvenal's *Satires* and Justin's *Epitome*.
[53] Most of the similarities between WP and the *Carmen* are tabulated by M&M, pp.98–108.

where he could be the 'guardian of the shore and sea'.[54] Similarly, Morton and Muntz believed that 'William of Poitiers had studied the battle in the *Carmen* minutely', and that he revised it with the intention of exalting the Conqueror's role even further, and of diminishing that of his French allies, and especially Count Eustace of Boulogne, compared with that of the Normans.[55] Professor Barlow, the latest editor of the *Carmen*, also thinks that it was known to William of Poitiers, just as Davis was prepared to believe the reverse to be true, as the *Gesta Guillelmi* 'has some passages which are undoubtedly reminiscent of the *Carmen*'.[56] As a royal chaplain, William of Poitiers would presumably have have had little difficulty in acquiring verse written by a bishop who accompanied Queen Matilda to England in 1068, and as a Latin scholar he would have been interested in doing so. His familiarity with the *Carmen* is therefore easy to credit. Yet there is a counter-case.[57] At least some of the similarities between the two sources might be explicable if it were thought that both men had spoken to witnesses (or heard songs or seen written sources) telling similar sorts of stories, and the differences between them might then be because the stories varied rather than because one had consciously modified the words of the other; that William took off his helmet when rallying his troops, for example, also appears both in the Bayeux Tapestry (illus. 21) and elsewhere, and may have been widely reported. Equally, it has been noted that verbal similarities between sources 'are often due to common knowledge of classical authors... do not imply direct imitation, and do not help to solve the problems of whether either author knew the work of the other'. Moreover, even if the strong possibility that William of Poitiers did know the *Carmen* is accepted, it does not necessarily follow that his own account of the battle depended heavily upon it, or had to become a refutation or modification of it, for as

[54] Engels, 'Once more', 6–9; similarly, Foreville's edition of *GG*, pp.xxxv–viii.

[55] M&M, pp.95–8.

[56] *Carmen*, pp.xxix–xxx, xl, lvii; Davis, 'The *Carmen de Hastingae Proelio*', p.83.

[57] For what follows, including the quotation and the view that 'WP's sources were almost entirely oral', see Chibnall's comments, *GG*, pp.xxviii–xxx.

a contemporary who may well have known (or at least met) many of the principal men involved, and an ex-soldier presumably with a lively interest in it, he could have had a great many sources, and the poem is not known to have been of such importance that he would have felt obliged to question or correct its statements.[58]

Simply taken as it stands, the *Gesta Guillelmi* provides the most detailed description of the battle to have survived, but of course this is not to say that all its features are credible. It has already been noted that legends can develop very quickly around famous events,[59] and the story of how the duke put on his mail-coat reversed may be something of the sort, while it has been suggested that 'the reality' of the gold offered for Harold's remains was William of Poitiers' 'memory of Achilles and the body of Hector';[60] this may well be so, for in the *Iliad* Achilles specifically tells the dying Hector that he would refuse a ransom of ten or twenty times its value or still more for the corpse, and that even if Hector's father Priam offered its weight in gold his mother would never lay him on a bier where he might be lamented.[61] There is, however, a possibility that eleventh-century figures sometimes acted in ways intended to imitate elements of stories known to them.[62] Had Harold's mother, too, heard of Achilles and Hector, and might she have felt that acquiring her son's remains in such a way was in itself a fitting memorial? Whether this is so or not, the *Gesta Guillelmi* contains details which are credible enough. The description of the battlefield (as with the *Carmen*) is perfectly

---

[58] Barlow, *Carmen*, pp.lvi–viii, seems to me to overstate the probable significance of the *Carmen* among WP's sources. Given the length of his account of the battle one can hardly agree that 'the details of the campaigns were not of much importance', and given the extent of the oral material probably available to him that the *Carmen* was used '*faute de mieux*'.

[59] Above, p.91–2.

[60] Davis, 'William of Poitiers', pp.103, 113; *GG*, pp.124–5, 140–1. WP, (*GG*, pp.134–5), as my pupil Jonathan Browning has reminded me, had already likened Harold to Hector and William to Achilles; compare also the possibility that the *Carmen* (see Barlow's comments, p.xxxii) intended to equate William with Achilles.

[61] *Iliad*, xxii. ll. 343–53. I am grateful to my colleague John Davie for this reference, which suggests that Guy of Amiens and WP (if he did not simply take it from the *Carmen*) had a knowledge of the *Iliad* which somehow went well beyond mere familiarity with the *Ilias latina* (above, p.98, n.44). Eventually, of course (*Iliad*, xxiv), Achilles did allow Priam to ransom Hector's body, but not for its weight in gold.

[62] A point made by Davis, 'William of Poitiers', p.114.

compatible with the present terrain, that of English fighting methods and weaponry, as far as it goes, is borne out by other evidence (including that of the Bayeux Tapestry), and the significance of the French retreat is a recurrent feature of the sources, even if William of Poitiers goes further than anyone else in describing one real withdrawal followed by two that were feigned.

In offering their works to the Conqueror William of Jumièges and William of Poitiers were adopting a practice not unusual among those who composed the Latin poetry and prose of the period. Some years later their contemporary Baudri, abbot of Bourgeuil near Tours, followed suit in addressing the poem known as the *Adelae Comitissae* (*To Countess Adela*) to King William's daughter Adela, wife of Count Stephen of Blois. Baudri was born near Orléans in 1046, studied probably in Angers and then entered the monastery of St Peter in Bourgeuil, eventually becoming abbot there in about 1089. After a failed attempt to obtain the bishopric of Orléans he was eventually appointed to the archbishopric of Dol in Brittany in 1107, but discovered that Breton manners were little to his taste and between that date and his death in 1130 made a number of journeys to Britain and Normandy. Over the course of his long life he also produced a considerable body of written work, including saints' lives, a history of the First Crusade and his *Itinerarium*, a description of his foreign travels. Of his more than 250 poems, which with one exception survive in their entirety in a single twelfth-century manuscript, and which were mostly written during his time in Bourgeuil, two were addressed to Adela. The first, the *Adelae Comitissae*, which refers to her husband as absent from home but still alive, can be dated between Count Stephen's departure on the First Crusade in 1096 and death in 1102, and perhaps specifically to 1101 or 1102.[63] It is a lengthy treatment of the purported furnishings and ornamentation of her great chamber, including a ceiling which depicted the heavens complete with the signs of the zodiac, stars and planets, and a floor which bore a map of the world divided

---

[63] On Baudri's life and the date of the poem, see Ratkowitsch, *Descriptio Picturae*, pp.19–20.

into Asia, Europe and Africa. Around the bed were statues of Philosophy and her seven disciples, the Quadrivium of Music, Arithmetic, Astronomy and Geometry being at its head, and the Trivium of Rhetoric, Dialectic and Grammar at its foot; a third group of figures represented Medicine, accompanied by Hippocrates and Galen. More significant in the present context are the wall hangings, worked in silks and gold and silver thread, embellished with pearls and jewels, and accompanied by titles (in a manner presumably similar to that of the Bayeux Tapestry). Their subject matter began with the Creation, the Garden of Eden and the Flood, followed by further scenes from the Old Testament and stories from Greek mythology (including the siege of Troy) and Roman history. Finally, a marvellous piece, which hung around Adela's bed, depicted the deeds of her father, with particular emphasis on the conquest of England. At the end of the poem Baudri asked for a reward from 'the goddess' which he evidently did not receive, as his request was eventually repeated in the second and (at thirty-two lines) much shorter composition he addressed to her.

The early scenes of the supposed Conquest sequence dealt with William's birth and the struggles of his minority, but moved quickly to Halley's Comet and a speech made by the duke to his magnates in which he set out his claim to the English throne (his consanguinity with Edward the Confessor, the latter's promise, his written confirmation of it as he lay dying and the broken oath of Harold – called simply 'a certain perjurer') and told them to prepare ships to be ready in the fifth month. Eventually, 3,000 vessels assembled and crossed the Channel, and the battle was apparently fought immediately; not for Baudri the lengthy preliminaries of some other sources, although he dwells on the building of the fleet and its embarkation. He says that the very large enemy army abandoned its horses and massed in a single dense formation whose spears looked like a forest, and which would have been impregnable had it held together. The duke sent his archers and crossbowmen against it and they inflicted the first casualties, as death seemed to the English to be falling from the sky. As French missiles inflicted further losses, in ranks so tight-packed that the dead were unable to fall, (some of) the enraged English broke formation to launch a counter-attack, while the Normans simulated flight and then intercepted and annihilated their pursuers. Eventually, the French rushed upon the enemy in disordered ranks and were put to flight, the rout being fuelled by the rumour that the duke had been killed. At this point William removed his helmet and made a speech which stressed the futility of withdrawal and the fact that victory was at hand. Then he spurred his horse and charged into battle, bettering the feats of both Hector and Achilles. Even so, much hard fighting followed, and the ground ran with the blood of the slain, until Harold was hit by an arrow[64] and his forces lost heart and began to retire, being harried mercilessly by the Norman cavalry until night-fall interrupted the slaughter. The following morning the duke made a speech urging his men to take no heed of booty until the war was won, and it was subsequently brought to a successful conclusion.

Baudri of Bourgeuil's *Adelae Comitissae*, which may have been intended for a wider audience than simply its subject,[65] belongs within a well-known classical, late antique and medieval tradition of depictions of both real and imaginary buildings and works of art, including Homer's account of the shield of Achilles and Virgil's of those of Aeneas and Turnus, the lines in Ovid's *Metamorphoses* which describe the palace of the Sun and the wonderful engravings of the earth, sea and sky which adorned it, and Ermold the Black's detailed account, in a piece addressed to the Carolingian emperor Louis the Pious, of the paintings to be seen in the early ninth century on the

---

[64] *Perforat Hairaldum casu letalis arundo, AC*, l. 463; *letalis arundo* is a reference to Virgil's *Aeneid*, iv. 73. Tilliette, 'La chambre de la comtesse Adèle', 167–9, notes other references to Virgil, to Lucan's *Pharsalia* and to Statius' *Thebaid*, and points out that for Baudri (as for WP, above, pp.98–9) 'on ne donnera une idée de l'importance de la bataille d'Hastings qu'en l'assimilant à la bataille antique de Pharsale ou aux combats mythiques devant les murs de Thèbes'. Ratkowitsch, *Descriptio Picturae*, pp.60, 73, notes also Baudri's use of the *Psychomachia* by the late Roman Christian poet Prudentius, and argues that in thus stressing that the duke was a Christian warrior he sought to portray him as the superior of Aeneas and Caesar.

[65] It is the only one of Baudri's poems surviving in part (ll. 749–946, on the world map) and in a variant text in a second manuscript, written in York in the fourteenth century. Ratkowitsch, *Descriptio Picturae*, pp.18, 29, follows the suggestion of Gautier Dalché and Tilliette, 'Un nouveau document', 247–8, that this variant goes back to the copy sent to Adela, while the other version is that kept by Baudri for insertion into his collected poems.

walls of the church and secular hall of the royal palace at Ingelheim;[66] the latter comprised scenes from both the Old and New Testaments and from antiquity: Cyrus, Phalaris, Romulus and Remus, Hannibal and Alexander all had their place, together with the Christian Roman emperors Constantine the Great and Theodosius, while the more recent triumphs of Frankish princes were represented by Charles Martel's victories over the Frisians, King Pepin I's over the Aquitanians and those of Charlemagne (Louis' father) over the continental Saxons.[67] Yet if the items decribed in Ermold's poem have a certain amount in common with those of the *Adelae Comitissae*, there are also significant differences between the two pieces. Ermold was a member of Louis' court and presumably familiar with the subject matter he was describing, while by contrast it is far from clear how well Baudri knew Adela (and others whom he addressed in familiar terms),[68] and his poem itself suggests that his account of the Norman Conquest hanging and therefore probably of the entire chamber is in fact entirely fictional.[69] Yet his description of the battle cannot be regarded in the same light. Whether he owed very much to other surviving sources is something upon which scholars have failed to agree. The figure of 3,000 for William's fleet could well have come from William of Jumièges, it is conceivable (but unlikely, see below) that he was familiar with the Bayeux Tapestry, and a great deal of his material can also be found in the *Carmen* and William of Poitiers, including that on the great density of the English formation, the duke's use of missile troops, the feigned followed by a real French flight (this being the version of the

[66] *Iliad*, xviii. 480ff; *Aeneid*, viii. 626–728, vii. 789–92; *Metamorphoses*, ii, 1–18. These examples and many others are given by Ratkowitsch, *Descriptio Picturae*, pp.9–11, 21–4.

[67] Ermold the Black, *In honorem Hludovici Pii*, ll. 189–284. On this poem and its context, see Godman, *Poetry of the Carolingian Renaissance*, pp.45–7.

[68] See Phyllis Abrahams' comments in her edition of *AC*, pp.xxiv–v.

[69] In ll. 567–70, Baudri says (in Herren's translation) 'If you could believe that this weaving really existed you would read true things on it, O writing paper. But you might also say: "What he wrote ought to have been; a subject like this was becoming to the goddess"'. See B&W, 26; Barlow, in *Carmen*, p.lx; Brown and Herren, 'The *Adelae Comitissae*', espec. 71–3; Tilliette, 'La chambre', 153, 170. On Baudri, and poems addressed by others to Adela, see van Houts, 'Latin poetry', 49–50. Tilliette (161) shows that some passages of the poem would be unintelligible to a reader not possessed of such considerable learning as was clearly attributed to Adela.

Carmen rather than the *Gesta Guillelmi*),William's removal of his helmet to halt it and personal prowess in the fighting,[70] and the belief that this continued until nightfall.[71] Nevertheless, Baudri was no slave to such sources even if he did know them, for unlike him they do not attribute to the duke speeches made as he landed in England and at the battle's close, and it is difficult to say when he was drawing upon them and when he was simply utilising oral traditions about the fight similar to their own. Moreover, if he had ever had any contact with Adela the authority of those traditions may have been good. It is of no small interest from this point of view that one of them had Harold killed by an arrow. Baudri did not take this from either the *Carmen* or the *Gesta Guillelmi*, which do not contain it, and there is no obvious reason to think that he drew it from the history of the Normans written in Italy *c.*1080 by Amatus, monk of Montecassino; this specifies that the English king was hit in the eye.[72]

[70] Ratkowitsch, *Descriptio Picturae*, p.72, notes that the removal of the helmet is 'ein altes episches Motiv, das bei mehreren antiken römischen Epikern anzutreffen ist', and suggests that Baudri modelled it on *Aeneid*, v. 670ff, and x. 368ff; but these are not precise parallels, and in the second, where Pallas atttempts to halt his routing Arcadians by making a speech similar to William's and then charging into battle like the duke, he does not first remove his helmet in order to be recognised. Note also the speech allegedly (*EE*, pp.20–1) made by EarlThorkell to rally Danish troops fighting the English at Sherston in 1016.

[71] Tilliette,'La chambre', 154, acknowledges the links withWP but thinks that 'nous sommes plutôt ici en présence d'une composition personnelle de Baudri à partir de la "version officielle" diffusée par les propagandistes de la nouvelle dynastie'. However, in concluding his discussion of the derivation of the other subject matter of the poem, he comments (160) that 'dans chaque matière, l'auteur a consulté l'autorité reconnue et mis en vers son enseignement'. Ratkowitsch, *Descriptio Picturae*, pp.59–61, is sure that Baudri usedWJ andWP and thinks he may have known the *Carmen*; she also suggests that he was familiar with Godfrey of Rheims' poem *Lux mores hodierna*, which includes a celebration of the virtues of the Conqueror and Adela; on this, see van Houts,'Latin poetry', 47–8.

[72] *Contre cestui* (Harold) *ala premerement Guillerme, et combati contre lui; et lui creva un oill d'une sajete, et molt gent de li Englez ocaist*; Amatus, *Storia de' normanni*, ed. Bartholomaeis, pp.11–12.The Latin text does not survive, but was translated into Old French in the early fourteenth century; the accuracy of this version (and therefore whether the statement about the arrow stood in Amatus' original) is not certain, although Bartholomaeis, its most recent editor, did not think the material on William's conquest of England interpolated. On Amatus, see Wolf, *Making History*, pp.88–9, who thinks the French version 'not hopelessly corrupt'; Albu, *The Normans in their Histories*, pp.109–10, judges it 'more an adaptation than a precise translation' and thinks use of it 'as if it were an eleventh-century Norman text' problematic. I am grateful to Dr Graham Loud for assistance on Amatus.There are similarities between Baudri and the Tapestry, but Abrahams (n. 61, pp.244–7) and Tilliette ('La chambre', 150–2) argue, convincingly in my opinion, that they are insufficiently compelling to indicate his knowledge of it; for a different view, see Brown and Herren, 'The *Adelae Comitissae*', and Ratkowitsch, *Descriptio Picturae*, pp.62–5, 74–6, but their case is weakened by the reference to the arrow in Amatus and above all by the probability that theTapestry did not originally show Harold struck by one (see the Appendix).

It looks as though the belief that Harold had been killed by an arrow, which is also to be found in twelfth-century sources, was one attached to the battle at an early date.

In 1075 Orderic Vitalis was born near Shrewsbury. The son of an English mother and a French priest, he was offered at the age of ten to the monastery of St Évroul in Normandy, and there he wrote the works upon which his reputation as one of the great Anglo-Norman historians of the first half of the twelfth century is based. From about 1095 he compiled a set of annals for his abbey, and it may have been at about the same time that he began revising the *Gesta Normannorum Ducum* of William of Jumièges; he had completed most of it by 1109.[73] Orderic's additions were very extensive, and sometimes he was concerned to correct the bias of his sources: unlike William of Jumièges and William of Poitiers, for example, he was prepared to write about the Conqueror's illegitimate birth, and when he dealt with England he took trouble to give a balanced account. On the events of 1066 he inserted details of the almost complete annihilation of the Norwegian forces at Stamford Bridge (while giving, wrongly, the date of 7 October) and also tells the story of how Harold's brother Gyrth attempted to dissuade him from being involved in fighting against the duke, a story which may have come from 'a lost account, probably poetical'.[74] On the battle of Hastings itself, he left William of Jumièges' text largely unaltered, but added to it a description of the difficulties experienced by the French during their pursuit of the fleeing English, when they rushed against an ancient rampart concealed by high grass, fell against each other and were crushed to death. William of Poitiers (whose work Orderic probably knew at this date, as he certainly did later) has a similar incident at the same stage in the battle, but he describes it in rather different terms, and it looks as if Orderic was drawing on an independent tradition.[75]

---

[73] For this and what follows, including comment on Orderic's additions and alterations to WJ, see *GND*, i. lxvi–lxxv.

[74] Orderic, in *GND*, ii. 164–71; Chibnall, *HÆ*, ii. xxiv.

[75] In his later work he amalgamated this story with that of WP, see further, below, pp.233–4.

Shortly after completing this work he turned to that known as the *Historia Æcclesiastica* (*History of the Church*), and spent about ten years on the book which includes a treatment of Hastings, the first he wrote, which was finished c.1124.[76] He reports that King Harold was a fine physical specimen and famed for his eloquence and bravery, but criticises him for usurping the English throne, and says that it was done without the consent of the people and that the ensuing reign saw much oppression. He then wrongly assigns the exile of Tostig to 1066, and claims that the earl visited Normandy and encouraged William to cross the Channel with an army. Next he moves to William's calling of a council and dispatch of an embassy to Rome (both drawn, with additions, from William of Poitiers), and to Tostig's adventures in England and supposed visit to Harald of Norway. An extended treatment of the affairs of St Évroul (where the abbot died at this time) intervenes, before Orderic returns to Tostig and Harald and the battle of Stamford Bridge, and then William's landing on the south coast and Gyrth's attempt to persuade his brother not to fight. From this point down to the finding of Harold's body and its burial his account follows that of William of Poitiers fairly closely, while reducing from 700 to seventy the number of English ships said to have been sent into the Channel to prevent the French escaping, and adding a number of details of its own: Thurstan, son of Rollo, is said to have borne the standard of the Normans, and the name of the place is correctly given as Senlac. William of Poitiers does not say when Harold was killed, and Orderic therefore followed William of Jumièges in stating that it was during the first assault, and he also repeated his own earlier account of the disaster which befell the French during the pursuit, this time fusing it with the version in the *Gesta Guillelmi*, and naming one of the dead (of perhaps the battle as a whole) as Engenulf of Laigle. If he had heard stories about how Harold died, and it is difficult to believe that he had not, he did not choose to repeat them.[77]

---

[76] *HÆ*, ii. xv. It had its origins as a history of his own monastery.

[77] *HÆ*, ii. 134–45, 168–79; on Senlac, see above, pp.56–8; on Orderic and the family of Engenulf, below, p.235, n.91. Like other sources, Orderic misnames the Norwegian king Harald Fairhair, information perhaps obtained when he visited Worcester, see *HÆ*, ii. 188–9, and Chibnall's note, 186, n.1.

A work contemporary with this book of Orderic's *Historia Æcclesiastica* is that known as the *Brevis Relatio de Guillelmo nobilissimo comite Normannorum* (*Brief History of the most noble William, count of the Normans*), in fact a history of Normandy and England from about 1035 to the early twelfth century written by an anonymous but probably Norman monk of Battle Abbey between 1114 and 1120, and surviving in what is believed to be the author's autograph. His work was carried out in the time of Abbot Ralph (d. 1124), who had known both the Conqueror (as a royal chaplain, like William of Poitiers) and Archbishop Lanfranc of Canterbury, and who may well therefore have been a good witness, even on events which he had not seen at first hand; these no doubt included the battle of Hastings.[78] His narrative of the Conquest is broadly similar to that of William of Jumièges and William of Poitiers, while containing a number of details which they do not. Harold, for example, is said to have sworn his oath on a reliquary called the Ox's Eye, and to have been crowned at St Paul's;[79] when, after his victory over his brother (Harald Hardrada is not mentioned), he heard of William's invasion, he came to London as quickly as possible and spoke to the English and Danes who were with him, holding his oath to the duke as nothing. Then he left London with all his army and came to the place now called Battle, reportedly saying that he had never done anything so willingly as come to this fight, and little knowing the punishment that almighty God was about to inflict upon his pride. William and the Normans came to a hill opposite that occupied by the English, and a speech said to have been made by the most Christian duke as he was putting on his armour is worthy to be transmitted to posterity. He was accidentally offered his coat of mail back to front, and calmly told the soldiers standing near him that if he

---

[78] See van Houts' comments, *BR*, pp. 7–15.

[79] *BR*, pp. 28–9. Van Houts thinks that the reliquary was among those bequeathed to Battle Abbey by the Conqueror on his deathbed, 'The Memory of 1066', 167–9. The *Chronicon Monasterii de Hida* account (see below, p. 123, n. 103), p. 290, which may have used *BR*, claims that the reliquary was one of St Pancras, a detail rejected by Lewis, 'The Earldom of Surrey', 334.

believed in omens he would not go into battle that day, but in fact he had never believed in such things, only in the Creator. Once armed, he asked a soldier standing near him where he thought Harold to be, and was told that he was believed to be in the very dense formation of men on the crest of the ridge (*in illo spisso agmine quod erat ante eos in montis summitate*), for the soldier thought Harold's standard could be seen there. William then called upon God to do him justice that day against Harold the perjurer, spurred his horse into the English ranks and killed one of their number. Not much later a Norman unit (*cuneus*) of almost a thousand horsemen attacked elsewhere and rushed upon the English with a great impetus as if wishing to slay them, but when they reached the enemy line pretended to flee as if they were afraid. The English believed they were really fleeing and set off in pursuit in the hope of killing them, but when they saw this the Normans, who were more cautious in war than the English, soon turned back and, placing themselves between the pursuers and their main line, quickly annihilated them. Thus the Normans and the English began fighting each other, but the battle lasted almost all day and into the evening, until the defeated English fled, and those who could not flee remained to die. In that battle Harold and his two brothers were killed, and with them the greater part of the English nobility, and in that place Duke William ordered an abbey to be built in memory of his victory and for the absolution of the sins of all those who had died there.[80]

There is little sign that this description of the battle owes much to any other that has survived, for although the story of the reversed armour could have come from William of Poitiers it may be that both writers had heard the same tradition, and frequent use in the *Brevis Relatio* of terms like 'they say' (*fertur*) suggests that its author's sources were often oral.[81] This is hardly surprising, as Abbot Ralph is unlikely to have been the only Battle monk with stories to

[80] *BR*, pp.31–3.
[81] A point made by van Houts, *BR*, p.22.

tell. It is also significant that while the feigned retreat appears here as elsewhere, the *Brevis Relatio* places it at the beginning of the fight, and does not share William of Poitiers' opinion that it followed upon a real rout which the duke managed to halt. It does share with other sources the belief that the fighting lasted virtually all day, but if the community at Battle knew anything of deaths in ditches, or of reverses of any kind suffered by the French forces, this author preferred to remain silent about them.

The final source which needs to be considered by the historian of the battle of Hastings is the longest and one of the most colourful, the *Roman de Rou* (*History of Rollo*) by Master Wace. A native of Jersey (then part of the duchy of Normandy) born *c.*1110, Wace was educated in Caen and Paris, and eventually returned to Caen, where he produced a number of verse pieces in the vernacular, including saints' lives and his two major works, the *Roman de Brut* and the *Roman de Rou*. The *Brut*, finished in 1155, was a translation into French of Geoffrey of Monmouth's history of the kings of Britain (written in the 1130s), while the *Roman de Rou* deals with the deeds of the Norman dukes from the earliest, the tenth-century Rollo, down to the battle of Tinchebrai (between the Conqueror's sons Duke Robert of Normandy and King Henry I of England) in 1106. More than 16,000 lines in length, it was begun in 1160, but Wace did not lay down his pen until the middle of the 1170s, when he says that King Henry II required him to hand the work over to a Master Benoît (probably Benoît of St Maur); this was after the king had made him a prebendary of Bayeux cathedral.[82] He was a cleric, but wrote in French probably to reach a lay audience which could not understand Latin; he also wrote to entertain, but this is not to say that he was not a serious historian too, for he knew and used a considerable number of the authors who have already received our attention – including William of Jumièges, William of Poitiers, Eadmer, Orderic Vitalis and William of Malmesbury; he may also

---

[82] I have followed Holden's account of Wace, iii. 15–18; van Houts, 'Wace as Historian', pp.103–6; and the introduction to the new translation by Burgess. See also Eley and Bennett, 'The Battle of Hastings', 54–68, who describe the battle as 'the centre of gravity of the entire work'.

have been familiar with the *Carmen* and the *Brevis Relatio*, and the Bayeux Tapestry, if it was in Bayeux in his day.[83] These sources, as he was aware, cannot always be reconciled, and this was something which he was prepared to bring to his audience's attention: when dealing with the reason for Harold's visit to Normandy during Edward the Confessor's reign, for example, he mentions the statements of the French sources, but adds the English version of events given by the Canterbury writer Eadmer and says that he does not know the truth of the matter.[84] Thus, while it may be necessary to acknowledge that his statements are based on what Round called 'a *congeries* of authorities, on tradition, and occasionally of course, on the poetic invention of the *trouveur*',[85] the fact remains that Wace went to some trouble to seek out information, and that his efforts resulted in the preservation of material which would not otherwise have survived. It has been suggested that he deliberately researched oral memories of the events of 1066, and that during his visit to the abbey of Fécamp in 1162 he was informed that the monk who acted as one of Duke William's messengers to Harold before the battle was named Hugh Margot.[86] On the size of the French fleet, he comments that as a boy he had heard his father say that 696 vessels sailed from St Valéry, but that he had also found it written as 3,000 (a figure given by both William of Jumièges and Baudri of Bourgeuil); he also seems to have had reliable information on the numbers of ships provided by some of the duke's magnates.[87] Accordingly, when he gives details which are his alone they cannot be dismissed simply on the basis of the relatively late date at which he worked; equally, there is no way of checking them.

The events of 1066 occupy a major place in the *Roman de Rou*, taking up more than 3,000 lines in all, while the account of the

[83] B&W, 28, think that Wace 'drew heavily on the Tapestry for his description of the Norman conquest'; others have been less convinced, *RR*, trans. Burgess, p.xxxiv.

[84] *RR*, ll. 5543–604; see above, p.29-30. On Wace's frequently expressed concern for truth, see *RR*, trans. Burgess, pp.xxxvi-vii.

[85] Round, 'Wace and his Authorities', 677.

[86] Van Houts, 'Wace as Historian', 114-5.

[87] *RR*, ll. 6423–32; below, pp.181-2.

battle of Hastings alone is about a tenth of the whole.[88] This gives a clear indication of the importance of this subject matter to Wace's audience, which was also thought to be very interested in the individuals involved: other sources mention few participants in the battle on the French side, but Wace refers to a great many Norman lords. His account of the events which were to be of such interest to their descendants begins with William hearing of Harold's usurpation of the English throne and assembling a council of his men, some of whom proved willing to undertake an expedition, others not. Eventually they agreed to serve, and the duke then called on areas bordering Normandy, promising lands and payment to those who would follow him. He also sent to the pope for support, and received from Rome a gonfanon (standard) and a most precious ring, which had beneath the stone a tooth of St Peter; at much the same time Halley's Comet appeared. A description of the building of William's fleet follows, and its assembly at St Valéry, voyage across the Channel and arrival near Hastings. Once there, the duke's men constructed a fort out of material they had brought with them, while the news of their landing was carried to Harold beyond the Humber. He quickly reached London, ordering an army to assemble from throughout England, and there encountered an envoy of William, the Fécamp monk Hugh Margot, who rehearsed his master's claim to the throne and urged Harold to relinquish it; in reply, his own envoy to the duke offered a large sum of gold and silver if the French would depart, or if not a battle on the coming Saturday. Wace then tells the story of how Harold's brother Gyrth attempted to dissuade him from leading the English forces, of Harold's refusal, and of his setting up of his standard on the site of Battle Abbey. He also had the place surrounded by a good ditch with entrances on three sides, and the following morning the two brothers rode out to reconnoitre the French positions.[89] The sight caused Harold to

---

[88] Bennett, 'Poetry as History?', 25.

[89] Eley and Bennett, 'The Battle of Hastings', 60–1, note that Harold and Gyrth are here 'a regular pair of heroic companions from the *chanson de geste*, inviting comparison with Vivien and Girart, Raoul and Bernier, Roland and Oliver'.

propose a delay until he had a larger army, but Gyrth rejected this because of the effect it would have on English morale, and they returned to camp to prepare for battle. Further negotiations followed in which William offered Harold all of Northumbria if he would submit and Gyrth all the lands of their father Earl Godwin; he also threatened any of the English who supported them with excommunication, much to their concern. However, their spirits were restored by a rousing speech from Gyrth (in Wace's version of events at least as significant a figure as Harold himself) and, the talking being done, both sides prepared to fight.

At this point Wace included William of Malmesbury's account of how the English spent the night before the battle carousing, while the French made confession of their sins. A lengthy speech by the duke in which he stressed the treachery of the English followed an arrangement that his forces should form three divisions, and we are then given the tale, also to be found in William of Poitiers and the *Brevis Relatio*, about William donning his armour reversed, while Orderic Vitalis' simple statement that the Norman standard was borne by Thurstan, son of Rollo, is elaborated into his carrying of the papal banner only after others had refused the honour.[90] Wace next, however, inserted material not from any known source: the duke instructed Roger of Montgomery[91] and William FitzOsbern to command one of the wings, containing the men of Boulogne and of the county of Poux in Picardy and soldiers of his own, while the other consisted of troops from Brittany, Poitou and Maine under the Breton Alan Fergant[92] and Aimeri, vicomte of Thouars; in the centre was William himself. As for Harold, he had summoned men from castles, cities, ports, villages and boroughs, and they included peasants armed with clubs, iron forks and stakes; none had come from north of the Humber, but the names of many of the shires and towns south of it are listed as having sent contingents. Wace at this point rejects the widespread belief that the English army was small, and

[90] See further, Bennet, 'Poetry as History?', 33.

[91] On Roger, see below, p. 119.

[92] A mistake for the Breton Alan Rufus, van Houts, 'Wace as Historian', 118.

gives it as his own opinion that their numbers equalled those of the French. They had, he says, erected a barricade to their front,[93] and Harold ordered the men of Kent to go where the first attack would be made, for it was the custom that the first blow belonged to them,[94] as it was also that the Londoners should be stationed around the standard and guard the king himself. As the French approached, Harold and Gyrth further disputed the wisdom of fighting, it being the latter's opinion that large as their army was (400,000 is the figure given) the peasantry was of questionable worth compared with troops of the quality which now opposed them. However, they took up position near the standard, and their men gave their battle-cries of 'Holy Cross' and 'God Almighty', while Taillefer rode before the duke singing of Charlemagne, Roland, Oliver and those who died at the battle of Roncesvalles, and asking for permission to strike the first blow. This he did before the English surrounded him, and as the lines closed there began the battle which is still, says Wace, of great renown.

The opening lines of his description of it consist of stock phrases enlivened only by the inclusion of the Norman battle-cry of *Deus aïe!* and the English one of *Ut!* ('Out!'), and the first concrete detail is of the Normans being pushed back upon a ditch which they had earlier crossed, and of horses and men being thrown into it; many of the English died there, and more of the Normans at that time than any other, as those who saw the dead said. Upon witnessing this the boys set to guard the baggage began to panic until Odo of Bayeux rode up on a white horse to rally them, before returning to a battle which raged from nine o'clock in the morning until three in the afternoon without either side gaining an advantage. It was then that the French archers began to fire into the air so that their arrows fell upon the heads and faces of their enemies, and Harold was struck on the right eye, which was put out; only after he was wounded, according to Wace, did

[93] These were the lines (7793–8) disputed by Round and his opponents in the 1890s, see below, p.141 and n.40.
[94] On this, see further, below, p.169.

the Normans stage a feigned flight to break up the enemy line. The English foolishly followed them, thus abandoning a position in which they could hardly have been defeated, and as their enemy turned to face them once again the *Roman de Rou* becomes for many lines a recital of fighting involving the alleged actions of 117 Norman lords, seventy-four of them simply designated by the territory which they ruled and without a personal name being given.[95] Even when names are supplied they sometimes refer to people such as Roger of Montgomery who are known not to have been present.[96] Yet, while one might believe that much of this catalogue of heroic deeds was invented by Wace to please the descendants of those supposedly involved, he may have eked out some of his comments with genuine traditions. He says, for example, that Robert son of Erneis broke through the English in an attempt to cut down their standard, but was surrounded, killed, and eventually found lying at its foot; these details cannot be confirmed, but a charter granted by his son to the monks of Fontenay does say that he was killed in England in the Conqueror's time.[97] Recently, Dr van Houts has gone further than this, and has suggested that Wace's details of the exploits of individual Normans, far from being largely fictional, were actually based on research among his contemporaries upon the nature of family traditions about the battle.[98]

Of the English themselves the men of Kent and Essex are supposed to have fought well and pushed the Normans back, until a charge led by Duke William finally broke their countrymen's resistance and his men penetrated at last to the English standard. There the wounded Harold still stood, until beaten down twice, first by a blow to his helmet and then by one which cut his thigh to the bone. His brother Gyrth fell under a blow from the duke himself,

[95] The figures are from Douglas, 'Companions of the Conqueror', 131; see also Bennett, 'Poetry as History?', 28–35, for the argument that Wace sometimes alludes to the politics of his own day.
[96] Douglas, 'Companions', 132, 143–4; OV, *HÆ*, ii, 210–1, says that the duke left Roger in Normandy to act as regent.
[97] Douglas, 'Companions', 142.
[98] Van Houts, 'Wace as Historian', espec. pp.109–16.

and then Harold too was killed, although Wace says that the press around the king was so great that he knew not the identity of the slayer. Even then, he reports that the English fought on until the close of day, until news of their king's death spread, and men began to flee, not stopping before they reached London. As for William, two horses had been killed beneath him, and as he removed his armour and his attendants saw the damage it had sustained they exclaimed that there had not been such a knight since the days of Roland and Oliver. He raised his standard and tent, took his evening meal and slept at the place where the English standard had been, and the following day the French buried such of their friends as they could find, while native noblewomen took the corpses of their relatives to be interred in village churches; Harold himself was borne to Waltham (in Essex) for burial.

Such are the surviving sources on the battle of Hastings. Those from the English (or, more strictly speaking, Anglo-Norman) side do not exist in any quantity until the first half of the twelfth century, when authors such as John of Worcester, William of Malmesbury and Henry of Huntingdon were influenced by native resentment at the effects of the Conquest, a tendency to make excuses for the defeat and the very common medieval belief that disastrous events could only be the judgement of God upon a sinful people. Nevertheless, these accounts are relatively straightforward compared with the problems posed by the significant body of almost contemporary material from French writers. The *Carmen de Hastingae Proelio* may well be the work of Guy of Amiens, but it and the writings of William of Jumièges, William of Poitiers and Baudri of Bourgeuil are panegyrics of Duke William, and shape their comment accordingly; neither substantial military difficulties experienced by the Normans nor anything else to the duke's discredit are likely to be reflected in their pages, and the temptation to draw parallels between the events of 1066 and those of the classical period may have led to distortion. Moreover, some of the similarities between the sources are the result of direct borrowing, thus reducing their value as evidence: Orderic Vitalis and Wace certainly used earlier material, for example, and the accounts of the *Carmen*, William of Poitiers and Baudri of Bourgeuil may well be related; similarly, both Baudri and William of Malmesbury may have seen the Bayeux Tapestry.[99] By the twelfth century, and the works of Gaimar and Wace, we are to an extent in the realms of history as fiction.

Nevertheless the picture is far from being an entirely negative one. Wace, despite the fact that he was writing a century later, probably had access to a certain amount of valuable information independent of our other surviving sources, and the same is true of most of his predecessors. Men who fought in the battle need not always have been particularly reliable witnesses, both because of genuine confusion as to what course events had taken and a desire to magnify their own achievements, but the likelihood that the three contemporary French authors (Guy of Amiens, William of Jumièges and William of Poitiers) had spoken to eye-witnesses is high; the designer of the Bayeux Tapestry and Baudri of Bourgeuil may have done so too. Moreover, one can hardly stress too much that there was once a very much greater body of evidence which has not come down to us. Some of this was committed to writing, for if Sigebert of Gembloux was correct in saying in the early twelfth century that Archbishop Lanfranc wrote a work about the deeds of Duke William,[100] it is likely that it referred to Hastings, and the fact that both Guy's *Carmen* and William of Poitiers' *Gesta Guillelmi* have survived by a hairsbreadth, and the full text of Baudri's *Adelae Comitissae* only in a single manuscript, is by itself a salutary warning of how much may have disappeared. The songs and stories of the period have certainly done so, but are known to have existed: Henry of Huntingdon says that as a boy he had heard very old men speak of King Æthelred II's massacre of Danes in England on St Brice's Day in 1002; William of Malmesbury that the magnificence of the

[99] But see n.72 above on Baudri, and for comment on WM and the Tapestry, below, p.220.
[100] I owe this reference to Barlow, *Carmen*, p.xiv, n.3, who comments that Sigebert's words are 'a good description of *GG*, usually ascribed to William of Poitiers'.

celebrations attending the marriage of Cnut's daughter Gunnhild to the future emperor Henry III in 1036 was still celebrated in songs in his own time; Wace that he had heard his father comment on the number of ships which sailed with the Conqueror from St Valéry.[101] It would be astonishing if one of the most celebrated battles of the age was not also the subject of song, and of an immense body of popular report, rumour and reminiscence which eventually passed away without ever having taken any sort of literary form. This being so, one should not be too ready to assume that similarities between different sources are necessarily the result of direct borrowing, for what such parallels may often reveal is that stories about the battle, wherever and by whomever they were told, tended to group around certain themes: the long and hard-fought nature of the conflict, the difficulty which the French had in breaking the densely packed English line, the significance of a real and/or a feigned retreat by William's men, the role of his archers, deaths in ditches during the battle and/or after it, and the importance of Harold's own death (in some versions through being hit by an arrow) late in the day. Moreover if these themes recur so frequently because they reflect what was commonly said, it is no great distance from this to the argument that what was commonly said was itself some sort of reflection of what had actually happened, or at least what was believed to have happened.[102] Historians of more recent conflicts are frequently able to establish a fairly precise timetable of events and say a great deal about the individuals involved in the fighting. It will never be possible to

---

[101] *HA*, pp. 340–1; *GR*, i. 338–9; Wace, *RR*, ll. 6423–8.

[102] Note, by way of contrast, Barlow's conclusion (*Carmen*, pp. xc–i) that that of the 'near-contemporary' sources 'all are variations on a common literary theme', and that if 'Guy of Amiens had not written his poem, the story would probably have been quite different'. Given the great fame of the battle, and the probable access of those responsible for the sources produced before *c.* 1100 to eye-witness testimony even if only at some removes, this elevation of the importance of the *Carmen* in the creation of later accounts seems scarcely plausible. In earlier work, Barlow was willing to allow a significant role to verbal witness in shaping the near-contemporary sources, although he also expressed considerable scepticism about the details they provide, and suggested that Hastings is 'almost as obscure' as Fulford and Stamford Bridge, 'The *Carmen de Hastingae Proelio*', pp. 189–90, 217; in *The Godwins*, p. 104, he states that 'we have very few facts' about it.

reconstruct Hastings on this kind of scale; its story can never be told as can those of Waterloo and of Gettysburg, of the first day of the Somme and of D-Day. Nevertheless, it is not completely beyond recovery as a historical event.[103]

---

[103] Some sources which refer to the battle have not been discussed in detail here. The *Chronicon Monasterii de Hida* account, pp.293–4, dates from *c.*1128–34 and was perhaps written by a Norman monk of the Cluniac priory of St Pancras at Lewes or by a Norman author working in the duchy itself; see Lewis, 'The Earldom of Surrey', 330–4, and Gillingham, 'Henry of Huntingdon', Appendix. The *Draco Normannicus* of Stephen of Rouen is a Latin verse treatment of Norman history derived from a number of earlier writers including WJ and composed in the late 1160s (ll. 1427–95 on the battle). On Benoît of St Maur's account, written after that of Wace, whom he replaced in Henry II's favour, see Eley and Bennett, 'The Battle of Hastings', 68–77, and more generally, Blacker, *The Faces of Time*, pp.45–52, 119–32, 185–90.

4

THE ENGLISH ARMY

No matter with which we have to deal is darker than the
constitution of the English army on the eve of its defeat.
F.W. Maitland, *Domesday Book and Beyond*

In the popular consciousness, Harold being hit in the eye by an
arrow at Hastings is one of the most famous of historical events, and
seemingly of a piece with other gems from the period: Alfred burning the cakes at a low point in his fortunes, Æthelred the Unready
foolishly paying the Danes to go away, all combine to give the
poorest of impressions of the military capacities of Anglo-Saxon
government. Nor is it a picture which a closer look might seem to
contradict. Between about 800 and 1066 England was the scene of
more fighting than at any other time in its history, apart probably
from the opening decades of the Roman invasion. In the ninth century, after an initial period of coastal raiding, the Vikings destroyed
the kingdoms of East Anglia and Northumbria, and also conquered
half of the midlands realm of Mercia; Alfred's alleged culinary misfortunes[1] occurred as they almost overcame that of Wessex too.

[1] On this legend, see *Alfred the Great*, ed. Keynes and Lapidge, pp. 197–202.

During the 870s, English rulers survived in England by only the narrowest of margins. In the late tenth and early eleventh centuries, by which time they were dealing with the united country created by Alfred's successors, the Scandinavians reduced the government of Æthelred II (the Unready)[2] to apparent impotence, and in 1016, after about twenty-five years of fighting, Æthelred's dynasty was deposed and replaced by that of the Danish Cnut. Exactly fifty years later, following the interval which saw the extinction of Cnut's line and the succession of Æthelred's son Edward the Confessor, Harold II was defeated at Hastings, and the country had the first of what was this time to prove a long line of foreign kings.

Moreover, if all this gives an impression of military ineffectiveness it is one which some of the sources would appear to confirm. Of all the battles fought in England in this period we have reasonable accounts of only three, and only one of those, King Æthelstan's engagement against a great coalition of his enemies at *Brunanburh* in 937,[3] was a victory. The other two were defeats – Hastings, and the fight between the local levies of Essex and a Viking army at Maldon in 991, during the reign of Æthelred. At Maldon the Vikings landed on an island, probably because it offered some protection to their ships, and found the English facing them at the other end of the causeway which connected it to the mainland. The native commander, Ealdorman Byrhtnoth, rightly or wrongly allowed them to cross the causeway without opposition so that the battle could take place on equal terms, and was subsequently killed, whereupon part of his army fled. According to the poem *The Battle of Maldon* the remainder then affirmed, in some of the most moving words in Old English literature, their determination to show their loyalty to their lord by dying where they stood.[4] Whether they

---

[2] The term is a later distortion of the soubriquet *unræd*, 'no counsel', which is probably contemporary, and was a malicious pun on the name Æthelred, 'wise counsel'.

[3] *ASC*, i. 106, 108–10. The location of the battle is not certain.

[4] The poem is incomplete at both beginning and end, and is known only from an eighteenth-century transcript, the manuscript having been destroyed by the fire in the Cotton Library in 1731. Perhaps composed shortly after the battle, its historical reliability has been much disputed; see briefly, *The Battle of Maldon AD 991*, ed. Scragg, pp. 34–5.

actually did so is not known, but certainly they were overcome, and the same year saw the payment of the first of the very large tributes for which Æthelred's reign is famous. At Hastings defeat came about, if William of Poitiers can be believed, through apparent indiscipline, when English forces three times left the position which had served them so well to chase a French army which then encircled and destroyed its pursuers. If there is added to this the depiction on the Bayeux Tapestry of figures who are clearly poorly armed peasants, anyone might be forgiven for thinking that Anglo-Saxon armies were little more than armed mobs which trusted to bravery and luck more than to elaborately organised logistics, military technology and tactical skill.

Yet this cannot be so, as can be readily demonstrated by a rather more detailed survey of late Anglo-Saxon history than that undertaken so far.[5] Alfred may in the late ninth century have saved Wessex by the narrowest of margins, but he did so by carrying out well-known reforms to its military system which ensured that Viking raiders received a rather warmer welcome in the later stages of his reign than they had done hitherto. His son Edward the Elder, in campaigns which are recorded in some of the most stirring and remarkable of all the entries in the *Anglo-Saxon Chronicle*, subdued East Anglia and Danish Mercia, and by 927 his grandson Æthelstan, virtually forgotten today but one of the great European figures of his time, was the first king of all England. In 934 he led both an army and a navy into Scotland in a campaign which foreshadowed those of Edward I over 300 years later, and received the submission of northern kings and princes; on some of his coins appeared a legend used by no other pre-Conquest king: *Æthelstan rex tot(ius) Brit(anniæ)* ('Æthelstan, king of all Britain').[6] Forty years later his relative Edgar, another of the great forgotten figures of English history, also achieved dominance over much of Britain, and perhaps of part of Ireland too, being rowed on the Dee at Chester by

---

[5] See, similarly, Hollister, *Anglo-Saxon Military Institutions*, pp.128–9.
[6] See Walker, 'A Context for *Brunanburh*?'.

six of his subordinates[7] after a coronation earlier in the year which may have been intended to emulate that of the western emperor, Otto I of Germany, crowned in Rome in 962. Of course, Edgar's son, Æthelred II, is not forgotten, and for the wrong reasons, but that there were great inherent strengths in the system of government which he inherited from his forebears, and was unable to employ effectively, is suggested by the career of the Danish Cnut, who after 1016 utilised English wealth and military resources to create an empire which embraced not only parts of Britain but Denmark, Norway and perhaps some of Sweden too. Like Edgar, Cnut copied the German emperors, for there is a contemporary drawing of him in which he is being given a crown which, with its arched bar, was a deliberate imitation of the German imperial crown, and his daughter married the future Emperor Henry III of Germany, who was eventually to request the help of the English navy against one of his enemies, Count Baldwin V of Flanders. In the same decade, the 1040s, King Swegen Estrithson of Denmark also asked Edward the Confessor for the assistance of English ships. If the late Anglo-Saxon military system was a farce, Swegen and Henry III had not heard of it.[8] Could it be then, that the defeats of the period were not the inevitable result of an organisation which was inherently chaotic, but accidental outcomes of personality and circumstance of the sort which can bring down even the most well-organised of military forces (for war is a risky business), and that it is to such organisation, as well as good leadership, that one should attribute the successes of Alfred, Edward the Elder, Æthelstan, Edgar and Cnut?

That this must to an extent be the truth can be powerfully suggested by momentarily turning aside from military matters to what is known about the late Anglo-Saxon period generally, and late Anglo-Saxon government in particular. In the last thirty years this subject has been revolutionised by the work of Professor James

[7] JW, ii. 422–5. John's source for this event may have been a tenth-century poem, Campbell, 'Asser's *Life of Alfred*', p.138.

[8] Hollister, *Anglo-Saxon Military Institutions*, pp.125–6.

Campbell.[9] He sees late Anglo-Saxon England as economically developed and therefore effulgent with the wealth which proved such a powerful attraction to invaders; the margin between the king's authority and that of the great lords may have been significantly greater than it was on the continent; so may the size of the political community (the number of people whose opinions in some sense mattered politically); government was not a remote force which impinged seldom and gently on the English people, but omnipresent in their lives; the division of the country into shires and their sub-units the hundreds ensured that the king's will could be made known and implemented at a very local level, the hundreds being used for the exercise of many functions, including the fiscal, judicial and military; these organisations probably ran alongside an extensive network of officials, the reeves, who profited from doing the king's business, and who seem in some respects to have been able to exercise a degree of control over people's lives which is somewhat startling; if so, this is because we are always prone to underestimate the capacities and achievements of so-called primitive systems of government.[10] Campbell's work has been complemented by that of numismatists,[11] who have shown that late in his reign Edgar introduced a coinage system of great complexity. This involved, among other things, issuing a new coin type every six years or so (after 1035 every two or three), probably so that the authorities could make a substantial profit by insisting on a favourable rate of exchange of old coins for new. One might think that the population would simply have ignored all this and continued using old coins, but the evidence is that they did not, presumably because there was a date beyond which the previous

[9] See P. Wormald, 'James Campbell as Historian', including the judgement (p.xxi) that 'Campbell's importance lies... in how he has taught historians of early times to think'.

[10] See especially Campbell, 'Observations on English Government from the Tenth to the Twelfth Century'; 'Some Agents and Agencies of the Late Anglo-Saxon State'; 'The Significance of the Anglo-Norman State in the Administrative History of Western Europe'; 'Was it Infancy in England? Some Questions of Comparison'; 'The Late Anglo-Saxon State: A Maximum View'.

[11] The literature is very extensive, but for an introduction see Stewart, 'Coinage and recoinage after Edgar's reform'.

type was no longer legal tender, and all significant purchases were witnessed by the king's officials. When tenth-century laws state that all trading must take place in towns before witnesses it is virtually certain that this was not legislation which was amusingly ambitious and ineffective, but deadly serious and strictly enforced. It is known what strict enforcement might involve. Confiscation of all one's possessions is a common penalty for wrongdoing in this period, and there are several examples of kings who ravaged parts of their own territory because the inhabitants had incurred their displeasure. When the people of Worcestershire killed two tax collectors Cnut's son Harthacnut despatched an army with instructions to burn Worcester itself, devastate the entire shire and kill all the men. These orders were partly carried out. Worcester was burnt and the shire (or at least some of it) ravaged, but few were killed: they had fled in all directions; if late Anglo-Saxon government was a farce, they had not heard of it. On the fifth day peace was restored, the royal anger appeased and the ravagers returned home, loaded with booty and doubtless glowing with virtue at their implementation of the king's wishes.[12] Given, then, the determination of kings to govern, and the evidence that they often did so very effectively indeed, and given also the need for defence against external enemies, which as noted earlier was very frequent, and must have seemed of overriding importance, what one might expect to find is a military system which was well-organised, well-equipped and a reflection of the intelligence and power to be found in other aspects of the late Anglo-Saxon state. Of course, these arguments are circumstantial: is there any evidence which will put flesh on their bones?

It is likely that some of the administrative features of the late Old English period had their origins in a remote past.[13] Certainly, remarkable feats of government were implemented before the time with which this study is mainly concerned. In the late eighth century, for example, the Mercian king Offa constructed a rampart of

<hr />

[12] The harrying of 1041 is noted by *ASC* C and D (i. 162–3); for most of the details, see JW, ii. 532–3.
[13] Campbell, 'The Late Anglo-Saxon State', pp.2–8.

considerable length on the Welsh border which may have availed itself of the services of 'very many thousands of diggers'[14] by the imposition of labour service upon his subject peoples. Nevertheless, a treatment of the military capacities of the army which fought at Hastings can reasonably begin with Alfred, and two elements of the reforms which succeeded in stopping the seemingly overwhelming Viking advance in the late ninth century. Firstly, there was the building, or perhaps renovation in some cases, of an extensive network of burhs (fortified towns and fortresses) and their manning by garrisons capable of looking after themselves; this meant that it became much more difficult for the enemy to overrun areas than it had been previously, as is evident from the entries in the *Anglo-Saxon Chronicle* for the 890s, when the attackers never succeeded in penetrating Wessex as they had done in the dark days twenty years earlier. Remains of some of these defences survive above ground, as for example at Wallingford and Wareham, and they do so together with a document, the Burghal Hidage, which reveals something of the way the authorities had them built and maintained. It lists many of the burhs, and says that if one hide (the Anglo-Saxon unit of fiscal assessment) supplies one man then every pole (that is about 5 yards) of wall would be manned or maintained – there are difficulties about the precise meaning of the word used[15] – by four men. It is possible using this formula and the other figures given to work out the size of the individual burhs mentioned in the document, and in a number of cases the result corresponds closely to the extent of the surviving defences of the places concerned. It is also possible to calculate the total number of

[14] Ibid., p.6. See most recently Hill, 'Offa's Dyke: Pattern and Purpose', who questions whether construction ran all the way along the border from sea to sea, as claimed a century later by Bishop Asser, the biographer of King Alfred.

[15] This word, the Old English *waru*, can refer either to physical defence or the discharge of fiscal obligations. Dr Rumble (*The Defence of Wessex*, ed. Hill and Rumble, pp.178–81) keeps the options open by concluding that the formula refers to the defence of wall 'in a military and/or a fiscal sense'; Campbell, 'Stenton's *Anglo-Saxon England*', p.272, thinks that the similarity between the formula and the Domesday Book entry on Chester (DB, i. 262d), which says that the city wall and bridge were repaired by one man from every hide in the shire, makes it 'nearly certain that what is in question is maintenance'.

men involved in their maintenance or defence – 27,671.[16] And this, of course, as Alfred had other men who were not involved in defending or maintaining burhs, immediately suggests a scale of activity involving tens of thousands, perhaps, dare one say it, many tens of thousands of men, which might seem surprising, but which other evidence does not entirely fail to confirm.

Alfred is also well known for his interest in the West Saxon navy. It is by no means clear that he founded it, or that the measures he took were particularly successful, but there is the explicit and contemporary statement in the *Anglo-Saxon Chronicle* that he was responsible for a new type of ship, 'neither of the Frisian design nor of the Danish, but as it seemed to himself that they might be most useful'. Some had sixty oars, some more.[17] Now craft of thirty oars a side may have been very large indeed, and are entirely absent from the archaeological record of the period, although this is far from being extensive enough to provide any substantial reason for thinking that they could not have existed. N.A.M. Rodger has accepted the possibility that these vessels had crews of two to three hundred men, being 'a massive application of money and manpower' and among the largest 'built in northern waters during the Middle Ages'.[18] Possibly so, but it does not necessarily follow that they were particularly rare. In the reign of Æthelred II, Bishop Ælfwold of Crediton bequeathed to the king a ship of sixty-four oars, 'all ready except for the rowlocks'.[19] If it were common for sources from the period to give precise information on the sizes of warships, and if such information usually referred to smaller craft, it would be reasonable to regard sixty-oared vessels as exceptional. But as such references are in fact very uncommon one is left

---

[16] Davis, 'Alfred the Great: Propaganda and Truth', pp.42–3. This seminal article is the foundation of the best modern scholarship on Alfred.

[17] *ASC*, i. 90.

[18] Rodger, *The Safeguard of the Sea*, pp.15–17; see also his very useful, 'Cnut's Geld and the Size of Danish Ships', *passim*. However, Rodger does not consider the possibility that 'so large a number of oarsmen (sixty or more) might have been accommodated in some manner other than simple alignment', for example with the oars double-banked; Swanton, 'King Alfred's ships', 13.

[19] *EHD1*, No. 122; Rodger, 'Cnut's Geld', 400, suggests, not very plausibly in my view given the Alfredian evidence, that some of the oars may have been spares.

wondering. Could it be that there were times when great battle-ships crewed by hundreds of men, the Dreadnoughts of their day, were by no means rare, and that this was not unconnected with the desire of King Swegen of Denmark and Emperor Henry III to seek English naval assistance in the 1040s?[20]

Alfred's measures included the use of troops who travelled on horseback so that they might more easily pursue Viking forces which did likewise, and further evidence of activity on a large scale is to be found in a law code of King Æthelstan which demands, in a provision which may relate specifically to the obligations of the inhabitants of burhs, that he be supplied with two well-horsed men from every plough. A 'plough' in this context may be an assessment unit rather than an actual object – in other words, however many ploughs a landowner actually had, it was not necessarily the same as the notional figure at which the government assessed him for tax, and which was presumably based on the perceived wealth of the land concerned. Domesday Book, compiled on the Conqueror's orders in 1086, mentions both ploughlands and ploughteams, although the results of associating Æthelstan's order with either of them are fairly staggering, for by the 1086 figures he would have been demanding at least 120,000 mounted men from the former and 160,000 from the latter.[21] Yet if association with these units is rejected, as it seemingly must be, one would still think that there must have been many 'ploughs' in his kingdom, and even if not all were related to the military obligations of burhs the likelihood that

---

[20] See further on the Anglo-Saxon navy, Hooper, 'Some Observations on the Navy in Late Anglo-Saxon England'; Strickland, 'Military Technology and Conquest: The Anomaly of Anglo-Saxon-England', 373–8, with the comment that it was 'the arm to which the Anglo-Saxons themselves attached great, if not supreme significance'; Rodger, *The Safeguard of the Sea*, pp.14–30. There were, of course, smaller vessels too. DB, i 1a, refers to the supply to the king of twenty ships for fifteen days a year, each of them containing twenty-one *homines*. Even if the latter were soldiers additional to the rowers they seem unlikely to have been in very large craft. I owe this reference to James Campbell.

[21] II Æthelstan 16, *Die Gesetze der Angelsachsen*, ed. Liebermann, i. 158; Darby, *Domesday England*, pp.95–136, 336. Abels, *Lordship and Military Obligation*, p.111. See also the note in *The Laws of the Earliest English Kings*, ed. Attenborough, p.208: 'the requirement stated here is exceptionally heavy; but the explanation probably is that cap. 13–18 seem to have been intended for *burgware*, who may be regarded as primarily a military caste'.

he was asking for many thousands of well-horsed troops seems high. Moreover, that reliable sources such as the Burghal Hidage and Æthelstan's law code suggest large figures makes one the more inclined to believe such totals in sources of a more dubious nature. In the second decade of the eleventh century the German bishop Thietmar of Merseburg recorded a report that when London was under siege by the Danes in 1016 it contained 24,000 coats of mail.[22] Rather significantly, he thought this incredible, but in the context of other very sizeable totals it may not be.

If one turns from the administrative evidence mentioned so far to accounts of actual campaigns (which are considerably more plentiful than those of battles), it is to be expected that the apparently great capacities hinted at in the one will also be found reflected in the other, and this is indeed so. Take, for example, the events of 917,[23] when Edward the Elder was in the process of reconquering the eastern midlands, partly by the building of burhs in enemy territory, from the Scandinavians who had settled there in earlier decades. In that year he ordered such works to be constructed at Towcester and *Wigingamere*, both of which then had to withstand sieges until in the case of the former reinforcements arrived. In the summer, a great force assembled from the men of nearby burhs and took by assault the Viking fortress of Tempsford, while in the autumn Colchester was captured by a great army consisting of garrisons and men from Kent, Surrey and Essex; at much the same time the enemy made an unsuccessful attack on Maldon in Essex, suffering 'many hundreds' of dead in fighting its reinforced garrison. The king himself then led a West Saxon army (thus far evidently inactive) to Passenham while Towcester was fortified in stone, and once these men had gone home another force assembled for the capture of Huntingdon. Perhaps it was the same army which then restored the defences of Colchester. In the same year Edward's sister Æthelflæd, Lady of the Mercians, captured the Viking stronghold of Derby. Even more

---

[22] Thietmar, *Chronicon*, ed. Holtzmann, pp.446–7; trans. *EHD1*, p.348.

[23] *ASC*, i. 101–3. I use the revised date for this entry of *EHD1*, p.214.

impressive in its way is the effort which Edmund Ironside, the son of Æthelred II, made against Cnut in 1016. Although it came at the end of a long period of military failure, in which the West Saxons themselves had been prepared to abandon their native dynasty and accept a Danish king, Edmund was able to call up all the people of England five times,[24] and at least three major battles were fought during the year, at Penselwood (probably in May or early June), Sherston (25 June) and *Assandun* (18 October), with possibly a fourth near the Forest of Dean before Edmund made peace and eventually died (30 November).[25] This capacity for engaging in repeated conflict is reminiscent of the fighting of 871, when the *Anglo-Saxon Chronicle* claims that there were nine engagements between the West Saxons and the Vikings; of these, the victory of Æthelred I and his brother Alfred at Ashdown followed a mere four days after they had suffered heavy losses at Reading, and was itself followed only two weeks later by a defeat at Basing.[26]

What emerges from such material, which of course must bring to mind the three battles of 20 September to 14 October 1066, is that pre-Conquest English military systems, far from being easily exhausted, were capable of producing battleworthy forces over an extended period, and despite loss and defeat. Of course, it might reasonably be objected that almost 200 years separated 871 and 1066, and that even the events of 1016 do not necessarily prove anything about the military resources available to Harold II fifty years later.[27] This is true, but those fifty years were far from uneventful, and such evidence as there is does not suggest a marked decline in the effectiveness of English forces. Cnut used them in Scandinavia at the battle of Holy River *c.* 1026 (perhaps a defeat in the midst of a successful campaign to repulse a Norwegian and Swedish attack on

---

[24] *ASC,* i. 151.
[25] On the Forest of Dean battle and the dates of Sherston and *Assandun,* see Lawson, *Cnut,* pp. 78–9, 143.
[26] *ASC,* i. 71–2.
[27] Abels, 'From Alfred to Harold II', argues that 'English military institutions eroded between the death of Alfred in 899 and the Battle of Hastings' and that Harold 'possessed a military system that was seriously flawed' (pp. 16, 29).

his position in Denmark), in conquering Norway in 1028, and doubtless also in securing the submission of other princes in the British Isles.[28] The reign of Edward the Confessor saw considerable fighting against the Welsh. In 1052 Gruffydd of North Wales raided Herefordshire and defeated local levies near Leominster; three years later he and Irish forces assisted the return of the exiled Earl Ælfgar of Mercia, overcoming local troops who had been made to fight on horseback under the king's (French) nephew Earl Ralph, and sacking Hereford. Earl Harold then gathered men from almost all England who provided a screen while he built an earthwork around the town, there was a reconciliation with Ælfgar and peace was made. Nevertheless, Gruffydd remained a problem, not least because he henceforth controlled all the Welsh. The following year he defeated and killed Bishop Leofgar of Hereford and in 1058 assisted Ælfgar in a second return from exile. But in 1063, after an interval about which little is known, he finally met his match. Harold advanced to Rhuddlan and burnt the palace there, subsequently sailing with a fleet from Bristol in a campaign coordinated with an army led by his brother Earl Tostig; this was too much for the Welsh, and on 5 August Gruffydd was killed by his own men and his head brought to Harold. Whether or not this was the most successful invasion of Wales since the Roman period and 'the rebirth of England as a military power',[29] it certainly suggests that there was little the matter with the country's military system, and this campaign was not the only successful venture of Edward's reign. In 1054 Earl Siward of Northumbria had invaded Scotland with a navy and an army which included some of the king's housecarls, and defeated King Macbeth in a battle in which both sides suffered heavy losses; having installed Malcolm as king of Cumbria and Lothian, he returned home laden with booty.[30] Nor should the

[28] Lawson, *Cnut*, pp.96–101, 104–7.
[29] Barlow, pp.211–2, and more generally on Edward and Wales, pp.204–13; also Barlow, *The Godwins*, pp.68–9. The main primary sources are the C, D and E versions of *ASC*, i. 176–91; JW, ii. 592–3; *LKE*, pp.86–7.
[30] *ASC*, C and D, i. 184–5; Barlow, pp.202–3. Malcolm showed little gratitude, ravaging Northumbria in 1061 and assisting Harald Hardrada in 1066; on housecarls, see below, pp.158–9.

general threat from Scandinavia be forgotten, and in particular the hostile fleet which came from Norway in 1058.[31] England was no safer in the Confessor's reign than in the previous tumultuous two and a half centuries, and it is not probable that those responsible for its defences were unaware of this, especially once it became clear that King Edward's death was likely to be followed by foreign invasion. Thus, the *Anglo-Saxon Chronicle* C text's statement that in 1066 Harold gathered greater land and naval forces than had ever been seen before is likely to be an accurate enough reflection of the scale of the preparations made to receive William.

Of course, the size and nature of the army which fought at Hastings is another matter. The battles of Fulford and Stamford Bridge had taken place very recently and had involved losses, although the known ability of English kings to assemble forces at short notice should give pause to those who would assume that it must on that account have been inadequate, and it should not be forgotten that most of the sources agree that fighting was hard and lasted all day. Yet any attempt to be more precise than this is fraught with difficulty, as will now become apparent. None of the eleventh- and twelfth-century writers give any sort of plausible figure for Harold's army.[32] Most of those from the English side tend to minimise its size, from the *Chronicle* E text's mild statement that he fought before it had all gathered to what look like the deliberate attempts of John of Worcester and William of Malmesbury to reduce the impact of defeat by suggesting that their countrymen stood little chance from the first.[33] The exception to this is the *Chronicle* D version's statement that it was a large force, a view with which the *Carmen*, William of Jumièges and William of Poitiers all concur. Naturally, the French writers can be accused of wishing to exaggerate the number of Duke William's enemies in order to magnify his victory, and even if the idea that their force was 'large'

[31] Above, p. 38.

[32] The *Carmen*, ll. 223–4, gives twelve hundred thousand, which *FNC*, iii. 741, thought 'the whole military population of England'; Wace, *RR*, ll. 7861–3, has Harold claim to have 400,000 men.

[33] Above, pp. 58–70.

were to be accepted there is no way of knowing what the word meant in eleventh century terms. Yet none of this has prevented historians of the battle from advancing opinions on the size of the English army which have often worn a rather greater appearance of certainty than the evidence actually warrants.

The most detailed scholarly treatment of Hastings remains that of Freeman's *Norman Conquest*. Freeman enjoyed visiting historical sites, and travelled to Battle from his home in Somerset on a number of occasions. On 2 June 1869 he walked over the ground in the company of Captain Edward R. James of the Royal Engineers, whose father Henry had been director-general of the Ordnance Survey since 1854, where he pioneered the reproduction of maps by photozincography. Thus it was that the publication of Freeman's third volume was delayed so that it could include a zincographed fold-out map of the battlefield produced by the Ordnance Survey; it showed the English army drawn up along most of the Battle Abbey ridge in forty-nine individual units, with housecarls in the centre and 'light-armed' on the wings; to their front was a palisade, and there was an 'outpost' (which may have owed something to awareness of Wellington's use of Hougoumont and La Haye Sainte at Waterloo) in what is now the area of Horselodge Plantation, on the south-western face of the ridge.[34] Freeman relied on Captain James to put the extent and arrangement of the palisade into a 'scientific military shape', and warned in his preface that:

> The relative position of the different divisions in the two armies seems beyond doubt, but the extent of ground occupied by each division must be matter of pure conjecture. The one absolutely certain point is the position of the English Standard and the fact that it was against that point that the main attack under William himself was made.[35]

[34] See above, pp.51-6, on the topography of the battlefield. On Freeman's map (opposite) 'b b b' represents the palisade and 'c c' the outpost; he commented on the latter, *FNC*, iii. 444, 477.
[35] Ibid., iii. vi–vii. Many years later James disclaimed all responsibility for the way in which the details of the battle had been shown, 'The Battle of Hastings', 19.

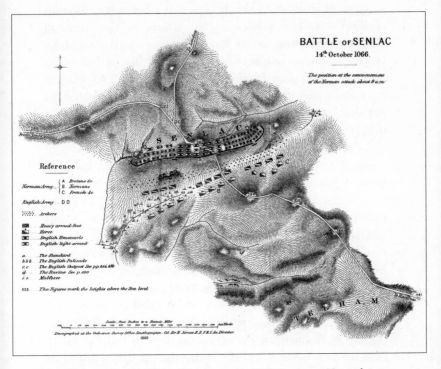

Freeman's map of the dispositions of the two armies, *FNC*, iii. opp. 433. Not to the original scale.

No one could quarrel with the final sentence, but elsewhere its author spoke of an 'immovable wedge of men which, as if fixed to the ground by nature, covered… every inch' of the ridge, and of 'ranks of men… ranged… closely together in the thick array of the shield-wall'.[36] Prudently, he gave no estimate of the numbers involved,[37] but there was an inconsistency between some of these comments and the map, whose neat little units bore no obvious relationship to an extended, densely packed line. Freeman died of

[36] *FNC*, iii. 471.
[37] Ibid., iii. 740–2.

smallpox in Spain on 16 March 1892; only a few months later his reputation, and in particular his account of the battle of Hastings, had come under attack (anonymously) from John Horace Round; within twenty years a very different view of the extent of the English deployment on the ridge, and therefore of the scale of the battle, had occupied a position from which it has not since been dislodged. Indeed, so unassailable has this position apparently been deemed that there has been no attempt to dislodge it.

The fact that Round never essayed a full and coherent account of the fight about which he was eventually to write a great deal did not inhibit some trenchant comment on what he took to be errors in that of Freeman, whose reputation for historical accuracy, along with that of the acclaimed *Norman Conquest*, he sought to destroy. Thus, he ridiculed both the adoption of the name Senlac for the battle as the 'truth is simply that the site of the battle had no name at all', and the idea that the English front was protected by a palisade, based on a (supposed) mistranslation of a poor authority, Wace's *Roman de Rou*;[38] further, he questioned the belief that the English had formed up with the heaviest troops in the centre and the lighter armed on the wings, as it would have been foolish of Harold to place such forces on his right flank, which Freeman had himself acknowledged to be the weakest point in his position. In Round's judgement, the most reliable native force, the shield-wall of 'heavy soldiery, clad in helmets and mail', would have occupied their entire front, with the 'half-armed peasants' behind it, able to throw missiles over the heads of their colleagues and back them up in repelling an attack.[39] There followed a bitter controversy between Round and those who took up the cudgels on Freeman's behalf, T.A. Archer and Kate Norgate, with the latter eventually accusing her opponent of acting dishonourably in

---

[38] *RR*, ll. 7793–804.
[39] Round, anonymous *Quarterly Review* article of July, 1892.

attacking from 'the shelter of his anonymity' a 'dead man who had given him no provocation'.[40]

The period of this debate also saw the publication of the German scholar Wilhelm Spatz's small book *Die Schlacht von Hastings*. This rejected both the notion that the English had employed such a difficult formation as a shield-wall and the claim that the French had used a feigned retreat, resulting, in Round's words, in the belief 'that both armies were little better than armed mobs... incapable of the simplest formation or manoeuvre'.[41] But Spatz also attempted to arrive at estimates of the sizes of both forces, and argued that as Harold had in the battle only the military strength of southern England, and as he would probably have attacked the French and not been defeated so heavily if his army had been larger than theirs, he therefore probably commanded no more than 6,000–7,000 men, the number which Spatz believed William brought against him.[42] Only two years later Sir James Ramsay's *The Foundations of England* appeared. This concluded that 5,000 Frenchmen 'would satisfy our ideas of what was at all likely: 10,000 men we should consider beyond credibility', and although he gave no estimate for the English he accepted that Harold fought before all his troops had arrived. He also accepted (from William of Poitiers) that they were

[40] Norgate, 'The Battle of Hastings. Part II', 76. See further Round, anonymous *Quarterly Review* article of July, 1893; 'Wace and his Authorities'; and 'Mr Freeman and the Battle of Hastings'; Archer, 'Mr Freeman and the "Quarterly Review"'; 'The Battle of Hastings. Part I'. These are only the main references in a controversy which lasted six years; a list of all the significant material produced between 1892 and 1898 is given in Round, 'The Battle of Hastings', 63. He had little difficulty in convicting Freeman of factual error (for he did not confine his assault to the battle), but emerged from the fray by no means unscathed, or innocent of error, himself; he did not respond, for example, to Miss Norgate's rejection of his views on 'Senlac', and was eventually refuted by W.H. Stevenson (above, p. 56); his stance on Freeman's supposed mistranslation of Wace was damaged when S.R. Gardiner, editor of the *English Historical Review*, produced letters from two 'eminent French authorities' supporting Freeman's belief that Wace's *escuz de fenestres e d'altres fuz* indicates 'bien un rempart, une sorte de palissade'; *EHR*, ix (1894), 260; Burgess has recently rendered the passage (*RR*, ll. 7793–7): 'they had made shields for themselves out of shutters and other pieces of wood. They had them raised before them like hurdles, joined closely together; from them they had made a barrier in front of them'.

[41] Round, 'The Battle of Hastings', 61; to a French audience he presented Spatz's rejection of the shield-wall as 'un exemple extrême de cette tendance à bâtir des théories en dehors des faits, à laquelle l'esprit allemand est souvent trop enclin', 'La bataille de Hastings', 70.

[42] Spatz, *Die Schlacht von Hastings*, pp. 33–4; for Spatz and the French army, see below, pp. 176–7.

so densely massed that the dead could not fall, and judged that this 'points to a formation many ranks deep'; referring too to John of Worcester on the narrowness of the site, and alleging that the Battle Abbey *Brevis Relatio* states that the Normans found the English in *illo spisso agmine quod erat ante eos in montis summitate* ('in that very dense formation which was before them on the crest of the ridge'),[43] Ramsay concluded that their line must have formed three sides of a square around that crest, with the rear 'being left open as sufficiently protected by the ravines, and in fact unassailable'.[44] In making the perfectly reasonable suggestion that the English left flank was turned back against the steep northern face of the ridge Ramsay may have recalled Round's comment that the line 'might, for all we know, have formed a crescent or semicircle, its wings resting strongly on the rear-slopes of the hill'.[45] It is not clear from this just where Round thought the English right could have been positioned, but the map (illus. 38) which accompanied Ramsay's book placed it roughly at the southern end of what is now Battle High Street. There is, however, nothing in this area that could reasonably be described as a 'ravine'. Round had judged Freeman's map of the battlefield in need of substantial revision, and Ramsay's version was quickly joined by another, that of F.H. Baring. The latter concurred with Ramsay in refusing to join Freeman in allowing the English a frontage along the entire length of the ridge, because Charles Oman had already suggested that if one combined with such a frontage Round's belief that their formation consisted of a continuous shield-wall then such a formation, if ten or twelve ranks deep, could have contained 25,000 men.[46] Baring thought that this was far more

[43] This was rather misleading, as *BR* in fact simply records a report that Harold's standard was to be seen there; above, p. 113.

[44] Ramsay, *The Foundations of England*, ii. 16–17, 22–6.

[45] Round, anonymous *Quarterly Review* article of 1893, 101; *Feudal England*, p. 366, n. 100. Round thought that Ramsay had made a 'fairly strong case' for his view that the English stood wholly 'on the little "plateau" of the summit of the hill' and were not more than 5,000 strong, without wishing to 'assert that the Normans were so few as this', 'The Battle of Hastings', 62. For the northern slope of the eastern part of the ridge, see illus. 62.

[46] Oman, *A History of the Art of War: The Middle Ages*, pp. 154–5; he also estimated that there were 2,000 to 3,000 housecarls around the standard.

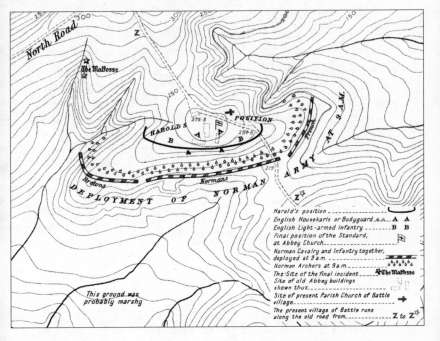

Detail from Baring's map of the dispositions of the two armies, *Domesday Tables*, end-paper. Not to the original scale, and with an abbreviated key superimposed.

than seemed likely, and therefore proposed a shorter front (if not quite as short as Ramsay's), arguing that as we are told that they were densely compressed this cannot have been true of a line of the length that Freeman had suggested, and that the English chronicles suggest an army that was not large. He also agreed with Ramsay and Spatz that the French army was not large (the figures given by William of Poitiers being 'not to be taken as arithmetic at all'), and thus arrived at an estimate of 10,000 to 13,000 for the English, 'many of them… rustics'. This allowed each man a front of two feet on a line 650–800 yards long, with ranks ten to twelve deep. The French he guessed at perhaps 8,000 to 10,000, while

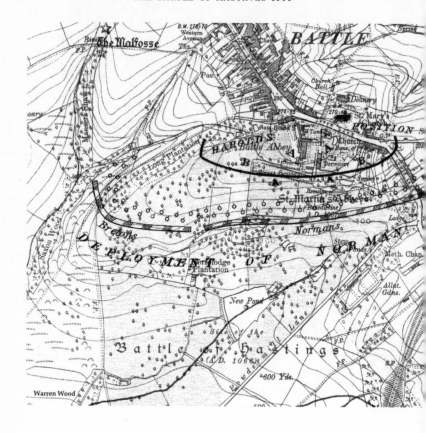

considering Ramsay's estimate of 5,000 'rather small, but not impossible'.[47] Baring reproduced a map made at a scale of 6 inches to the mile in 1907 for Major-General Edward R. James, who as a captain had walked the field with Freeman nearly forty years earlier; this was naturally better than the earlier map (which had used a scale of 4 inches to the mile and much less informative contouring) on the relief, and of course showed the smaller English

[47] 'The Battle Field of Hastings', 65–70; 'On the Battle of Hastings', 217–20. But in n.2 to p.219 he added on the English: 'I incline to a position 600 yards long, rather than 800, and to 10,000 men or less, rather than 12,000 or 13,000'.

Baring's map of the dispositions of the two armies superimposed on the OS 6-inch map of 1931, and centred on Battle parish church. Not to the original scale.

frontage.[48] Like Ramsay, Baring thought that its left did not extend fully eastwards along the ridge, where the slope is less severe, but was turned back so that it was protected from envelopment by the steep gradient to the north; the English right he placed a little further west than Ramsay, but agreed in showing it bent back towards (but some distance from) what is now Battle High Street. However,

[48] The map, which showed the English deployment upon which both evidently agreed, was first published in James' article 'The Battle of Hastings', in which he acknowledged 'much kind assistance' from Baring. Comparison with modern OS maps suggests that it is not completely accurate, pushing the lower reaches of the stream which runs west out of New Pond, for example, rather too far to the south.

he knew that Ramsay was mistaken in positing the existence of a 'ravine' in this area, and commented instead that:

> a brook runs close behind the ridge and at 400 yards from the church the bank at the back, though not so formidable as it is further west, is already 20 feet high; it has too a wide trench at its foot, cut by the head of the little stream, so that there is quite enough to prevent any effective attack from the rear at this point by the Norman horse.[49]

As will become evident shortly, this was not particularly convincing. Even so, Baring's basic guide to the extent of the English deployment was to carry all before it, being apparently adopted in Sir Frank Stenton's influential and widely read *Anglo-Saxon England* in 1943, and featuring in many other treatments of the battle down to the present day, including R. Allen Brown's article from 1980, which reproduced his map with little comment.[50] It is, of course, a concomitant of this that the relatively small numbers first advanced by Spatz have also

---

[49] 'On the Battle of Hastings', p.218.

[50] Stenton, *Anglo-Saxon England*, pp.594–5. With typical caution Stenton described Baring's frontage and referred to his map without specifically accepting them, having already warned, in words reminiscent of Freeman's, that the only certainty about the English dispositions was the location of Harold and his standard; Brown, 'The Battle of Hastings', 4–5, 10–11. Lemmon, 'The Campaign of 1066', p.96, shows an English front about 900 yards long, but with a western flank not bent back towards the 'brook': 'to refuse the flanks at all was really unnecessary because medieval attacks on a flank were usually frontal' (p.100); similarly, Beeler, *Warfare in England 1066–1189*, p.18. Fuller, *The Decisive Battles of the Western World*, i. 377, opted for a slight curve, turning the English right back to the 'brook', while there are varying degrees of curve in Morillo, *Warfare under the Anglo-Norman Kings*, p.163, and *The Battle of Hastings: Sources and Interpretations*, ed. Morillo, pp.xxiii–xxx; Oman, who had once accepted Freeman's long line, eventually went further than Ramsay and Baring in showing the English position as almost a semicircle, with the western flank extending over the 'brook', *A History of the Art of War: The Middle Ages*, i. opp. 164. Bennett's recent maps (*Campaigns of the Norman Conquest*, pp.38, 42) do not trouble overmuch with the streams, as the flanks of the short English front are shown resting upon two strategically placed patches of woodland for which there is no evidence.

become part of the staple diet of those who read about the battle.[51] Yet that this should be so is not because of any overwhelming evidence in their favour, for the truth, at least as far as the English army is concerned, is that its size is simply not known; consequently there is a wide range of possibilities, and the tens of thousands of men who lie in the outer reaches of that range may in fact be no less plausible a figure than the few thousand who inhabit the inner reach. To the possibility of tens of thousands, spread over a considerably greater area than the mere crest of the ridge, indeed to something not very unlike Freeman's position, it is now necessary to turn.

Firstly, it must be noted that the location of the English right wing is not quite so straightforward as a casual reading of Baring's comments might suggest. The phrase 'the bank at the back... already 20 feet high', which he used to describe the area where that wing rested, implies an almost vertical drop when in fact there is no such feature in this vicinity, as is evident from the 10-foot contour lines on his map.[52] Moreover, the 'head of the little stream' actually

---

[51] Oman, who originally guessed 25,000 English and 10,000–12,000 French horse and 15,000–20,000 French foot, eventually spoke cautiously of 'many thousands' of English and perhaps 12,000 French, *A History of the Art of War*, pp.154–6, and (2nd edn) i. 156–8; most other estimates have been closer to Spatz's roughly 7,000 a side, *Die Schlacht von Hastings*, pp.26–34. Stenton, *Anglo-Saxon England*, p.593, wrote of 7,000 English and rather fewer French; similarly his earlier *William the Conqueror*, p.196, and Douglas, *William the Conqueror*, pp.198–9. Burne, *The Battlefields of England*, pp.37–8, suggested nearly 9,000 Normans and 'the English about the same at the start, with considerable reinforcements flowing in during... the battle'. Lemmon, *The Field of Hastings*, p.24, averaged eleven earlier estimates to arrive at 8,800 English and 8,000 French; similarly, his 'The Campaign of 1066', p.102, followed by Beeler, *Warfare in England*, pp.16–17. Morillo, *Anglo-Norman Warfare*, p.58, thinks the 'best estimates of army size are between 5000 and 7000'; Delbrück, *History of the Art of War*, iii. 152, guessed 7,000 French and 4,000–7,000 English; Lot, *L'Art Militaire*, i. 284–5, announced that the English could not have been more than 8,000 to 9,000 strong, but probably did not reach half that, while the French numbered 7,000. Barlow, *The Godwins*, p.101, thinks that for the French '20,000 men and 500 ships would seem to be the top limit; ten thousand effectives is probably closer to the mark'. Brown, *The Normans and the Norman Conquest*, p.150, n.47, warned that figures of about 7,000 a side 'are more or less rational guesswork'. The belief that medieval armies were almost always small, widely held since the days of Delbrück (to whom Spatz's book was dedicated) and Lot, remains so, see Verbruggen, *The Art of Warfare in Western Europe*, pp.5–9. On the size of the French army, see further below, pp.176–86.
[52] In his 1905 article, 'The Battle Field of Hastings', 66, Baring had stated that 'the bank at the back, though not so formidable as it is further on, is already over *thirty* feet high' (my italics).

contains very little water. The 6-inch Ordnance Survey sheet to which he referred,[53] and current maps, although they do have a stream rising on the northern edge of this part of the ridge, place its source rather further from the abbey gatehouse than did Baring,[54] and examination on the ground shows (illus. 53-5) that it is in fact not here a stream at all, but what would be better described as a drainage channel; as it is so near the top of the ridge it is virtually impossible for it to contain any substantial body of flowing water, and even in the very wet autumn of 2000 it did not do so, producing little more than a trickle;[55] if there was a signifi- cant obstacle to French cavalry seeking to outflank the English in this area, the 'head of the little stream' can hardly have been it.

It is very likely from what is known of the battle that Harold did occupy a position which William found difficult to turn, and that this is why the conflict appears to have consisted of repeated frontal attacks; it is thus not unreasonable to speculate on where his flanks may have lain, and it might be said that as far as can be told from the existing ground there seems a rather better position than the one selected by Baring and widely accepted ever since, which one could think rather too easy to simply ride around, despite the undeniable gradient; it is to be found further south (illus. 56), at the western end of the ridge, where there is a slope due west of just over 1 in 8, and the ground falls into the area of Saxon Wood. It also happens to be Freeman's position. It is by no means impossible that in 1066, as today, there was dense vegetation in this area, where the water to nourish it collects and drains from the Wadhurst Clay, and that this prevented the English position being outflanked. However, there is, of course, no certainty about this, and our igno- rance of the precise extent of whatever woodland or undergrowth

---

[53] No. 57 N.E.; Baring, 'On the Battle of Hastings', p.217, n.2.

[54] On the OS Explorer Sheet 124, the stream is shown rising just below the 65-metre contour line, to the top left of the 'B' of 'Battle Abbey', and just to the west of Long Plantation.

[55] It is noteworthy that James' article on the battle argues for the same deployment, which had been 'the subject of the most careful consideration on the actual ground by Mr. Baring and myself', but says nothing of any stream, speaking instead of a slope of '1 in 8 on the right rear', 'The Battle of Hastings', 26.

there may have been elsewhere obviously makes it very unsafe to place much weight on such an argument when attempting to fix the extent of Harold's deployment.

In any case, there is a better one to hand. The Bayeux Tapestry (see illus. 45-6) has a scene in which the French attack a hillock, prefaced by the inscription *Hic ceciderunt simul Angli et Franci in prelio* ('Here the English and the French fell at the same time in the battle'). To the left, under the word *simul*, is a body of water, and to the left of that a French horseman faces left, and thus has his back to the sequence which follows; this may well be the Tapestry designer's way of indicating that the said sequence is quite distinct from the scene (illus. 19) showing the deaths of Harold's brothers Gyrth and Leofwine which precedes it. To the right of the water two horses have been upended in one of this source's most powerful images; to the right of them a mailed English foot-soldier holding a spear is pulling down a horseman by seizing his mount's girthstrap, and another horseman apparently prepares to hurl a spear at the defenders of the hillock. These consist of two men with neither armour nor any kind of weapon tumbling down the slope evidently in death, three men with moustaches who have spears and shields but no helmets or coats of mail, and a soldier with a beard but no moustache who holds a spear and is receiving a spear-thrust from a French horseman who has his weapon couched underarm.[56] On the ground at the foot of the hillock there is a figure equivalent to this last except that he has no beard and is regarding the enemy with obvious trepidation, and to the left of him appears a man of a rather different type, without armour, but holding an axe, wearing a sword and with a very prominent moustache. To the right of the hillock (illus. 20-1) Bishop Odo is seen comforting the boys and Duke William removes his helmet, almost certainly to prove that he is still alive, as recorded by several of the written sources. The fact that Odo is turned away from the hillock scene may or may not indicate that these events were thought distinct from it.

---

[56] As noted earlier (above, p.81) the reliability of this element of the scene is suspect.

This part of the Tapestry is important because it can be located on the battlefield with a reasonable degree of plausibility, because this has important consequences for the debate on the extent of the English deployment, and because elements of it bear upon their fighting methods in ways that are also of no small significance. Freeman identified the hillock as the area of Horselodge Plantation, part of the subsidiary ridge to the south-west of the main one, covered today with bushes and small trees, and to the north of what is now New Pond; he also suggested that Harold stationed troops there from the outset to protect the approach to the main English position at a point where the gradient is relatively easy.[57] However, he thought that the water lay beyond the western end of the ridge in the vicinity of Saxon Wood, and that the Tapestry scene itself showed men cut off on the hillock during the annihilation of those of the English who left their positions to pursue the fleeing French, a view apparently supported by a passage in William of Malmesbury's *Gesta Regum* referring to the occupation of a *tumulus* at that point in the battle.[58] In fact, it seems much more likely that both water and hillock are really part of the same scene, as Round noted,[59] and that the former is not only that which flows west in the area of New Pond and to the south of Horselodge Plantation, but may also be identifiable with the 'sandy brook' (if that is what the word Senlac means)[60] which according to Orderic Vitalis gave the battle its name; it is, at least, as is especially noticeable today west of New Pond (illus. 44), distinctly sandy. Furthermore, it is by no means certain that the men shown on the hillock did end up there during the wreck of the pursuit, for while some can undoubtedly be

---

[57] *FNC*, iii. 444, 477; on this part of the battlefield, see above, pp. 51–2.

[58] *FNC*, iii. 490–1; *GR*, i. 454–5; among those who have followed Freeman on the location of the hillock are Lemmon, 'The Campaign of 1066', 96, 106, and *The Field of Hastings*, p.48; Morillo, introduction to *The Battle of Hastings*, ed. Morillo, p.xxvii; and Bennett, *Campaigns of the Norman Conquest*, p.38.

[59] Round, anonymous *Quarterly Review* article of 1893, 78–80.

[60] But this may not be the most likely interpretation, see above, pp.57–8; other commentators have also located the water in this area, for example, Lemmon, *The Field of Hastings*, p.48. The maps in Burne, *The Battlefields of England*, p.25, and Barclay, *Battle 1066*, p.58, marked the stream as 'Sandlake Brook' and 'Sandlake Stream' respectively.

described as 'half-armed peasants'[61] the distinctly well-provided men with moustaches look far more like a specialist group of light infantry, and the moustaches themselves 'as if some special significance attached to them'.[62] Perhaps this is a 'picked company' of the sort mentioned in the *Anglo-Saxon Chronicle* poem on King Æthelstan's great victory at *Brunanburh* in 937.[63] If so, then their light equipment, so suited to the broken ground upon which they are found,[64] suggests that they were indeed deployed there from the beginning of the battle, an idea which would be powerfully reinforced if Sir David Wilson is correct in thinking that the serrated shapes above the water to the left represent 'a defensive work of sharpened stakes';[65] this would, of course, also go a long way to explain why the French horses are in such spectacular difficulties, and together with the mailed English infantryman pulling down an enemy horseman would indicate that not only the Horselodge Plantation area but also that now occupied by New Pond, and perhaps ground further west and south-west too, was held in strength against the French. The construction in 1815 of New Pond (illus. 30-2),

[61] Brown, 'The Battle of Hastings', 20.

[62] *The Bayeux Tapestry*, ed. Stenton, p.175. Moustaches appear on Englishmen, including King Harold, elsewhere in the Tapestry, and are almost certainly an indication of social status. Note also Norgate's comment ('The Battle of Hastings', 73) on the 'light-armed warriors, whose accoutrement was respectable enough to give them some title to rank as regulars'.

[63] *ASC*, i. 108. The Old English *eóred-cist* is translated as 'picked company' here on the assumption that the first element (sometimes used as the equivalent of the Latin word *legio*) refers to troops of any kind and that the second derives from the verb *céosan*, to choose; see Plummer's glossary, ibid., 328, and *The Anglo-Saxon Chronicle*, trans. Swanton, p.108, n.1. The word *cist* can, however, also denote a company, and *eóred* often refers specifically to a group of horsemen (hence its use by J.R.R. Tolkien for the squadrons of the Riders of Rohan in *The Lord of the Rings*); thus, 'mounted companies' is an alternative (adopted by *EHD1*, p.219). Swanton states that *eóred* derives from *eoh*, 'war-horse'.

[64] Note also the comments in John of Salisbury's *Policraticus* on Harold's use of light infantry against the Welsh in 1063, cited by DeVries, 'Harold Godwinson in Wales', pp.83–4.

[65] *BT*, pp.192–3. It is, of course, impossible to be sure that they are not vegetation of some sort: Brown, 'The Battle of Hastings', n.120, suggested 'tufts of marsh grass'. Abels, *Lordship and Military Obligation*, Figs 6–7, notes that 'the defenders of the hill are well-armed', accepts the identification of the shapes in the water as stakes, and makes the point that they indicate deployment on the hillock before the battle began. Fortunately, all the essential elements of the events near the water and on the hillock are present in the earliest drawing of this part of the Tapestry by Antoine Benoît (see the Appendix). Wilson's suggestion was anticipated in 1816 by Hudson Gurney's comment ('Observations on the Bayeux Tapestry', 370) on 'foot seeming to defend a kind of entrenchment against horsemen'.

which has an overflow which allows water into the channel to the west only when the Pond itself is full, must have greatly reduced the wetness of this area, but in the early eighteenth century the marsh which eventually extended down to Powdermill is known from Budgen's estate map of 1724 (illus. 33) to have begun due south of the westernmost part of the main ridge, that is at the point now occupied by the easternmost part of Warren Wood, and this ground can be very boggy even today. It is perfectly possible that Harold rested his right flank upon that marsh,[66] and that the Tapestry is showing French attempts to dislodge his men from that area. Maps made before the construction of New Pond do not suggest that the rather narrow stream (illus. 44) need have been any wider in 1066 than it is today, and if the Tapestry is reliable in showing fighting around a considerable body of water this may have been just to the north-east of the modern Powdermill Lake, that is west of the track which today forms the western boundary of the English Heritage site, and which separates the rest of Warren Wood from its eastern tip.[67] However, this is far from certain, for the earliest detailed map of the area (that of 1724) is still subsequent to the creation of the three Stew Ponds east of New Pond and directly south of the abbey buildings which inhibit the flow of water in the upper reaches of the little valley, and there may at the time of the battle have been marshy pools in that vicinity; certainly, Budgen marked what later became the site of New Pond as 'Weanyer's Pond', although no body of water is actually visible on his map, and there is even today a fairly extensive area of marshy ground east of the point where two separate little streams feed into the Pond (illus. 57-8).

If all this is to push the Tapestry's evidence fairly hard, there would seem to be good grounds for doing so. It is far from unlikely that Harold, who knew that he would be facing heavy cavalry and must have considered how he might best do so, decided to employ field defences against them, and the hillock scene was presumably

---

[66] As the map published in Behrens, *Battle Abbey under Thirty-Nine Kings*, p.18, suggested.

[67] The estate map of 1811 (ESRO, BAT 4435) shows a regularly shaped and therefore probably man-made pond distinct from Powdermill Lake in this area.

thought readily recognisable by the Tapestry's audience, some of whom may have witnessed the fighting depicted. It is also arguably very significant that what is probably our earliest detailed source on the battle, the *Carmen*, says that the English occupied not only a *mons* ('hill') and rough ground, but also a *vallis* ('valley'),[68] and although its author Guy of Amiens did not elaborate on what happened in that area, and William of Poitiers, who preferred to stress the reluctance of the English to meet William on level ground,[69] did not refer to it at all, their silence can plausibly be filled by those writers who speak of deaths in ditches during the battle. William of Malmesbury, in the passage noted by Freeman, says that the English occupied a *tumulus* from which they hurled missiles and rolled down stones on the enemy, killing so many of them near a deep ditch that the bodies made it level with the plain;[70] Henry of Huntingdon has the duke's men falling into a large and well-concealed ditch during their simulated flight and the English also suffering heavy losses there as they retired;[71] Wace mentions ditches several times, and says that during the battle the Normans were pushed back to one which they had previously left behind them, more dying at that time than any other, as those who saw the dead said.[72] Of course, these details are not completely consistent, but there is a good chance that at least some of them reflect memories of fighting in the drainage areas south of the main ridge. If so, there is an even stronger likelihood that the initial English deployment extended to those areas, and was not restricted to the crest of the ridge as Ramsay and Baring argued, and their many followers have long believed. Moreover, this deployment to the south, if it was not simply restricted to the area immediately below the later abbey,

[68] *Carmen*, ll. 365–8.

[69] *GG*, pp.126–7, 170–1.

[70] On WM's possible use of the Tapestry, see below, p.220.

[71] *HA*, pp.392–5.

[72] *RR*, ll. 6969–72, 7847–8, 8079–96. But, of course, Wace probably used both WM and HH and possibly knew the Tapestry. To the west of New Pond there is visible today a series of mounds which extends for something like 300 metres. While there are other and more likely explanations of their origin, there is clearly a possibility that they are grave mounds. See below pp.249–50 and illus. 65–9.

may support Freeman's contention that English troops also occupied much of the ridge itself. More radically, and remembering that the only certain point is the location of Harold's standard, one might wonder whether it was not simply that he rested his right flank on the easternmost reaches of the marsh, but whether very significant fighting may not also have taken place to the south-west of Horselodge Plantation, in the relatively flat countryside which extends for just over half a kilometre down to Powdermill Lake.

If there is a good chance that the scholars who wrote immediately after Freeman were mistaken about the extent of the English position, could they have erred on the question of numbers too? This is a much more difficult matter, and one ultimately incapable of resolution. Even so, discussion of it is not entirely fruitless. It is known from Domesday Book that before the Conquest Berkshire sent a man to the army from every five hides and that he was given four shillings from each one as his maintenance and wages for two months.[73] It has been thought probable that the same system operated throughout much of England, and that in the shires in the Danelaw assessed in carucates six of these units fulfilled the same function.[74] Thus, if the assessment of England as a whole was something like 80,000 hides[75] they ought to have supplied about 15,000 five-hide men, and such men were probably well-equipped, for when Æthelred II raised a fleet in 1008 he required that every eight hides should provide a helmet and a coat of mail.[76] This

---

[73] DB, i. 56c.

[74] Hollister, Anglo-Saxon Military Institutions, pp.38–52, building on earlier work such as Round, Feudal England, pp.67–9, and Maitland, Domesday Book and Beyond, pp.156–7. Hollister (pp.52–3) thought the system in East Anglia impossible to reconstruct. Abels, Lordship and Military Obligation, pp.108–15, is less convinced of the universality of the five-hide and six-carucate rules (similarly, Delbrück, History of the Art of War, iii. 160–1) but notes (p.113) that the Domesday evidence suggests that Bedfordshire 'must have had some standard rule, similar to that practiced in Berkshire'.

[75] For the Domesday figures, including the totals for individual shires referred to shortly, see Darby, Domesday England, p.336. They come in all to just over 69,000 hides, but Domesday does not deal with lands north of Yorkshire, London and Winchester are omitted, and for many of the boroughs no figures are given: compare the lists in ibid., pp.364–8 and Ballard, The Domesday Boroughs, p.65. Thus, 80,000 may not be far from the true total.

[76] ASC, i. 138. The Chronicle, of course, uses the Old English word for mailcoat, byrne, the equivalent of the Carolingian (and Germanic) brunia. No Anglo-Saxon mailcoat of this period has survived, above, p.79, n.109. Contamine, War in the Middle Ages, p.51, estimates the number of men available from the five-hide system as 20,000.

levy system survived for some time after the Conquest, and in 1094 William II (Rufus) is said to have summoned 20,000 men for service in Normandy and then turned them back at the coast after taking the half pound (ten shillings) each man had with him. This sum suggests a uniform system of support recognisable from the Berkshire Domesday, while the figure of 20,000 is far from implausible on the five-hide calculations just mentioned.[77] Moreover, such totals might also seem to fit an event such as the battle of *Æthelingadene* in 1001, when the Vikings killed eighty-one men of Hampshire,[78] for on the five-hide reckoning the defeated force would have numbered about 550 men, raised from a shire assessed at 2,785 hides.

Other evidence such totals do not fit. It is very difficult, for example, to believe that the peasants armed only with spears depicted on the Bayeux Tapestry had been supplied by units of five hides,[79] or that all the forces raised by individual shires were made up in this way. There are many examples in the *Anglo-Saxon Chronicle* of invaders being met by the men of one shire only, and in some cases the totals produced by the five-hide rule carry little conviction. In 1010, for example, the levies of East Anglia and Cambridgeshire were defeated by a Viking force described as 'immense' when it arrived the previous year. Yet if the English thought that they stood a chance of being victorious by engaging with only just over 1,000 men the eleventh-century meaning of 'immense' was curious indeed.[80] In fact, it is possible that some local forces could summon every able-bodied man if necessary, and on the Welsh border that is

---

[77] *ASC*, i. 229; similarly, Bachrach, 'William Rufus' Plan', p.55; Hollister, *Anglo-Saxon Military Institutions*, pp.43–4, regarded 20,000 as 'a gross exaggeration'.

[78] *ASC*, i. 132.

[79] Abels, who does not believe that all freemen may have been liable for military duty in 1066 (see below) or had ever been so, implies (*Lordship and Military Obligation*, pp.178–9) that the Tapestry's figures can be equated with minor landholders of the type known to have fallen in the battle; this seems to me most implausible. For general criticism of Abels' thesis, see the review by Professor Loyn, *EHR*, cvii (1992), 164–5, and for something close to an earlier statement of it on the battle of Hastings, Delbrück, *History of the Art of War*, iii. 154–6.

[80] *ASC*, i. 139–40. Cambridgeshire was assessed at 1,297 hides in 1086, Norfolk at 2,423 carucates and Suffolk at 2,411 carucates. On the five-hide and six-carucate rules this would have produced around 1,065 men.

what elements of the Domesday evidence suggest.[81] Thus it would not be surprising if in critical circumstances national armies were assembled in a similar way, for when the *Chronicle* says that Edmund Ironside called up all the English nation five times against the Danes in 1016 it is probably referring to a higher rate of summons than one man from every five hides.[82] The flexibility of early medieval administrative methods would have allowed infinite variation in what was required, as one is reminded by material from Carolingian Francia, which had a system of government sufficiently like that of the late Anglo-Saxon state for its evidence to be worth noticing. In 806 Charlemagne ordered that in military action in Spain or against the Avars five of the (continental) Saxons were to equip a sixth, in the case of action in Bohemia two were to equip a third, but if there was fighting against the neighbouring Sorbs one and all were to come; similarly, when the Frisians were summoned counts, royal vassals and horsemen were all to be present, but of the poorer men six were to equip a seventh.[83] In the circumstances of 1066 Harold seems likely to have asked for more men rather than fewer, and this is the implication of such scanty evidence as survives. Domesday Book records that two of the three holders of an estate of four hides and one virgate at Tytherley in Hampshire were killed at Hastings.[84] It is possible, but seems unlikely, that these two men were representing lands assessed at a total of ten hides. If they were not, then the Hampshire levy was made up of more soldiers than the five-hide reckoning, if it was ever used in the shire, would have produced. Two other Domesday entries give the same sort of impression. A freeman who held only twelve acres at Winfarthing in Norfolk

[81] Hollister, *Anglo-Saxon Military Institutions*, p.29, and on what Hollister called the 'great fyrd' generally, pp.25–37.

[82] *ASC*, i. 151. While one has to agree with Abels (*Lordship and Military Obligation*, pp.176–7) that the entry cannot refer to the summons of every able-bodied man in England, it does not seem likely that Edmund's armies 'differed only in the number of shires involved, not in the personnel called forth'.

[83] *Capitularia*, ed. Boretius, i. No. 49, c. 2; *Charlemagne*, trans. King, p.257.

[84] DB, i. 50a.

also died in the battle, along with Breme, another freeman who possessed 1½ carucates at Dagworth in Suffolk.[85]

Moreover, it is doubtful whether all those who served in Anglo-Saxon armies did so because of the requirements of the hidage system or of a more extended summons. In some cases they fought as one of the duties of a relationship of mutual obligation between them and a lord. Very early in the ninth century Charlemagne ordered that men summoned from the counties were each to come with spear, shield and a bow with two strings and twelve arrows, but that bishops, counts and abbots were to bring *homines* in possession of metal body armour and helmets.[86] The *homines* of these lords were clearly distinct from men levied from the land, not least in being rather better equipped, and such a distinction may well have been evident in English armies too. When the men of Essex assembled to face the Vikings in battle at Maldon in 991 their leader, Ealdorman Byrhtnoth, positioned himself, according to the poem *The Battle of Maldon*, where he knew his *heorðwerod* ('household companions') to be most loyal. Following his death his thegn Offa was killed, yet he had accomplished what he had promised his lord, and lay by his side as a thegn should.[87] When a thegn died he was required to give (or more probably give back) military gear to his lord in what was known as the heriot. Late in Edward the Confessor's reign Ketel, a thegn of Archbishop Stigand of Canterbury, provided for the return of a horse, shield, spear, sword, helmet and coat of mail, while the laws of Cnut had required that the heriot of a king's thegn consist of four horses (two saddled and two unsaddled), a helmet, a coat of mail, two swords, four spears and

---

[85] DB, ii. 275b, 409b. There is no way of knowing that these men did not have other and more extensive lands elsewhere. The other casualties listed by Domesday are Edric the Deacon, a man of Harold, who held an unspecified amount of land at Cavendish in Suffolk, and Ælfric, who held sixteen hides in Huntingdonshire from the Abbot of Ramsey (DB, i. 207a, 208a; ii. 449a). See also, below, p.237.

[86] *Capitularia*, ed. Boretius, i. No. 77, c. 9; *Charlemagne*, trans. King, p.244. The precise nature of Carolingian metal body armour, usually denoted by the words *brunia* or *lorica*, is unclear, see Coupland, 'Carolingian Arms and Armor in the Ninth Century', 38–42.

[87] *BM*, ll. 23–4, 288–94. See Hollister, *Anglo-Saxon Military Institutions*, pp.127–8; Abels, 'English Tactics, Strategy and Military Organization in the Late Tenth Century', 146.

four shields.[88] Doubtless thegns who served in the army also often represented five hides of land,[89] but this need not always have been so, for there may have been household companions of great lords who held no land at all, and if so they would not have been dissimilar to many of the most famous soldiers believed to have fought on the English side at Hastings, the mercenaries known as housecarls.

Whether their fame is justified is another matter. Anglo-Saxon kings had probably paid specialist troops at least since the days of Alfred, who according to his biographer Bishop Asser set aside part of his revenues each year to be given to his *bellatores* ('fighters'),[90] but on his accession in 1016 Cnut was once thought to have introduced a military fraternity of regularly paid élite troops governed by strict rules. Two Danish writers of *c*.1200, Sven Aggeson and Saxo Grammaticus, say that they consisted of 3,000 men (Sven) or 6,000 in sixty ships (Saxo) and give the regulations using versions of the *Lex Castrensis* (*Law of the Retainers*), which according to Sven he had translated into Latin from a vernacular record produced by Archbishop Absalon of Lund and believed to reflect the practices of Cnut's time.[91] Unfortunately, the *Lex Castrensis* is now thought worthless as a source for the eleventh century,[92] and this means that it is necessary to depend on the sparse and unsatisfactory contemporary and near-contemporary evidence. Housecarls became (or at least the word was applied to) men who were more than simply hired fighters. They are found in Domesday Book holding land and looking very like thegns, and in Harthacnut's reign collecting taxes.[93] Yet that they could also be important militarily there is no doubt. The Domesday entry for Wallingford, which refers to fifteen acres where

---

[88] See Brooks, 'Arms, Status and Warfare in Late-Saxon England', who argues (p.89) that Cnut's rates had been in force under Æthelred II; Ketel's will is translated *EHD2*, No. 189.

[89] Hollister thought that they always did so, *Anglo-Saxon Military Institutions*, p.64.

[90] Asser, p.86. Payments were also made to his *ministris nobilibus*, i.e. probably thegns.

[91] Sven Aggeson, *Lex Castrensis*, ed. Gertz, i. 64–92, at 68–9; Saxo, *Historia*, ed. Christiansen, i. 36–44.

[92] For a revision of Larson, *The King's Household in England before the Norman Conquest*, pp.152–71, see Hooper, 'The Housecarls in England in the Eleventh Century', 166–9; Abels, *Lordship and Military Obligation*, pp.161–70; and note also Eric Christiansen's comments, Saxo, i. 154–5, and *The Works of Sven Aggesen*, pp.7–11.

[93] Lawson, *Cnut*, pp.179–80.

housecarls stayed, hints at the existence of housecarl garrisons.[94] John of Worcester says that almost all Harthacnut's housecarls participated in the ravaging of Worcestershire in 1041 and the D text of the *Anglo-Saxon Chronicle* that some of the Confessor's were killed during Earl Siward's invasion of Scotland in 1054.[95] Nor was the king the only lord to be served by such men. Some of Siward's own housecarls died on the Scottish expedition, as did those belonging to Earl Tostig in the Northumbrian revolt of 1065, while Domesday Book mentions individual housecarls of the earls Leofwine, Ælfgar and Waltheof.[96] Doubtless both the royal housecarls and those of Earl Gyrth, Earl Leofwine and other lords took part in the battle of Hastings, but that is just about as far as one can go; they must have been the 'stipendiary and mercenary soldiers' who according to William of Malmesbury bore the brunt of the fighting,[97] but if their deeds were ever celebrated they made little impact on the authors of most of the sources which have survived; if Wace had heard anything of them, he did not choose to tell. Still, their numbers and those of the household thegns would have added to those levied from the land by means of the hidage and the more extended levy systems.[98]

To discuss the size of the English army and its deployment in the battle is to discuss a range of possibilities. The inadequate and tendentious nature of the evidence means that it is impossible to prove Ramsay, Baring and others wrong in believing that Harold had no more, and perhaps many less, than 10,000 men, who defended a restricted position around the crest of the ridge. Indeed, the witness of the *Chronicle* E text, John of Worcester and William of Malmesbury would all tend to support this view, and because the clay of the western part of the field retains water very well it could

---

[94] Campbell, 'Some Agents and Agencies of the Late Anglo-Saxon State', p.204, n.18.

[95] JW, ii. 532–3; *ASC*, i. 185. The more contemporary C text does not mention them.

[96] *ASC* C, i. 190; Larson, *The King's Household*, p.164.

[97] *GR*, i. 422–3.

[98] Bachrach, 'Some Observations on the Military Administration of the Norman Conquest', 4, 24–5, suggests that Harold had 50,000 men or more at his disposal late in 1066, at least 14,000 being from the five-hide system along with 'several thousand first-class warriors' in the followings of the king and great lords.

be argued that fighting around the Bayeux Tapestry's watercourse took place in the vicinity of a large pond on the main ridge, and that the Tapestry's hillock is not Horselodge Plantation but a feature on that ridge;[99] this interpretation would also be likely to think of the battle's name of Senlac as referring to a sandy channel in the area of the road known today as Lower Lake, and east of the location of Harold's standard;[100] it could also be stressed that there are so many streams and eminences in the vicinity that it is hazardous to identify any with those in the Tapestry, or even suggested that the designer in this instance created a scene which bore little relation to actual events. Yet whether such arguments offer the most plausible interpretation of all the surviving source material is another matter. The insistence of post-Conquest English authors like John of Worcester and William of Malmesbury on the inadequacy of the English forces may be the result of a desire to minimise their countrymen's defeat at a time when the effects of the Conquest were still a very sensitive issue.[101] Moreover, it is not only contemporary French writers like Guy of Amiens and William of Poitiers who say that the English army was large, but the D text of the *Anglo-Saxon Chronicle* as well. The latter also has them under attack before they were properly ordered, and if this was so when there had been time for the construction of field defences this would seem more likely to have been a problem experienced by a large army than a small one. Furthermore, the area of low-lying land south of the main ridge, containing a stream which is distinctly sandy, and which before the construction of New Pond would probably have passed through an area much more marshy than is the case today, is despite all doubts a distinctly plausible location for the Tapestry's water, and the statement of the *Carmen* that the English occupied not only a hill but also a valley is also of the greatest significance from this point of view.

---

[99] Bradbury, *The Battle of Hastings*, p.189, suggests that it 'is the artist simply showing the main hill of the battle' in a different view; similarly, Barlow, *Carmen*, p.lxxxi. Burne, *The Battlefields of England*, p.29, n.2, thought the scene 'refers to the closing stage of the battle when the English position was contracted and attacked from each side'.

[100] Above, pp.57–8.

[101] Above, pp.60–70.

1 King Edward and two of his men (one is usually assumed to be Earl Harold) at the beginning of the Bayeux Tapestry, before Harold leaves for Normandy. Earlier representations of the Tapestry show that the word *Edward* is not original.

2 William gives arms to Harold in 1064. The audience of the Bayeux Tapestry would have seen this as evidence that Harold had become William's man. See p.27.

3 Harold swears the oath to William, one of whose men points to the word *sacramentum*. See pp.28–31.

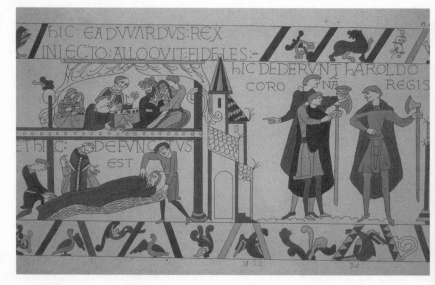

4 King Edward speaks to his followers on his deathbed and Harold is given the crown. The way in which the figure with the crown points to the deathbed scene seems to indicate that Harold's accession was related to it. See p.33.

5 King Harold sits enthroned. The presence of Archbishop Stigand of Canterbury, whose position was not recognised by the papacy, is probably intended to suggest that he had carried out the coronation, and thus question its legitimacy (see p. 63). On the right men marvel at Halley's Comet.

6 The English point to Halley's Comet in April 1066, while Harold sits uneasily on his throne. See p.34.

7 One of the men involved in William's embassy to Count Guy of Ponthieu in 1064 is named by the Bayeux Tapestry as Turold. The appearance of his name, and of those of Vital and Wadard elsewhere, suggests that these followers of Bishop Odo of Bayeux formed part of the Tapestry's audience. See pp.76-7.

8 A cleric and a woman named Ælfgyva near Duke William's palace in 1064, with a naked and erect man gesturing in the lower border. This famous scene, which has defied modern attempts to understand it, is a powerful reminder of how much the Tapestry's audience knew that we do not.

9 Norman cavalry attack the castle at Dinan during the Breton campaign of 1064. Although doubtless delightful to the aristocratic audience for which the Tapestry was made, it is questionable whether their role in assaulting fortifications, or in the battle of Hastings, was quite as important as this source suggests. See p.212.

10 The French transport weapons and barrels of wine to their ships in September 1066.

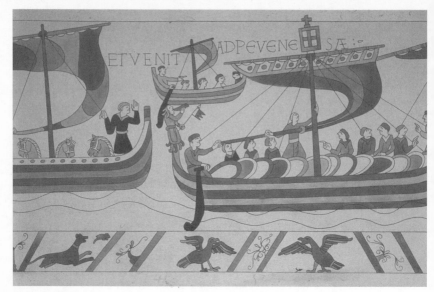

11 Duke William's vessels cross the English Channel on their way to Pevensey.

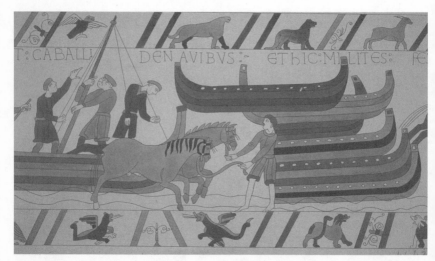

12 French horses disembark in England. This scene is a warning against trusting the Bayeux Tapestry too far, as it is improbable that war-horses were carried across the Channel in vessels of such shallow draught as these. See p.79, n.108.

13 Bishop Odo blesses a meal at the French camp on the coast of Sussex. This and illustrations 7 and 20 are among the scenes which have encouraged historians to believe that the Bayeux Tapestry originated within Odo's circle.

14 The building of the French castle at Hastings shortly after Duke William's landing. See p.189.

15 An English scout announces the presence of William's army to King Harold.

16 French cavalry about to go into action in the battle of Hastings. Within the constraints of the medium, the Bayeux Tapestry's depictions of the appearance and equipment of such men seem likely to be accurate, but this may not be true of the impression that they played a dominant role in the fighting. See pp.79-81, 212-4.

17 Duke William's archers (the figure in mail may be a crossbowman) advance into battle at Hastings flanked by cavalry. These are the only French missile troops shown in the main register of the Bayeux Tapestry. See p.80.

18 The English shield-wall at Hastings fronted by a single archer. See pp.165–8.

19 The deaths of Harold's brothers Leofwine and Gyrth. This scene in the Bayeux Tapestry may be evidence that English heavy infantry sometimes fought in loose order. See pp.80, 165, 223.

20 Bishop Odo comforts the boys, perhaps at a crucial stage of the battle. On the left, a French trooper transfixes an English peasant defending the hillock. See also illustrations 45-6 and p.81.

21 Duke William removes his helmet during the battle, presumably to prove that he is still alive.

22 Edward Augustus Freeman. Regius Professor of Modern History in the University of Oxford, 1884–1892; author of *The History of the Norman Conquest of England*.

23 The steps leading to the high altar of Battle Abbey. The ground in this area was levelled after the battle in order to facilitate the construction of the abbey buildings. See p.50.

24 The slab which today marks the site of the high altar of Battle Abbey, the place where what was believed to be Harold's body was found after the battle. See p.50.

25   The inscription upon the slab marking the site of the high altar of Battle Abbey.

26   The area immediately south of the high altar of Battle Abbey, with the ruins of the monastic dormitory.

27 The abbey terrace looking east.

28 View from the abbey terrace with the drainage channel which feeds into New Pond in the middle distance.

29 The westernmost of the two ponds on the northern edge of Horselodge Plantation, containing water in November 2000. The area is usually dry. See p.52.

30 New Pond from Horselodge Plantation.

31, 32 New Pond, built by Sir Godfrey Webster in 1815, looking west (above) and east (below).

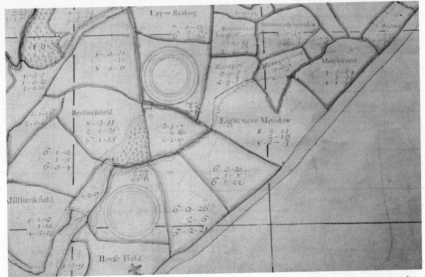

33 Richard Budgen's map of the area south of the western part of the Battle Abbey ridge, 1724. The Stew Ponds are visible at top right while the later New Pond covers some of the same area as Weanyer's Pond. The track which leaves the Catsfield road and runs along the south-western side of Eight-acre Meadow still exists, and can be seen on the 1931 OS map, pp.54-5.

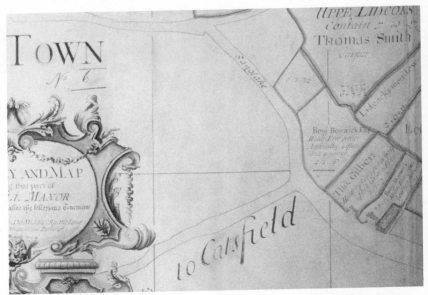

34 Richard Budgen's map of the eastern part of the town of Battle, with the road now called Lower Lake marked as 'Sanglake'. See p.57.

35 The geology of the Battle area according to the British Geological
Survey 1:50,000 Series, Sheet 320/321, *Hastings and Dungeness*. Dark green:
Wadhurst Clay; Yellow: Tunbridge Wells Sand; Lemon: Alluvium; Blue-grey:
Ashdown Beds; Grey: Head. Not to the original scale. See pp. 57-8.

36 Detail from Ramsay's map of the dispositions of the two armies, *The
Foundations of England,* ii. opp. 24. Not to the original scale, and with the
key superimposed. See pp. 141-2.

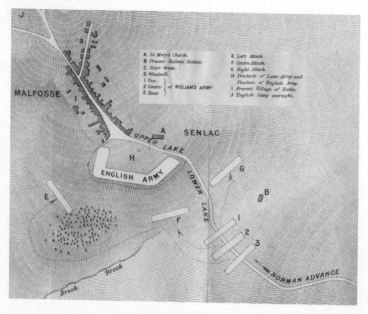

37 The easternmost of the large ponds on the northern edge of Horselodge Plantation. See p.52.

38 The western part of the battlefield on the Battle tithe map of 1859, see p.51.

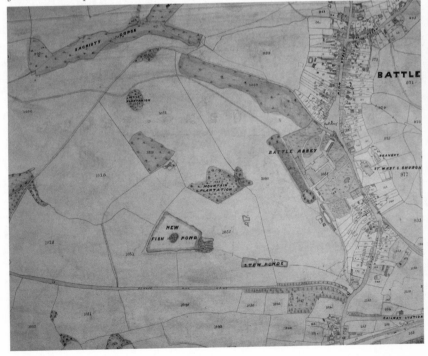

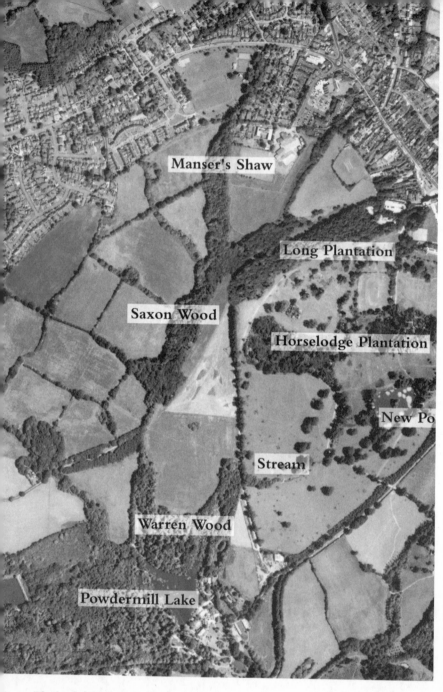

Manser's Shaw

Long Plantation

Saxon Wood

Horselodge Plantation

New Po

Stream

Warren Wood

Powdermill Lake

39 The battlefield from the air. See pp.49–58.

Upper Lake

Marley Lane

Battle Abbey

Lower
Lake

Stew Ponds

Starr's Green

nd

Railway
Line

40 The mound which formed part of the motte-and-bailey castle built by William the Conqueror in York in 1068, surmounted today by the later Clifford's Tower rather than the original wooden palisade. Its size is suggestive of the scale of Norman military operations. See p.245.

41 Horselodge Plantation from the south-east. The sandy nature of the ground can be seen at bottom right, and may be connected with the name Senlac by which the battle came to be known. See pp.58.

Top: 42 New housing on the probable site of the battle of Stamford Bridge. In these fields an army commanded by King Harold II annihilated the troops of King Harold Hardrada and gained one of the greatest victories of the late Anglo-Saxon state. See pp.39-40.

Above: 43 The extreme western end of the Battle Abbey ridge under a covering of light snow, January 2002.

Right: 44 The sandy stream (the Senlac after which the battle was named?) west of New Pond in summer. See pp.58, 150.

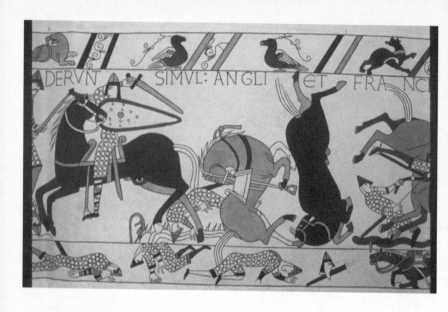

Above and below: 45, 46 Hand-coloured engraving of the Bayeux Tapestry's watercourse and hillock scene, as published from the drawing of Charles Stothard by the Society of Antiquaries in 1819. See pp.149–52.

47 The road from Hastings (Lower Lake, see p. 58) climbs the southern face of the Battle Abbey ridge. The gradient here is less severe than further west. See p. 53.

48 The Hastings road (Lower Lake) runs south near the Chequers Inn.

La région de Troarn vers 1760.
(Carte de Cassini. feuille 27.)

Sieren, phot.

49 The estuary of the river Dives in Normandy as it was in the eighteenth
century, Sauvage, *L'abbaye de Saint-Martin de Troarn*, opp. p.246. Bavent, near
to which Wace says the river entered the sea, is to the west of the island of
Robehomme. The likely extent of the Dives estuary in 1066 can be used in
support of the idea that Duke William assembled a large number of vessels within
it, see pp.182–3.

50 A wall incorporating part of the wall of the south aisle of the eleventh-century abbey church, the only part of that building still standing above ground level.

51 The site of the abbey cloister.

52 The relatively flat top of the western part of the Battle Abbey ridge viewed from just south of the abbey terrace.

53 The upper part of the drainage channel on the western side of the Battle Abbey ridge as it turns east into Long Plantation (on the left); Saxon Wood in the centre. Baring argued that this channel could have been a significant obstacle to French cavalry. See pp. 145-9.

Above: 54 The same channel passing into Long Plantation beneath the modern track.

Right: 55 The channel inside Long Plantation, photographed on 15 October 2000 after a period of very heavy rain.

Below: 56 The western drainage channel further south, where the ground falls more steeply into Saxon Wood; this area would have offered better protection to the English army's right flank than the location suggested by Baring.

57 The small pond to the east of one of the inlets to New Pond; this may be an artificial pond built to help control the flow of water to the Battle gunpowder mills. However, it demonstrates the wetness of the area.

58 The area of boggy marsh to the east of New Pond which may have been the location of the fighting depicted in the Bayeux Tapestry's watercourse and hillock scene. See p.152.

59 The flat top of the western part of the Battle Abbey ridge. If this ground was not occupied by the English army it may have provided terrain ideally suited to French cavalry. See p.214.

60 The modern-day view of the southern slope of the eastern part of the Battle Abbey ridge, north of Battle railway station. See p.53.

61 A modern-day view of the extreme eastern end of the Battle Abbey ridge, looking west. Compare illustration 45.

62 The northern slope of the eastern part of the Battle Abbey ridge, with Caldbec Hill on the horizon and in the foreground the drainage channel which Freeman thought the site of the Malfosse incident. See p.235, n. 91.

Above and below: 63, 64 The former Battle primary school, where the modern road is cut into the ridge and there was probably originally a steep slope to the east. It is possible that the English left flank rested in this vicinity. See p.205.

68 Similar features on the north bank of the stream west of New Pond, near the most easterly section of Warren Wood.

Above: 69 The man-made features pictured in illustration 68 from another angle.

Opposite top, middle and bottom: 65, 66, 67 The stream west of New Pond with man-made features on the south bank which are probably the result of dredging but could be indications of the burial of the French dead. See pp.249-50.

70 The central part of the Battle Abbey ridge under light snow, January 2002. The high altar is behind the ruins of the monastic dormitory at top right, while in the foreground is one of the three Stew Ponds. Feature J of the English Heritage *Survey*, which may be the remains of fieldworks used during the battle is clearly seen running from right to left half-way down the slope. See also illustration 72 and p.250.

71 Apparently artificial features on the eastern edge of Saxon Wood which may be no more than the remains of the root mantles of fallen trees. See p.250.

72 Immediately to the right of the small clump of vegetation, Feature J runs almost imperceptibly south-west near the westernmost part of the Battle Abbey ridge. See also illustration 70 and p.250.

73 Immediately north of the easternmost surviving part of Feature J and south of the abbey buildings, a depression in the ground may represent the site of French burials. See pp.251-2.

74 Drawing of the Harold death scene by Antoine Benoît, 1729. From a photograph loaned by Dr David Hill and John McSween; reproduced by permission of the Bibliothèque Nationale, Paris. On this and illustrations 75-7 see the Appendix.

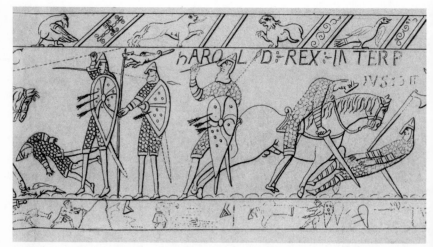

75 The engraving of Benoît's drawing of the Harold death scene published by Bernard de Montfaucon in 1730.

76 The engraving of Benoît's drawing of the Harold death scene published by Antoine Lancelot in 1733.

77 The engraving published from Charles Stothard's drawing of the Harold death scene in 1819.

78 Harold's death scene in the Bayeux Tapestry after restoration in the nineteenth century.

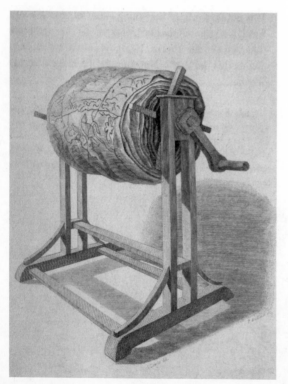

79 The drum upon which the Bayeux Tapestry was stored in the early nineteenth century, from Dibdin, *A Bibliographical Antiquarian and Picturesque Tour*, i. 377. See pp. 262-3.

All this may well imply that Freeman was correct in thinking that Harold's men occupied a great deal of the ridge too. Criticised after his death because of the extent of the English deployment shown on his map, the Tapestry's mailed English infantryman pulling down a French horse near the water is only part of the evidence that in fact he posited a deployment that was not, in at least one respect, extensive enough. How large a 'large' army may have been there is no way of knowing. The losses at Fulford and Stamford Bridge so soon before Hastings may have limited the numbers Harold could assemble, but the facility of the Anglo-Saxon military system for dealing in surprisingly large numbers, at least in the days of Alfred and Æthelstan, must to an extent call this into question, as must also its known resilience.[102] It is worth noting in this respect that Mercian military resources may not have been exhausted by the battle of Fulford, as a landowner from Worcestershire was evidently killed at Stamford Bridge. Had the shire sent one contingent to join Earl Edwin when he heard of the Norwegians' arrival, and then another to fight alongside Harold?[103] If he, like Edmund Ironside, called up 'all the English nation' to deal with the French, at a rate of considerably more than one man for every five hides, then one could be in the area of tens of thousands, especially as such a call-up would have been supplemented by both the sworn followings of great lords and numbers of the not-dissimilar housecarls. At the very least, tens of thousands are a possibility, and possibilities are all that there is, for the only certainty is that there is no warrant for accepting without demur the cosy consensus established in the late nineteenth century and hardly questioned since. The truth is that we do not know how large or small the English army was, and that ignorance should be friend to many possibilities.

---

[102] Above, pp.131-5.

[103] DB, i. 177d, speaks of an uncle of the abbot of Evesham who died *in bello Heraldi contra Norrenses* ('in Harold's war against the Norse'). Of course, he need not have been a member of a second Worcestershire levy, perhaps having joined Harold after fighting at Fulford, or holding land elsewhere in England and marching with the men of another shire; see *FNC*, iii. 361.

Whatever its size, what was its nature? Were Anglo-Saxon troops of the period largely a poorly armed rabble of ill-disciplined peasants strengthened by the better weaponry of the five-hide men, thegns and housecarls, or is there evidence for a much greater degree of professionalism than this? On circumstantial grounds, one would expect so. If any group in the early medieval west showed great skill in the waging of war it was the Vikings, for this was how they earned their daily bread.[104] They profited in many ways from their operations, by plundering, by being given tribute so that they would avoid plundering and the terror and devastation that were doubtless its usual accompaniment, by ransoming captives, by selling captives into slavery, and by serving foreign kings as mercenaries; and all this depended on their ability to defeat any who took the field against them. This was why opposing forces found them very difficult to deal with, and why it is probable that those which eventually gained a measure of success did so by achieving a level of professionalism which matched or at least approached that of their enemy. The sheer extent of the military measures taken by Alfred, in terms of manpower, ships and fortresses, has already been mentioned, as has the obvious scale of the forces deployed by his son Edward the Elder in the reconquest of the Danelaw. Yet it is almost certain that the military system utilised by them and their successors also contained an array of refined and important details of which nothing is known not because they never existed, but because of the inadequacy of the sources. Like Charlemagne's campaigns against the continental Saxons, the wars of Alfred and his son often involved attacks on fortified sites which probably included the use of siege machines. The more plentiful Carolingian sources mention them, the English ones do not.[105] Moreover, Charlemagne's order that his army was to

---

[104] On Viking methods, see below, pp. 170-1.

[105] In the nineteenth century Benjamin Thorpe's note to his translation of Lappenberg (*A History of England under the Anglo-Saxon Kings*, ii. 297, n.1) suggested that the *lignis imposita saxa* (literally, 'stones placed on pieces of wood') which WP (*GG*, pp.128-9) describes the English as hurling at the French referred to the use of field artillery. Unfortunately, 'stones tied to sticks' seems more plausible.

be provided with *fundibulas* ('slinging machines') and 'such men as know how to make them throw well' and 'stones for these on twenty pack-saddles'[106] is only part of one of a number of pieces of legislation which established in very precise terms what he expected of his subjects in this sort of area. He also, as has already been noted,[107] required the men from the counties and the *homines* brought by the lords to be equipped in a certain fashion, including in the latter case the possession of helmets and metal body armour. Nor were logistics neglected: tools were to be taken in abundance, while the provisions of the king, and of his bishops, counts, abbots and magnates, were to be transported in carts, and to include flour, wine and bacon.[108] The war-carts supplied by royal estates were to be well-constructed and to have coverings of skins sewn together in such a way that when crossing rivers there would be no ingress for water. They were to contain twelve *modii* of flour, and twelve *modii* of wine were to be carried in the carts designated for that purpose; each cart was also to have a shield, lance, quiver and bow.[109] The stewards of the royal estates were additionally to take great care of the horses, almost certainly because these had a military role,[110] and counts were to reserve two thirds of the grass in their counties for the needs of the army.[111]

English sources cannot match provisions as detailed as these, but plausible extrapolation from what there is can take us quite a long way. When Cheshire supplied one man from every hide to repair the walls of Chester in the eleventh century,[112] for example, it would be strange if they were not expected to appear with specific tools. In 1066 the provisions of the forces which Harold stationed on the south coast ran out early in September, just as those of the West

[106] *Capitularia*, ed. Boretius, i. No. 77, c. 10; I have used the translation of *Charlemagne*, trans. King, p.245.

[107] Above, p.157.

[108] *Capitularia*, ed. Boretius, i. No. 77, c. 10; *Charlemagne*, trans. King, pp.244–5.

[109] *Capitularia*, ed. Boretius, i. No. 32, c. 64; *The Reign of Charlemagne*, trans. Loyn and Percival, p.72. This document, the *Capitulare de Villis*, may be attributable to Charlemagne's son Louis the Pious.

[110] Ibid., cc. 13–15; trans. Loyn and Percival, pp.66–7. On the breeding of war-horses in this period, see below, p.192.

[111] *Capitularia*, ed. Boretius, i. No. 77, c. 10.

[112] DB, i. 262d.

Saxons besieging a Viking army had done in 893,[113] but provisions there had been, and one assumes that they had been transported to the required localities as a result of concrete administrative orders and by methods which must have included carts and draught animals. Similarly, it is not unlikely that those Anglo-Saxon soldiers who travelled on horseback found, like their Carolingian counterparts, that provision had been made for the feeding of their mounts, and that when Æthelred II ordered that every eight hides were to provide a helmet and coat of mail for his navy[114] this reflected a world in which the five-hide man from Berkshire marched to the army not only with his four shillings from every hide but also with clearly specified military equipment. If this resulted in a degree of uniformity in the weaponry of English soldiers it would match the evidence of the Bayeux Tapestry. The men in its shield-wall, for example, almost all have coats of mail and helmets, kite-shaped shields and spears, and this is hardly surprising in view of the evidence of heriots that helmets and mailcoats were the normal gear for men of status (and doubtless housecarls).[115] Similarly, the moustachioed light infantry on the hillock all have spears and shields, and their peasant companions simply spears. Even clubs could have been standard weapons, for Charlemagne's instruction that his men were to have a bow rather than a cudgel implies that the latter had once been acceptable and perhaps indeed required equipment; it may still have been so in England in 1066.[116]

Of course, this is perhaps to push the Tapestry's evidence a great deal too far; even so it has other features which are arguably significant. It is noteworthy, for instance, that the heavily armed English

[113] *ASC* C, i. 196; *ASC* A, i. 85–6.

[114] *ASC*, C, D and E, i. 138.

[115] One of the shield-wall men holds a small axe along with spears and a shield, another only a large axe, and one of the standard-bearers simply his standard; see illus. 18. Whether the Tapestry's shield-wall men are intended to represent housecarls is unclear. Another piece of evidence on the uniformity of equipment is JW's story (ii. 530–1) of how the ship given to King Harthacnut by Earl Godwin to atone for the murder of the ætheling Alfred contained eighty picked soldiers, each with a *loricam trilicem* ('triple coat of mail'), a sword, a Danish axe, a shield and a spear; on heriots, see above, p. 157–8.

[116] *Capitularia*, ed. Boretius, i. No. 77, c. 17; *Charlemagne*, trans. King, p. 245.

fighting only with axes and those with round shields are operating in looser order than the shield-wall men (illus. 19). This may be nothing more than the quirk of a designer who wished to glorify the French cavalry by showing them in individual combat with armoured Englishmen,[117] or merely a depiction of a phase in the battle when the shield-wall had been broken. Yet it may also be that the designer knew that the nature of a soldier's equipment sometimes reflected the role that the man was expected to perform, and that the troops who comprised English armies and the formations which they adopted extended beyond simply the shield-wall. The round shield with its large boss may have been particularly suited to heavy infantry fighting in open order, giving more all-round cover than the kite-shaped variety,[118] while the space required to swing a large axe with two hands strongly suggests that many of its bearers must have been intended to fight in this way too. Armoured men with spear and sword might also have operated thus, as the individual defending the watercourse against French cavalry indicates. Equally, the single archer who fronts the shield-wall (see illus. 18) could be taken as representative of lines of missile troops who skirmished in front of the heavy infantry before retiring to the rear as the enemy approached.[119]

Yet if English armies contained specialist light infantry, missile troops and heavy infantry who fought in formations other than densely packed units, the fact remains that the shield-wall is of considerable importance, and a matter (for once) upon which a certain amount of information survives. Its use by the English went back at least to the time of Alfred, when according to Asser's account of the battle of Ashdown in 871, based on that of the *Anglo-Saxon*

[117] For the designer's bias towards cavalry, see above pp.79–81, and below, pp. 212–3.

[118] See the comments of Peirce, 'Arms, Armour and Warfare in the Eleventh Century', 244.

[119] The fact the Tapestry shows only one archer has often been remarked, and may be evidence of Harold's lack of such troops. But there is a danger of being misled here by the source's limitations. Lines of skirmishing English archers would not have been easy to represent in such a medium, especially considering the danger of confusion with the many French bowmen in the lower border. The designer also seems to have had little interest in depicting troops of modest social origin.

Chronicle, the Vikings split into two divisions, forming shield-walls of equal size, and the West Saxons did the same, while at Edington in 878 Alfred advanced *cum densa testudine* ('with a ?particularly dense formation') to fight against the pagans and won the victory;[120] similarly, at Farnham in 893 his son Edward is said to have used an *agmine denso* against the enemy.[121] The shield-wall appears again at Maldon in 991,[122] and at Hastings, where the insistence of the more detailed sources on the impenetrability of the English lines must refer to a body or (on the analogy of Ashdown) bodies of this type, which are represented after a fashion in the Bayeux Tapestry. The Latin word used by Asser to translate the Old English *ge-truma* is *testudo*, originally meaning 'tortoise', but also denoting a formation used by Roman legionaries in which they used their shields to protect themselves on all sides, and from above.[123] It was doubtless the implications of this parallel that caused Wilhelm Spatz to deny the use of the shield-wall at Hastings in significant terms:

Nur ein in langwierigen militärischen Exerzitien geschultes, also aus taktischen Körpern zusammengesetztes Heer würde imstande sein, eine so ausserordentlich schwierige Formation, wie sie ein lang fortlaufender, gerader Schildwall ist, zu bilden.[124]

---

[120] *ASC*, A, i. 70; Asser, pp.28–30, 45–6; trans. *Alfred the Great*, ed. Keynes and Lapidge, pp.79, 84.

[121] *The Chronicle of Æthelweard*, ed. Campbell, p.49. This entry in Æthelweard's translation of the *Anglo-Saxon Chronicle* into Latin (of *c*.1000) is believed to be based on a revision made in the reign of Edward (899–924) of the original *Chronicle* entry, see pp.xviii, xxviii–ix.

[122] *BM*, ll. 101–2, 242, 277. The words used here are the Old English *wihaga* ('battle-hedge'), *scyld-burh* ('shield-fortress') and *bordweall* ('shield-wall'). The last is also employed of the Viking formation in the poem on the battle of *Brunanburh* in 937, *ASC*, i. 106.

[123] The *ASC* entry for 871 says that the Vikings split into two *ge-fylce*, translated as *turmas* by Asser, and that Alfred and his brother King Æthelred then attacked their two *ge-truma*. *Ge-fylce* appears again in the same entry of the Viking units involved in the fighting at *Meretun*. WM (*GR*, i. 452) also uses the word *testudo*, in the phrase *conserta ante se scutorum testudine*, to describe the English shield-wall at Hastings.

[124] Spatz, *Die Schlacht von Hastings*, p.45. 'Only an army trained in protracted military exercises, such as an army made up of tactical corps would be, would be capable of forming such an extraordinarily difficult formation as a long, continuous shield-wall'. I am grateful to my colleague Paul Collinson for verifying the translation of this passage. 'Tactical corps' was a term adopted by Spatz from Delbrück and used to describe highly trained troops.

Exactly so. The Tapestry's depiction of the Hastings shield-wall is inadequate to the extent that it almost certainly fails to convey the formation's depth, which was presumably of many ranks, and if so such assemblies must have taken time to organise. When Asser says that Alfred's assault at Ashdown only took place *testudine ordinabiliter condensata* ('when the shield-wall had formed up properly') he had a particular and probably fairly elaborate process in mind, and it may be that at Hastings William was shrewd enough to begin proceedings before Harold's men had completed it, for this could well be the meaning of the *Anglo-Saxon Chronicle* D text's claim that the English were attacked *ær his folc gefylced wære* ('before his army was properly ordered'). Nor, whether it was employed defensively as at Hastings or offensively as at Ashdown, would it be easy to maintain in the stress of battle, as the ranks adapted to the loss of the dead and wounded. Neither is it likely that fighting in such units was solely the province of the well-equipped household troops of great lords, or of the mercenary housecarls, as the Tapestry's depiction of an armoured line might lead one to think, for it is clear from its use by the men of Essex at Maldon and probably from the Alfredian references that it was employed by levies raised from the shires too. If so, it is virtually inconceivable that they did not receive a considerable degree of appropriate training before being required to face the enemy.[125] English commanders may have been familiar with the *Epitome of Military Science* by the Late Roman writer Vegetius, and have reflected not only on his maxim that if you want peace you must prepare for war, but also on that which stated that if you want victory you must train soldiers diligently.[126] There may be an oblique reference to such training in the statement of *The Battle of Maldon* that Ealdorman Byrhtnoth

---

[125] Burne, *The Battlefields of England*, pp.24–5, judged the 'interlocked shield-wall... a poetic fantasy'; Lemmon, *The Field of Hastings*, p.43 (similarly, 'The Campaign of 1066', p.101), that the 'formation was obviously designed to give maximum cover from missiles. For 'in-fighting' it would have to be broken up'. This is, however, neither the implication of the literary references nor of the scene in the Bayeux Tapestry (illus. 18) in which English infantry are clearly receiving French cavalry attacks with overlapping shields and (mainly) spears used overarm.

[126] Vegetius, *Epitome*, p.63. The *Epitome* rivals Pliny the Elder's *Natural History* in terms of the number of manuscripts surviving from before 1300 (p.xiii).

told his men how to stand and asked that they should hold their shields properly, later asking them to form the 'war-hedge'.[127]

Indications of the sort of methods used to form up dense bodies of infantry have survived from the ancient world. Spartan hoplites fought in close order with shield and thrusting spear in a manner probably not dissimilar to that of the shield-wall, and in Xenophon's time a hoplite *mora* was made up of four *lochoi*, each of the latter having two *pentekostyes* of two *enomotiai* apiece.[128] The *enomotia* may have consisted of thirty-six men and if so the *lochos* had 144.[129] Yet, whatever the precise numbers, it is the mere existence of sub-units which is important, for it was these which enabled the phalanx to form up and manouevre, as was also the case with the constituent parts (cohort, maniple and century) of the Roman legion. Thus, it would be surprising (indeed, almost incomprehensible) if the shield-wall did not contain equivalents, and worth noting that Old English terms like *eóred-heáp*, *eóred-þreát*, *eóred-weorod*, *heáp*, *scild-truma*, *truma* and *weorod* may occasionally have had much more precise meanings than the simple 'troop' and 'company' which is as far as one can get in translating them today.[130]

Points such as these may (or may not) be half-answers on the many complexities of the Old English military system, but there is a great range of questions which can hardly be answered at all. When a shire levy faced the enemy alone, for example, how much provision was there for specialist troops such as archers[131] and light

---

[127] *BM*, ll. 17–20, 101–2.

[128] Xenophon, *Spartan Society*, trans. Talbert, p.178. I am grateful to Mr J.R.M. Smith for these references.

[129] P. Connolly, *Greece and Rome at War*, pp.39–41. However, this is speculation, and it should be noted with regard to Xenophon's remarks that 'the size and precise relationship to one another of the units mentioned both here and later are obscure', Talbert, p.187.

[130] See the entries in *An Anglo-Saxon Dictionary*, ed. Bosworth and Toller, and *Supplement*. King Alfred's translation of Orosius equates *truma* with the Latin 'cohort'; *scild-truma* eventually became 'sheltron', and was sometimes equated with the Latin *testudo*; see *OED* under 'trume' (rejecting a connection with the Latin *turma*) and 'sheltron'. Delbrück, *History of the Art of War*, iii. 153, denied any similarity between the capacities of the Greek phalanx and those of the English shield-wall.

[131] *BM*, l. 110, refers to the use of bows at Maldon apparently by both sides. Whether ll. 70–1 and 269–70 also refer to archery depends upon whether the word *flán* is translated 'arrow' or 'missile'.

infantry, and were all the rest of its men part of the shield-wall? If so, is it to be assumed that those who did not have shields, like the peasants depicted in the Bayeux Tapestry bearing only spears and clubs, fought in the rear ranks? In national armies where were the followings of great lords and the housecarls deployed, and the specialist units referred to by the term *eóred-cist*, and from which men were these units drawn? Did the Anglo-Saxons ever make use of cavalry?[132] When the levies of different shires coalesced in national armies how did they form up on the field of battle? Upon this, at least, there is just a little more to go on than the mere belief that some sort of system there must have been, for John of Salisbury's *Policraticus*, written *c.*1160, says that the English army's order of battle is that the men of Kent form the first line and those of Wiltshire, with Devon and Cornwall, come next.[133] Not long afterwards Wace made a similar statement about the Kentishmen, and added that the men of London formed the king's bodyguard,[134] both of course with reference to the deployment at Hastings. It is curious, and at the same time probably significant, that these late comments about the prestige of the men of Kent find a distinct echo in the report of Edward the Elder's harrying of Danish East Anglia given by the *Anglo-Saxon Chronicle* for 903. When he eventually wished to withdraw he told the whole army that they were to set out together (the levies of different shires had apparently separated) but the Kentish force lingered, despite having received seven messengers, and was caught by the Danes. In the bloody conflict which followed they lost several of their leaders, including two ealdormen, and were driven from the field, but inflicted heavy casualties on the enemy, King Eohric and Edward's renegade

---

[132] Glover, 'English Warfare in 1066', was ahead of its time, if inclined to place too much weight on the appearance of English horse in Snorri Sturluson's account of Stamford Bridge; see more recently, Hooper, 'The Aberlemno Stone and Cavalry in Anglo-Saxon England', 192–6; Bennett, 'The Myth of the Military Supremacy of Knightly Cavalry', 310; Strickland, 'Military Technology and Conquest', 359–60; and for the possible use of cavalry at *Brunanburh* (noted by Hooper) and the term *eóred-cist*, above, n.63.

[133] Campbell, 'The Late Anglo-Saxon State: A Maximum View', p.24.

[134] *RR*, ll. 7819–30.

cousin Æthelwold being among the dead.[135] If this reveals nothing else it speaks of the pride (and perhaps greed for booty) of some shire levies, who doubtless carried their own standard into battle, and whose men may have formed up beneath the banners of the shire's individual hundreds.[136] And if those levies sometimes contained peasants armed with no more than spears or clubs one should not be too ready to assume that such men had no military value.[137] Were this so it is doubtful whether a polity as concerned with warfare as the late Anglo-Saxon state would have had them there at all,[138] and if the Bayeux Tapestry shows them looking apprehensively at the approaching enemy[139] this may be no more than a reflection of the social prejudices of its patrons. Nor should one forget the known achievements of levies under professional direction at other times. It was the modern conscript equivalents of the armed peasantry of the Anglo-Saxon period who in 1918, with the assistance of artillery, tanks and ground-attack aircraft, in one of the greatest of all the victories of English arms, broke the elaborate German defence system known as the Hindenburg Line.

Raised, equipped and probably trained in elaborate ways, how elaborate were the tactical skills employed by those who led Old English armies into battle? Presumably they varied in quality at different times and under different commanders, but in considering these matters it is useful to note the important article on early medieval warfare which Professor Leyser presented to a conference on the battle of Maldon in 1991, and which was published only after his death. This is what he had to say about the fighting methods of the Vikings in the late ninth century, as they emerge from sources written on the continent:

---

[135] *ASC* A, i. 92, 94. I have used the date for this annal of *EHD1*, p.208, which suggests that these events actually took place late in 902.

[136] Campbell, 'The Late Anglo-Saxon State: A Maximum View', pp.24–5.

[137] An extreme example of this tendency is furnished by Delbrück, *History of the Art of War*, iii. 154, who suggested that the hard-fought nature of Hastings was proof enough that the English army was not composed of peasants, who would either have overwhelmed the enemy with their mass or immediately taken to flight.

[138] Hollister, *Anglo-Saxon Military Institutions*, p.130, makes a similar point.

[139] Above, p.149 and illus. 46.

The Northmen... possessed some very special skills of their own. They could and frequently did use ground which Frankish armies always avoided if possible. They massed, hid and then emerged from woods... More important still was the Northmen's habit of retreating into a stone building, a church, a house or, on one occasion, the palace of Nymwegen, and turning it into a fortress from which they could burst forth at their chosen time when it looked as if they were at bay. Now and again they attacked at night. Above all they had the capacity, the tools and the skills to erect quick and effective field fortifications, dykes fortified by stakes, palisades and advanced ditches. Time and again their enemies were hampered by these works. The great count Henry, one of their most ubiquitous assailants and admired everywhere as a great warrior, came to grief when he rode into what might today be described as a tank trap. As he tried to get out, momentarily helpless and at a severe disadvantage, he was slain.[140]

There is much that is important here. It is hardly surprising that some of these features appear in the English sources, although given their relative lack of detail on military campaigns the harvest in this respect is inevitably scanty. Even so, there is the fondness for taking the enemy by surprise (it was an unexpected attack in the middle of winter which brought Alfred to his knees and almost finished him off in 878) and the use of woodland, for in 893 the Vikings employed the forestry of the Weald to screen themselves from English forces, and in 1009, during Æthelred II's reign, they passed through the Chilterns on their way from London to Oxford. Some of their methods the English adopted (or were already familiar with) themselves: Asser says that in 878 a force of West Saxons surprised and defeated a besieging Viking force by bursting out from their defences at dawn; in 893 Alfred's men launched attacks on them by both day

[140] Leyser, 'Early Medieval Warfare', pp.48–9. Margrave Henry of Neustria was killed in 887. Note also the future king Olaf of Norway's alleged use of deep, narrow trenches against Breton cavalry in the early eleventh century, WJ, *GND*, ii. 24–7. Vegetius warned his readers against sudden irruptions by those under siege, *Epitome*, p. 138.

and night;[141] in 1066, Harold took Harald Hardrada by surprise at Stamford Bridge, and is believed to have attempted to do the same to the French three weeks later.[142] If he also used field defences on the battlefield,[143] the 'dykes fortified by stakes' mentioned by Professor Leyser, this is simply another indication of the intelligence with which the Anglo-Saxons waged war. That Duke William remained in the vicinity of Hastings awaiting the arrival of the enemy, and moved cautiously even after his victory, is a sign not only of his own military skill but also of the respect which he had for the foe.[144]

It would be both foolish and impossible to argue that the late Anglo-Saxon military system always worked like clockwork, for there is no doubt that it did not. In 1009 Æthelred II assembled a very large fleet at Sandwich to prevent further Viking attack, but it returned to London having achieved nothing after a major disagreement between the king's magnates; in 1066 Harold's forces on the south coast eventually had to disperse when their provisions ran out. Nevertheless, the more that becomes known about the ways in which English armies assembled and fought in this period the more it may become apparent that it saw the mobilisation of the country and its resources for war to an extent that was not to be repeated until the total wars of the twentieth century. The ability to continue fielding forces despite loss and defeat, the employment of conscript soldiers in dense and complex infantry formations, the existence of élite companies, the use of field defences – none of these were issues which an enemy could afford to regard lightly, and all may do much to explain why Hastings was so hard fought. Overcome the Anglo-Saxons may sometimes have been, for their enemies too were formidable, war is always a lottery, and few systems are immune to problems of personality and circumstance. Yet contemptible their military capacities were not.

---

[141] *ASC*, i. 74, 84, 139; Asser, pp.43–4.

[142] *ASC* C and D, i. 197–8; *Carmen*, ll. 279–83; *GND*, ii. 166–7; WP, *GG*, pp.124–5.

[143] Above, pp.151–2.

[144] Glover, 'English Warfare in 1066', 2–4; Hollister, *Anglo-Saxon Military Institutions*, p.129. Burne, *The Battlefields of England*, p.19, contrasted William's behaviour with that of Julius Caesar in 54 BC, who 'pushed inland in search of his enemy on the very day of his landing'.

5

THE FRENCH ARMY

The army which was defeated at Hastings was the product of a complex, wealthy and powerful system of government which had a long history of success behind it; the one which overcame it was not. It was an *ad hoc* force, assembled for the purpose not only from Normandy but also from other parts of France and perhaps even further afield. The earliest sources insist on this. Guy of Amiens' *Carmen* tells how before the battle the duke addressed men of Francia, of Brittany and of Maine, as well as Normans, apparently including men from their settlements in southern Italy, and later of the Normans fighting in the centre and the French and Bretons on the wings.[1] William of Poitiers lists men of Maine, Frenchmen, Bretons, Aquitanians and Normans, and has Breton horse and infantry and other auxiliaries on the left, apparently Duke William and the Normans in the centre, and presumably the French on the

---

[1] *Carmen*, ll. 250–60, 413–4. However, Barlow (p.xxxix), while prepared to accept the possibility that men from southern Italy were involved, prefers to emend the text so that they are referred to as subjects of the Normans rather than their comrades; the Norman conquest of Sicily, begun in 1061 but planned as early as 1059, was not finally completed until 1091, Loud, *The Age of Robert Guiscard*, pp.146–73. A horseman from Maine appears in *Carmen*, ll. 485–6; the messenger who announces William's arrival to Harold (ll. 159–60) speaks of Gauls and Bretons.

right.[2] The annalist of Nieder-Alteich on the Danube also affirms the presence of Aquitanians, as does the twelfth-century chronicle of the abbey of St Maixent, in Poitou.[3] William of Jumièges says nothing of the make-up of the duke's forces, but when Orderic Vitalis revised his work he described it as a great army of Normans, Flemings, French and Bretons; when he proceeded to write his *Historia Æcclesiastica* they became men of Gaul and Bretons, Poitevins and Burgundians, and other peoples from north of the Alps.[4] Wace, whose *Roman de Rou* contains much (if of questionable reliability) on the identities of the duke's companions, says that he cannot list the names of all the Norman and Breton barons in the company, and that there were also many from Maine and Anjou, from Thouars and Poitou, and from Ponthieu and Boulogne, together with soldiers from many lands, some there for land and some for money.[5] John of Worcester, more succinctly, claims that William brought with him auxiliaries from the whole of Gaul, while when the Bayeux Tapestry twice describes his men during the battle of Hastings they are on both occasions *Franci*: French.[6]

There is nothing inherently unlikely in these statements about the cosmopolitan nature of his forces. He already had a reputation as a successful soldier and England was known to be very wealthy. Even, therefore, if it is allowed that some of his non-Normans joined him because they were political allies, like the Bretons, or

---

[2] *GG*, pp.126–31. William rode *in medio* of the cavalry which formed his third line, doubtless with other Normans; Bretons and Aquitanians are also mentioned as being among his forces after his coronation (pp.160–1). It is not certain from the phrase *pedites pariter atque equites Britanni, et quotquot auxiliares erant in sinistro cornu*, whether the foot and auxiliaries on his left wing as well as the horse were Breton. WP does not specify the composition of the right wing, but has the Norman Robert of Beaumont fighting there; Barlow (*Carmen*, p.lxxvi, n.252) notes that he was heir to land in the French Vexin and could have been brigaded with other French troops.

[3] Above, pp.35–6; *La Chronique de Saint-Maixent*, ed. Verdon, pp.136–7; see Beech, 'The Participation of Aquitanians in the Conquest of England 1066–1100', 16–20. WP refers to Aimeri of Thouars (in northern Poitou) as an Aquitanian (*GG*, pp.148–9), and it is possible that Poitevins were the only such men present.

[4] *GND*, ii. 164–7; *HÆ*, ii. 144–5.

[5] Above, p.119; *RR*, ll. 8659–68.

[6] *JW*, ii. 604–5; the word *Franci* could be used in two senses at this date: for men who inhabited the land around Paris controlled directly by the French king, and for those in the area which roughly comprises modern France. The Tapestry seems to use this second sense, the authors mentioned above (WP has *Francigenae*) the first.

subordinates, like the men of Maine, this still leaves room for numbers of opportunists ready to make their fortunes. Europe contained many such men in the middle of the eleventh century. Tostig Godwinsson, for example, was able to enlist Flemings in the forces with which he attacked England from Flanders in 1066, and there is no difficulty in believing William of Poitiers' statement that as news of the duke's expedition spread, warlike men flocked to him, attracted by his very well-known generosity and confident in the justice of his cause.[7] They would have been further encouraged when they heard of the granting of the papal banner, and in fact an obvious parallel to their reaction is the assembly of the international armies of the First Crusade thirty years later, forces which were motivated not only by piety but also by a strong interest in the taking of booty. That very few of Duke William's non-Norman troops are known by name – one cannot get much further than Count Eustace of Boulogne, Guy of Amiens' nephew Hugh of Ponthieu, the Poitevin Aimeri of Thouars, the Breton Alan Rufus and perhaps Robert, son of Giffard[8] – is not of any great significance, for most of the surviving names of those who fought in the battle come from William of Poitiers and Wace, both writing for Norman audiences, and it is thus hardly surprising that they are predominantly Norman.[9] It is in fact rare to have more than a handful of names for participants in any battle of the period before the crusades, and the number of identifiable Normans is not only greater than that of non-Normans, but also greater than that of their known English opponents. It is not therefore reasonable to argue that William had few external auxiliaries simply because their precise identities cannot be established.[10] If the repeated assertions of

---

[7] GG, pp.102–3; in one of his passages in praise of the duke, WP later claims (pp.142–3) that he conquered England without much outside help.

[8] Above, p.90, n.9.

[9] On Wace's list, see above, p.119.

[10] There is a detailed treatment of this subject in Körner, *The Battle of Hastings*, pp.218–55, who rejects the idea that 'William's army contained thousands of volunteers from all parts of Europe' on much these grounds. I agree with Bachrach ('The Military Administration of the Norman Conquest', 3, n.5) that Körner's approach was 'aggressively hypercritical'. It is a curious kind of argument, for example (p.234), which acknowledges the presence of Eustace of Boulogne but allows him not a single man from his own county; on Flemish involvement, see Nip, 'The Political Relations between England and Flanders (1066–1128)', 151–3.

contemporary sources about the presence of such men on the expedition are to be rejected, it must be on other grounds.

Even so, there is no way of knowing what sort of proportion of the ducal army they formed, and when one comes to the question of its total size there are dilemmas of a familiar kind to be faced.[11] The sources do have figures to offer: the *Carmen* speaks of 150,000 men, William of Poitiers of 50,000 in France and 60,000 just before the battle, and the Poitevin chronicle mentioned earlier of how 'they say' that William had 14,000 men; William of Jumièges gives no size for the army, but says that it sailed in 3,000 ships.[12] Nobody would believe the *Carmen* here and hardly anybody William of Poitiers and William of Jumièges, for large round numbers look rhetorical and thoroughly unreliable. Even 14,000 has on the whole been thought beyond the bounds of possibility,[13] for in the last decade of the nineteenth century the scholars who favoured limiting the size of the English army to less than 10,000 men performed the same service for the French, and on what have long seemed plausible grounds. Wilhelm Spatz's *Die Schlacht von Hastings*, published in 1896, went into the matter in what appeared a scientific manner and came up with the conclusion that William led nothing like 14,000 men into battle. His reasons, in addition to the general observation that medieval armies were smaller than modern ones, were as follows: as William of Poitiers stresses that the forces delayed at Dives for a month by contrary winds were so well supplied that they did not plunder the surrounding country they cannot have been large; if William's fleet is estimated at 1,500 vessels, this and the Tapestry's evidence that they carried an average of seven men produces a total of 10,000–12,000; they landed at Pevensey in a single day when in 1854 the disembarkation in the Crimea of 60,000 men,

---

[11] Note not only the discussion of the size of the English army in the previous chapter, but also a recent attempt to assess the numbers of those who went on the First Crusade, upon which far more sources survive; France, *Victory in the East*, pp. 122–42.

[12] *Carmen*, ll. 96–7; *GG*, pp. 102–3, 116–7; *GND*, ii. 164–5.

[13] It is accepted by Bachrach, 'Some Observations', 3–4, providing that it included 4,000 noncombatants and represents the number present at Dives in the summer of 1066; he allows William 8,000 for the battle.

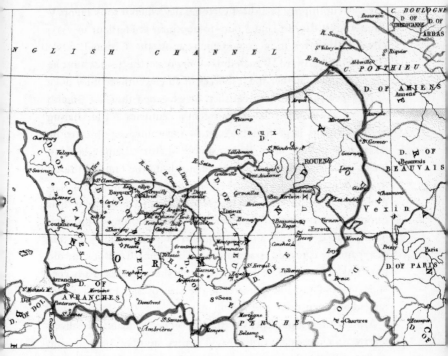

Detail from Freeman's map of Normandy and the surrounding states, *FNC*, ii. opp. 163.

just over 1,000 cavalry and 128 cannon took five days in good weather; an army of 40,000 to 50,000 men could not have marched the 11 kilometres from Hastings to Battle in the early morning of 14 October 1066; Domesday Book suggests that the Conqueror provided about 4,000 Norman warriors with land in England, and even allowing that some probably returned home and that many may have been killed in the fighting, this suggests a force of no more than 7,000–8,000; but as he must have left men to protect his camp, William probably had no more than 6,000–7,000 against Harold.[14] Not much later Sir James Ramsay judged that 5,000 'would satisfy our ideas of what was at all likely', and for similar reasons: the entire

[14] Spatz, *Die Schlacht von Hastings*, pp.27–30.

force was unshipped in a short October day when it took Henry V three August days to land 8,000–10,000 men at Harfleur in 1415; Edward III never took 10,000 men across the Channel, while Henry V and Edward IV each did so only once: the 'reader must be left to decide' whether the resources of an eleventh-century duke of Normandy could have equalled or exceeded those of English kings of the thirteenth or fourteenth centuries.[15] F.H. Baring agreed that the large figures given by the sources are 'not to be taken as arithmetic at all', being simply 'rhetorical equivalents' of 'many', and endorsed Ramsay's evidence from the Hundred Years' War and Spatz's points about the speed of the French disembarkation and the significance of a march of 'at least six miles from their camp' before the battle began. He also added a point of his own: having traced William's route to London after the battle by the trail of apparently damaged estates recorded by Domesday Book, he did not think it considerable enough to imply the activities of any very large army. Thus, his estimate of the size of the French forces ranged between 5,000 and 10,000 men.[16]

Most of these arguments, so attractive on first acquaintance, disintegrate on close examination, based as they are upon premises and evidence far too flimsy to support them. Baring's analysis of the valuations of Domesday estates, for example, has recently been revealed as seriously flawed when it comes to reflecting the line of William's march (and therefore the size of his army).[17] Similarly, Spatz's use of the numbers of Domesday landholders of Norman origin proves little, given that those who received land did so over a period of twenty years, and that there is little difficulty in believing that very large numbers of the rank and file never did so, and may never have expected to.[18] William of Poitiers stresses the wealth of England, and

[15] Ramsay, *The Foundations of England*, ii. 16–17. A slip, of course, for 'fourteenth or fifteenth centuries'.

[16] Baring, *Domesday Tables*, pp.207–20, 227.

[17] Palmer, 'The Conqueror's Footprints in Domesday Book'. Note, for example (p.29), that the Oxfordshire figures 'provide no evidence whatsoever that the Norman army passed this way, and strongly imply that it did not. Yet we know that it did'.

[18] See Douglas' comments on the use of Domesday evidence, 'Companions of the Conqueror', 132–3.

says that after his coronation King William gave part of it to those who had helped him win the battle;[19] nor should one forget the booty stripped from the dead, or the plunder taken from the land before the fight and probably after it. Other points can be disposed of even more easily. It may well be true that only a small force could have marched from Hastings to Battle before 9 o'clock in the morning, but there is actually no good reason to think that this is what William's army did, rather than awaiting Harold in the immediate vicinity during the preceding night.[20] Nor can one take seriously statistics based on average ship capacity as deduced from the Bayeux Tapestry when it is obvious that this source's represen-tations of numbers were never intended to reflect real totals; thus, it is no more plausible to believe that William's vessels carried an average of seven men than it is to suppose that they consisted of only eighteen ships, or that there was only a single English archer in the battle, or that only two men fled on horses at the end of it.[21] Moreover, when it comes to the question of the speed of the French disembarkation it should be noted firstly that the fact that William is said to have arrived on a particular day does not neces-sarily imply that he got all his troops ashore in a matter of hours, and secondly (and more significantly) that if we are to play the heady and dangerous game of historical analogy there is an event not referred to by Spatz and Ramsay which rather puts those of the Hundred Years' War and the Crimea in the shade. In 54 BC Julius Caesar, with five legions and 2,000 cavalry (that is, probably something over 25,000 men) in over 800 ships, reached the British coast about midday, landed without opposition (as did the Conqueror, as far as is known), chose a suitable place for a camp and marched against the Britons before midnight. It is thus neces-sary to be very careful before using evidence from other periods

---

[19] GG, pp.152–3.

[20] Below, pp.196–200.

[21] I have included in these totals the empty ships which have been beached. The third fleeing horseman on the present Tapestry the Benoît drawing (see below, p.228 and the Appendix) shows to have originally been an infantryman. James, 'The Battle of Hastings', 21–2, was also inclined to take the Tapestry's depictions of ship capacity literally.

to argue about what William could or could not have done in 1066, because that evidence may cut two ways, and be insufficiently analogous to be worth very much in any case.[22]

This leaves only the point that he could not have supported tens of thousands of men in France without them plundering the countryside around, if William of Poitiers' statement that they did not is to be credited. A recent analysis by Professor Bachrach has suggested the scale of the logistical problems involved in supporting an army of 14,000 men and perhaps 3,000 war-horses for a month; he estimates that about 2,340 tons of grain would have been required (including 1,500 for the horses), together with 1,500 tons of hay and 155 tons of straw, while someone would also have had to cope with 5 million pounds of equine excreta and 700,000 gallons of equine urine.[23] However, these figures have been seriously challenged: R.H.C. Davis, who thought the horses considerably smaller than does Bachrach, concluded that William's forces may have needed no more than 300 tons of grain and the same of hay while they were at Dives.[24] This not only shows the complexity, and to an extent invalidity, of the assumptions involved in such elaborate statistical exercises, it is also a reminder that there are actually no figures on the resources of northern France, particularly in terms of population levels and the production of livestock and foodstuffs, available to indicate that Duke William's forces could not have been substantially bigger than 14,000 men. Nevertheless, Bachrach's article is a powerful indication of the logistical problems that William would have faced, and even if his totals are too high it is worth noting his conclusion that scholars:

[22] Caesar, *The Gallic War*, v. 8–9, pp. 242–5. Caesar does not say in so many words that he marched against the Britons on the day of his landing, but it is strongly implied, and in line with his customary tactic of coming upon the enemy unexpectedly whenever possible. Of course, he disembarked on an open beach, whereas William's vessels probably entered harbours in the main; see further on the French landing, below, pp. 189–90.

[23] Bachrach, 'The Military Administration of the Norman Conquest', 11–15.

[24] Davis, 'The Warhorses of the Normans', 69, 80. The considerable discrepancy between the figures is partly, as Davis noted, because Bachrach miscalculated: a daily requirement of 14 tons of grain and the same of hay does not produce monthly totals of 1,500 tons of each, but 434 tons for 2,000 horses and 620 tons for 3,000.

have not fully appreciated the great resources in both wealth and organisation that were available in Normandy only a generation before the massive European-wide operations that sustained the first crusade.[25]

There is one aspect of Conquest logistics, however, upon which what looks like an administrative document, complete with some rather startling statistics, does survive – the size of the duke's fleet. William of Jumièges' assertion that it consisted of 3,000 ships looks impossible, if not quite as ludicrous as Geoffrey Gaimar's 11,000, and what seems a much more plausible and very precise figure is offered by Wace, who says that his father told him when he was a boy that 696 ships, excluding the ships, boats and skiffs carrying arms and harness, sailed with the Conqueror from St Valéry.[26] However, to this evidence can be added that of the text known as the Ship List of William the Conqueror. It survives in a hand of c.1130–60 in the Battle Abbey manuscript which also contains the oldest copy of the house's *Brevis Relatio*,[27] and is a list of the number of vessels owed to Duke William in 1066 by fourteen of his followers, together in the cases of four of them with the number of *milites* also due. Until recently treated with care because of the date of the manuscript and the rather surprising nature of its evidence, it has been rehabilitated in the work of Professor Hollister and Dr van Houts, the latter believing that the copy goes back to a text created in c.1072 or perhaps as early as December 1067 at Fécamp on the basis of information compiled just before the Conquest by monks of that abbey in the ducal service.[28]

---

[25] Bachrach, 'Military Administration', 21.

[26] Above, p.73-5 on Gaimar; *RR*, ll. 6423–32. Wace also notes WJ's figure. I have followed Edgar Taylor's translation of Wace here, but Burgess takes the (apparently ambiguous) meaning of the *RR* to be that the vessels carrying arms and harness were included in the total of 696. I am grateful to my colleague Marie-José Gransard for advice on Wace's Old French.

[27] Oxford, Bodleian Library, MS e Museo 93; see *BR*, pp.8–9; van Houts, 'The Ship List of William the Conqueror', 164–6; and compare Bachrach's comments on the probable keeping of written administrative records in 1066, 'Military Administration', 19–20.

[28] Hollister, 'The Greater Domesday Tenants-in-Chief', pp.221–6; van Houts, 'Ship List', 166–8. It did not, of course, escape Freeman's notice, *FNC*, iii. 378–80.

The duke's half-brothers, Robert of Mortain and Bishop Odo of Bayeux, owed 100 and 120 ships respectively, others fewer, but the (unstated) total comes to 776 and 280 *milites*. The list then says, wrongly (though its enumeration of magnates may have become truncated during transmission) that the total was 1,000, and that the duke also had many other ships from certain of his men, according to their means. Now Wace, too, had heard of William's magnates supplying specific numbers of vessels, and like the list assigns sixty to William FitzOsbern and unlike it forty to Bishop Odo, adding that the bishop of Le Mans provided thirty vessels and their crews (thirty being a number which appears once in the list, attributed to Walter Giffard). As Dr van Houts has said, Wace and the list differ sufficiently to appear independent of each other, and despite the inconsistency in the numbers assigned to Bishop Odo this tends to bolster confidence in their general reliability.[29] On this reckoning, then, the duke's fleet was sizeable, for if the list's statement that he was owed 1,000 ships by a portion of his men and more by others is accepted, and the likelihood considered that some of his continental allies (including the Aquitanians involved in the alleged naval battle of 1066)[30] supplied their own craft, then William of Jumièges' total of 3,000 does not look quite so ridiculous as it once did.

Moreover, such a conclusion might be supported by what is known of the anchorages employed. William of Poitiers says that the fleet assembled at the mouth of the river Dives *and neighbouring ports* (my italics), was delayed for a month by unsuitable winds and then blown by westerlies to St Valéry at the mouth of the Somme. Now the Gulf of Dives may at this date have provided a very large harbour indeed, for Wace claimed that the river flowed into the sea close to Bavent, which is some five miles from Dives-sur-Mer, where the entrance to the English Channel is situated today;[31]

---

[29] *RR*, ll. 6119–22, 6163–7; van Houts, 'Ship List', 161–4, 168.

[30] Above, p.36.

[31] *GG*, pp.102–3, 108–9; *RR*, II, l. 2882; Gillmor, 'Naval Logistics of the Cross-Channel Operation, 1066', 107; Bachrach, 'Military Administration', 6, 10–11 (his useful map has an inaccurate scale); the form of the lower Dives at this date is not, of course, known with any precision; see R.N. Sauvage, *L'abbaye de Saint-Martin de Troarn*, pp.245–52, who thought it *un vaste lac envahi par les marées*, and the eighteenth-century map of the area, illus. 49.

together with the 'neighbouring ports' it may have been able to shelter many hundreds of vessels. The same is true of the Somme estuary at St Valéry, and probably of the harbours around Pevensey where William landed. The presence of sand and alluvium in localities that are today well inland shows that they were once prone to flood or were open water, and Domesday Book records the existence of salt-pans, and thus presumably of salt-water, at (from west to east, in a clockwise direction) Eastbourne, Willingdon, Bowley, Hailsham, Netherfield, Ashburnham, Wartling and Hooe.[32] Hailsham is now 5¼ miles from the seashore. One reconstruction of the coast that William found (and doubtless knew that he was going to find) shows the bay itself with an entrance four miles wide and penetrating inland for about six miles, while the anchorage at Bulverhythe, west of Hastings, may have had an entrance about two-thirds of a mile wide and a penetration of about 2½ miles.[33] While all this is far from certain, as much of Pevensey Bay may in fact by 1066 have been saltmarsh,[34] what matters is the likelihood that there was more than enough space and protection for the French ships. Did William use such large anchorages because the size of his expedition required it?[35]

Even if there were a reliable figure for the numbers of vessels in his fleet we could not deduce the numbers it carried without negotiating the quicksand of average ship capacity, a matter upon which our ignorance of the nature and range of eleventh-century vessels prohibits any worthwhile conclusion; even so, just how far wide of the mark Spatz's estimate of seven men per ship might be is demonstrated by the account of a miracle said to have taken place in the time of Abbot Baldwin of Bury St Edmunds (1065–1097/8) involving a vessel carrying almost sixty men, thirty-six beasts and

---

[32] DB, 20c, 21a, 22b, 22a, 18d, 18b, 18a, 18a; see the map in Darby and Campbell, *The Domesday Geography of South-East England*, p.457. In the case of Netherfield, at least, the salt-pans were probably some way from the village, although alluvium reaches to Penhurst, a mile and a half to the south.
[33] These calculations have been made from the map prepared by J.A. Williamson and reprinted M&M, p.110. Seventeenth-century maps show a significant inlet at Bulverhythe.
[34] Brandon, *The Sussex Landscape*, p.111.
[35] The use of St Valéry may not have been part of his original plan, below, pp.187-9.

sixteen horses laden with merchants' baggage.[36] Still, this is not quite the end of the Ship List. Professor Hollister noted that William of Poitiers' *Gesta Guillelmi* names seven prominent Norman lay magnates who gave the duke the benefit of their counsel during 1066, and that if Richard, count of Evreux, is replaced by his son William, who fought at Hastings and is named in the list, then the seven correspond precisely with the eight (including Odo, a bishop) premier suppliers of vessels according to the List; thus one 'might almost suppose that William of Poitiers was writing with some such ship list at hand'.[37] Certainly one might, and one might also compare his comment that Agamemnon set out with 1,000 vessels but the duke had more with the list's total of 1,000 and 'many other ships'.[38] Such ideas could be taken further. If monks of Fécamp were with William's army keeping records (and one is said to have acted as a messenger to Harold before the battle)[39] could this be where William of Poitiers obtained his figures of 50,000 for the number supported by the Conqueror at Dives and 60,000 for those he commanded just before Hastings? The credibility of numbers like 60,000 is very difficult to ascertain. Ferdinand Lot noted that 60, 600, 6,000 and 60,000 appear frequently in medieval chronicles, and nor are they absent from works by Julius Caesar which William of Poitiers was eager to imitate.[40] But this is not to say that he was in this matter influenced by Caesar or simply made use of random round numbers, for what

---

[36] Herman the Archdeacon, *Liber de Miraculis Sancti Eadmundi*, ed. Arnold, i. 72. Herman wrote after Abbot Baldwin's death. I owe this important reference to James Campbell. Bachrach, 'On the Origins of William the Conqueror's Horse Transports', argues for vessels carrying twenty men and horses plus crew.

[37] *GG*, pp. 100–3; Hollister, 'Greater Domesday Tenants-in-Chief', p.223.

[38] *GG*, pp.110–11. WP could have been thinking of WJ's 3,000, although there is little evidence that he used WJ on the events of 1066, Davis, 'William of Poitiers', p.78.

[39] *GG*, pp.118–21; van Houts, 'Ship List', 168. Wace, *RR*, ll. 6757–61, claimed that the Fécamp monk Hugh Margot was sent by William to Harold in London.

[40] Lot, *L'Art Militaire*, i. 285, n.2; *The Gallic War*: 60: v. 5, 23; 600: ii. 15, 28; iii. 22; v. 2; 6,000: i. 27, 48; ii. 29; iv. 37; viii. 17; 60,000: ii. 4, 28; v. 49; vii. 83; pp.238–9, 262–3, 108–9, 126–7, 168–9, 234–5, 40–1, 78–9, 126–7, 226–7, 540–1, 94–5, 126–7, 298–9, 502–3. WP (*GG*, pp.170–1) gives a figure of 100,000 for the men who accompanied Caesar on the expedition of 54 BC, a figure which is exaggerated if WP knew the size of a Roman legion (Caesar says that he had five); note also Round, *Feudal England*, pp.290–2.

might seem like random round numbers also appear in early medieval assessment systems and lists which were not works of exaggeration and fantasy, but intended for the levying of taxation of various kinds, always a serious matter requiring precise records. Thus, the Anglo-Saxon document known as the Tribal Hidage deals repeatedly in recurrent round numbers of varying orders of magnitude including 600, while 60 appears six times in the Ship List (including one reference to *milites*) and is known also from the *Cartae Baronum* of 1166, believed to record the quotas of knights which William required from his tenants in England.[41] If 60,000 was not the number of men he actually had in 1066, it could have been the total recorded by a scribe in his service as the number he thought he ought to have had.

It is fair to say, however, that most historians would regard this as an impossible figure for the size of his army, many of them being wedded to the idea that medieval military forces can be safely assumed to have been small unless there is overwhelming evidence to the contrary, an idea which owes much to the views of the German scholar Hans Delbrück, to whom Spatz's book on Hastings was dedicated. On the face of it, of course, this is reasonable enough, but in a period where overwhelming evidence of any kind is often in short supply there is a danger that the occasional existence of armies of tens of thousands of men may be masked by the limitations of the sources, especially when they are linked to the assumption that any large figure cannot be trusted. Also, while analogies can prove nothing about the size of the French forces in 1066, it is worth noting two cases where the dismissal of large figures as simply wild exaggeration is not completely convincing. In 1106 the Conqueror's sons, Robert and Henry, met in battle at Tinchebrai in Normandy. The latter's forces were much the bigger, and were described shortly afterwards in a letter by a priest of Fécamp as having gone into battle in two lines of infantry, the second containing King Henry and his barons; 700 horsemen were placed with each line, and on the flanks were forces from Maine and Brittany of

---

[41] Dumville, 'The Tribal Hidage', 227; Round, *Feudal England*, pp.249, 251, 253.

about a thousand horse; the whole of Henry's army, says the priest, was about 40,000 men, compared with his brother's 6,000 and 700 cavalry.[42] Is an author who gives plausible figures for the cavalry really wildly inaccurate on the size of the forces as a whole? Similarly, it is possible to believe from contemporary sources that of the numbers engaged in the Wars of the Roses battle at Towton in Yorkshire in 1461 some 28,000 were left dead on the field.[43]

Of course, Duke William may have been well aware that the Late Roman military writer Vegetius warns against using forces that are over-large, commenting on the logistical difficulties of keeping them supplied, and stating that the ancients wished to have armies that were not so much numerous as well-trained.[44] Ultimately, one can only conclude that the duke would have had a better idea than ourselves of the size of the English force he might have to meet in battle, and presumably thought that he was taking with him enough men to offer a chance of victory. They may have numbered the 7,000 or so that is all most historians have been willing to allow, but considering the widespread territories from which they were drawn and the evidence that the fleet which carried them was very sizeable, tens of thousands are within the realms of possibility, as indeed is the case with the forces fielded by their opponents. It is perhaps also worth bearing in mind that contemporaries insist that the Norman invasion of southern Italy in the same period was motivated partly by over-population at home, that there is other evidence that the duchy's population was expanding at the same time as an economic boom was taking place, and that such phenomena may also have had their effect on the events of 1066.[45]

According to William of Poitiers, William took counsel with his men when he heard of Harold's usurpation of the English throne,

---

[42] Priest of Fécamp, *Letter on the Battle of Tinchebrai*.

[43] *Blood Red Roses*, ed. Fiorato *et al.*, pp. 15, 25; note also, by way of exception, K.F. Werner's estimate of the numbers available (from a very large area, of course) to Carolingian rulers in the ninth century as 35,000 cavalry and 100,000 infantry, as against earlier suggestions of about 5,000 in all (cited Contamine, *The Art of War*, p.25); also Bachrach's criticisms ('William Rufus' Plan', p.62) of medievalists who are 'in the thrall of Hans Delbrück's obsession for small numbers'.

[44] Vegetius, *Epitome of Military Science*, pp.64–5.

[45] Loud, *The Age of Robert Guiscard*, pp.84–5; Bates, *Normandy before 1066*, pp.96–8.

disregarded their opinion that a military expedition was beyond the resources of Normandy, and oversaw the building and equipping of the ships. He supplies no details of the mechanics of this process, to which the Bayeux Tapestry devotes some of its most interesting scenes, but Orderic Vitalis adds that clerics and laymen expended their energy and wealth in construction, and this seems to tie in with the evidence of the Ship List.[46] From there the sources move swiftly to William's embarkation. William of Poitiers, after recording the capture of an English spy and the duke's further refusal to be swayed by the doubts of his men, is the only contemporary source to give any very detailed account of the circumstances in which the French crossed the Channel; they were, he says, delayed for a month at the mouth of the Dives by contrary winds, and subsequently blown by westerlies to the port of St Valéry at the mouth of the Somme, a number of vessels being wrecked on the way. William then had the body of the saint brought from the church in an attempt to secure a favourable wind, and eventually it blew.[47] According to the *Carmen*, which also mentions the unfavourable conditions which held him in Normandy, bad weather kept him in the Somme estuary for a fortnight; William of Jumièges, however, says nothing of Dives or of contrary winds at St Valéry.[48] It is not, therefore, surprising that some historians have disbelieved this element of the accounts by William of Poitiers and the *Carmen*, arguing that the six weeks' delay was deliberate, and useful in allowing the duke to organise, provision and train his motley force while Harold waited to no purpose on the south coast of England.[49] It may also be

---

[46] GG, pp.100–3; *HÆ*, ii. 144–5. Note also WM, GR, i. 448–9, and BR, p.29; these references are given by van Houts, 'Ship List', 159–64, who also discusses the account of William's councils in Wace's RR. Councils were held at Lillebonne, Bonneville and (in June) Caen; Douglas, *William the Conqueror*, pp.184–5.

[47] GG, pp.102–3, 108–11.

[48] *Carmen*, ll. 40–77; GND, ii. 164–5.

[49] GG, pp.xxiv–vi; Gillingham, 'William the Bastard at War', p.155, notes the suggestion of Gillmor, 'Naval Logistics', 124, that the move to St Valéry came when William heard of the dispersal of Harold's forces on 8 September. It may also be a matter for concern, considering Guy of Amiens' and William of Poitiers' love of classical parallels (see above, pp.97–9), that both Caesar's crossings to Britain took place at night (as the Conqueror's is said to have done, see below) and that in 54 BC he was delayed by contrary winds for about twenty-five days, *The Gallic War*, iv. 23, v. 7–8, pp.210–11, 244–5.

that William knew of Harald Hardrada's expedition and hoped, as proved to be the case, that by delaying he would eventually face a weakened enemy, whether English or Norwegian. Yet none of this is certain. Purposely delaying a Channel crossing until late September would have been taking very considerable risks with the weather if conditions had been suitable earlier, and it has been argued on nautical grounds that the diversion to St Valéry was unintentional, as William of Poitiers implies, and put the duke in a thoroughly unenviable position.[50] It is true that it offered a shorter crossing to England than did Dives, but this may have increased the risk of interception by the English fleet, and sailing from the latter would have given him the option of striking east to Pevensey Bay or Chichester Harbour, west to Portsmouth or Southampton, or further west still to Poole, one of the biggest natural anchorages in the world. On the other hand, a longer crossing may also have meant, if the time necessary for embarkation and disembarkation is added, that men and animals would have had to spend two nights on board rather than one, something which all may have wished to avoid.[51] Even if William's fleet was a very large one the south coast of England offered many possibilities, and Harold covered them as well as he could by stationing himself centrally on the Isle of Wight, and levies 'everywhere along the coast'.[52] If William sailed for that coast in the middle of September and was instead blown to St Valéry, incurring losses on the way, then his entire enterprise

[50] C. and G. Grainge, 'The Pevensey Expedition'; the arguments which these authors adduce from WP and the *Carmen*, together with their stress on the nautical dangers of the lee shore which the area around St Valéry represented in the prevailing westerly winds, seem convincing.

[51] I am grateful to my colleague Stephen Lowden for this point. However, it may be, as Herman the Archdeacon's casual reference to a vessel carrying over fifty beasts rather implies (above, pp.183-4), that historians have tended to overestimate the problems the French faced in transporting their horses.

[52] *ASC*, C, i. 196; WP makes a similar statement about the levies, *GG*, pp.106-7; OV, *HÆ*, ii. 168-9, specifically names Hastings and Pevensey as being among the ports that Harold guarded. Note also Cnut's use of Wight as a naval base in 1022, Lawson, *Cnut*, pp.92-4. The Grainges, 'The Pevensey Expedition', pp.133-4, 140, find it puzzling in nautical terms, but may underestimate French willingness to beat against westerly winds to reach Portsmouth or Poole, or at least Harold's fear that they might do so; it is difficult, of course, knowing how far the vessels were rowed as well as sailed. In the prevailing westerlies, being on Wight would also have put him advantageously to windward of ships attempting a crossing to the east.

came somewhere near to disaster, and it says a great deal for his powers of leadership, not to mention ultimate good fortune with the weather, that he was eventually able to make a successful crossing a fortnight later. There must have been times when he remembered how his father's naval expedition against England had been brought to nothing by the elements.[53]

The accounts of the crossing given by the *Carmen* and William of Poitiers are very similar. The former implies that the French set sail late in the day, and says that nightfall was already close when William's vessel forged ahead of the rest; the fleet was then ordered to heave to until dawn, and once under way again made its landing in England at 9 o'clock as a comet prophesied the defeat of the English. William of Poitiers agrees that they anchored at sea, adding that William's ship subsequently became detached from the others, whereupon he calmly had a good meal as he waited for them to appear; when they had done so, they were all carried by a favourable wind to Pevensey, and there and at Hastings they built fortifications to protect themselves and their ships; William of Jumièges reports that those at Pevensey were strongly entrenched and that William went rapidly to Hastings to build the structures there; the *Carmen*, which gives no place-names, says that they repaired the remains of earlier defences.[54] The Bayeux Tapestry, having shown the building of ships and weapons and provisions being carried down to them (illus. 10), says that William himself sailed in a great ship and depicts a number of vessels, most of which contain horses, landing at Pevensey; the soldiers then hurried to Hastings to seize food, and after they had enjoyed a meal blessed by Bishop Odo began building a castle there (illus. 13-14). The D version of the *Anglo-Saxon Chronicle* reports that William came from Normandy to Pevensey on Michaelmas Eve, 28 September, and the Battle Abbey *Brevis Relatio* concurs; the E text says that he landed at Hastings on the following day, that of St Michael; the *Carmen* agrees that Michaelmas

[53] WJ, *GND*, ii. 76-9; above, p.20.
[54] *Carmen*, ll. 78-126, 140-4; *GG*, pp.110-15; *GND*, ii. 166-7; the Grainges, 'The Pevensey Expedition', p.135, think that William would have left St Valéry at high tide.

was approaching when the weather changed for the better, and William of Poitiers (followed by Orderic Vitalis) has him leaving on Michaelmas Day.[55] These dates are not, of course, entirely consistent, especially if he left in the evening and arrived the following morning. Only at a later stage in his account does William of Poitiers mention men who came ashore at Romney by mistake and were scattered by the English after heavy losses on both sides, a clear indication both that the crossing did not go entirely smoothly and that parts of the coast were defended despite Harold's absence in the north.[56]

The great bulk of the French force probably consisted of experienced soldiers, few of whom are likely to have been as poorly equipped as English peasants bearing no more than spears or clubs.[57] However, nor should one think of William's army as consisting principally of well-armed men in chain-mail. The Bayeux Tapestry suggests that most of the archers did not wear armour, and the same may have been true of much of the rest of his infantry. It is not at all clear that there existed at this date in Normandy a military system by which troops were levied from landholders by means of fixed quotas imposed from above by the ducal administration. Nevertheless, the duchy 'was full of vassals and mailed knights' and of mercenaries and the military households of the duke and the great lords;[58] when William needed to field an army he summoned men to his service,[59] and just as he expected his magnates to provide ships for his expedition to England in 1066 (as his father Duke Robert had when he decided to support the brothers Edward the Confessor and Alfred against Cnut)[60] he must also have expected them to provide men, although it is likely that many of these troops anticipated some sort of remuneration for their activities sooner or

---

[55] *ASC*, D and E, i. 198–9; *BR*, pp.29–30. *Carmen*, ll. 76–7; *GG*, pp.168–9; *HÆ*, ii. 170–1.

[56] *GG*, pp.142–3, and n.6.

[57] Above, p.149.

[58] See Chibnall's very useful, 'Military Service in Normandy before 1066', (p.66 for the quotation); and for reservations about the translation of the word *miles* as 'knight', below, p.224.

[59] Note, for example, WJ's comments on his assembly of Normans from all sides to deal with the rebellion of Thurstan Goz in *c.*1043, *GND*, ii. 102–3.

[60] Above, p.189, n.53.

later. The penitential drawn up for the army shortly after the battle of Hastings appears more lenient to those who fought in a public war (i.e. presumably as a result of an order from the duke) than to those who fought merely for gain (i.e. probably as mercenaries), and clearly some and perhaps many of William's men came into this second category.[61] However, this is unlikely to have meant that their leader regarded them as free agents. During hard campaigning in England over the winter of 1069–70 men from Anjou, Maine and Brittany asked to be discharged, but William refused, and when he did eventually dismiss his army, which received lavish rewards, he detained the fainthearts for an extra period.[62] Many of those who sailed with him had doubtless served previously, at least in the expeditions against Maine in 1063 and Brittany in 1064, and would have comprised a range of troop types – archers and crossbowmen, engineers and miners[63] capable of laying siege to fortifications, light and heavy infantry, and of course heavy cavalry. Such men were probably just as skilled in military methods as their English opponents, even if far too little evidence survives on Norman warfare before 1066 to make possible even the sort of treatment attempted for those opponents in the previous chapter; it is a particular problem that there is little evidence on how infantry were deployed in battle. Even so, the tactic of bursting from a fortress to take besiegers by surprise, noted by Professor Leyser as characteristic of the Vikings, is known to have been used by the Norman garrison of Tillières against a besieging force in the time of Duke Richard II, by Bishop Odo of Bayeux when defending Dover against the English in 1067, and by the men holding the castle at Exeter during the English revolt of 1069.[64] Along with evidence of their cavalry's ability to feign flight (see below), this can reasonably be taken as typical of the

---

[61] *Penitential articles issued after the Battle of Hastings*, c. 5. Douglas, *William the Conqueror*, pp. 191–2, used this as evidence that most of the duke's non-Norman troops were 'simple mercenaries'. There is doubt over the precise meaning of this chapter, in a corrupt text.

[62] OV, *HÆ*, ii. 234–7, probably using the lost ending of WP; see Chibnall, 'Military Service', pp. 89–90.

[63] OV, *HÆ*, ii. 212–3, speaks of attempts to undermine the walls of Exeter in 1068.

[64] Above, p. 171; WJ, *GND*, ii. 22–5, 176–9; OV, ii. 228–9. De Boüard, *Guillaume le Conquérant*, p. 205, suggested that the rapid mobility characteristic of Norman warfare in the eleventh century was a legacy of their Viking forebears.

professionalism, intelligence and competence with which the Normans waged war.

What sort of proportion of William's force the heavy cavalry formed there is no way of knowing.[65] Their dominant role in the Bayeux Tapestry should not lead to overestimation of their numbers, and certainly the suggestion that a third of the entire army was cavalry is difficult to credit; analogies prove nothing, but it is worth noting that probably under 10% of the men whom Caesar led against Britain in 54 BC were horsemen, and that if the priest of Fécamp's figures are accepted far less of King Henry's army fought as cavalry at Tinchebrai.[66] Yet whatever their numbers the threat posed by William's horse was something the English must have known they would have to take seriously. Mounted on expensive animals probably bred for the purpose, it is likely enough that they were highly trained and operated in units of perhaps five or ten known as *conrois*.[67] Doubts have sometimes been expressed whether they would have been capable of carrying out the feigned retreat which many of the sources on Hastings describe, but they are not very reasonable doubts given extensive evidence of the use of such manoeuvres in the early medieval period, and in particular William of Jumièges' statement

[65] Bachrach, 'On the Origins of William the Conqueror's Horse Transports', n.4, stresses that 'there is no source that even comes close to providing a reasonable figure'.

[66] Above, pp.185–6. Morillo, *Warfare under the Anglo-Norman Kings*, p.122, suggests an army of 5,000 to 6,000 men, including 2,000 cavalry possessed of 'perhaps 3000–6000 horses', i.e. three horses per man. Brown, *The Normans and the Norman Conquest*, p.150, wrote of probably 2,000 to 3,000 horsemen out of perhaps 7,000 men; Bachrach, 'Military Administration', 5, reckons with 2,000 to 3,000 horses. It might be objected, of course, that 54 BC is not a fair comparison, as the Normans valued cavalry more highly than did Caesar, who relied on heavy infantry; Vegetius, *Epitome*, p.65, suggests that cavalry might ideally have made up a fifth of Roman armies; also, while Henry and his barons fought on foot at Tinchebrai, this was clearly regarded as unusual.

[67] Verbruggen, *The Art of Warfare in Western Europe*, p.12, gives evidence on the training of heavy cavalry under the Carolingians; see also the valuable discussion of Carolingian cavalry by Bullough, '*Europae Pater*', 84–90. The history of the *conroi* before 1066 seems thoroughly obscure, for the word is a vernacular one and does not survive so early; Chibnall, 'Military Service', pp.87–8, states that 'not until the vernacular became the language of narrative does the *conroi* clearly emerge from the classical verbiage', and that knights were trained in 'small groups of five or ten, combined in larger units under their *magistri militum*'; Morillo, *Warfare under the Anglo-Norman Kings*, p.70, n.145, rejects the idea that there was 'decimal organization for small groups of cavalry'. On the horses themselves, see Davis, 'The Warhorses of the Normans', who suggested that the standard size may not have been more than fourteen hands tall.

that during fighting against the troops of King Henry of France in 1053 Normans led some of them into a trap by feigning flight.[68]

The duke himself, almost forty at the time of the battle, had been gaining experience of the stratagems of war since his youth. However, this did not include the frequent command of sizeable forces in set-piece conflicts, for in fighting in northern France in the middle of the eleventh century these were relatively rare events. Professor Gillingham has stressed the reluctance of commanders to stake their all on such hazardous throws of the dice, and argued that as William was junior to King Henry in their defeat of Norman rebels at Val-ès-Dunes in 1047, and as Varaville (against Henry and Geoffrey of Anjou) in 1057 was 'in fact not a battle', William had 'no previous experience of command in a set battle'.[69] This is going a little far. It is true that William of Poitiers seems to exaggerate the duke's role at Val-ès-Dunes as against that of Henry, and that William of Jumièges gives the impression that the French king was the senior partner;[70] nevertheless, he says that they launched a counter-attack together, and if William was not in sole command he was at least present and presumably responsible for the direction of his own men in a serious engagement of great consequence. At Varaville, William of Jumièges says that King Henry had crossed the river Dives and that the incoming tide prevented the second part of his army following him, whereupon William, who arrived upon the scene with alacrity, cut them to pieces before his enemy's eyes; as a result the latter withdrew.[71] He might have been surprised to know that he had not witnessed a battle, and one in which his opponent had seized a passing opportunity with great determination. Nor

---

[68] *GND*, ii. 104–5; cited by Brown, *The Norman Conquest*, pp.51, 171–2 (n. 147), and Gillingham, 'William the Bastard at War', p.154, who notes that the duke had long practised 'a type of warfare... dependent upon good group discipline' and that 'it is hard to envisage a type of warfare in which tricks like feigned flights would be more natural and more frequently practised'; for such flights more generally, see Bachrach, 'The Feigned Retreat at Hastings'. I agree with him in rejecting Lemmon's belief ('The Campaign of 1066', pp.109–10) that medieval accounts of such events are merely the covering up of real flights.

[69] Gillingham, 'William the Bastard at War', pp.143–4.

[70] WP, *GG*, pp.10–11; WJ, *GND*, ii. 120–3.

[71] WJ, *GND*, ii. 150–3; similarly, WP, *GG*, pp.54–7.

should the parallel with Hastings, where William is said to have attacked the English before they were properly ordered,[72] pass unnoticed. It might also be pointed out that sieges of fortifications, while not field engagements, did often see heavy fighting.[73]

When he arrived in England the duke took a step that was very unusual up to that time, at least among leaders intent upon conquering the whole country: he established a fortified camp (in the best Roman[74] and Viking tradition) by building defences at Pevensey and Hastings, and waited for Harold to attack him. This contrasts with Harald Hardrada's immediate advance on York, but whereas the latter had hopes that the Northumbrians would throw in their lot with him,[75] William probably judged that he was not likely to achieve much until a decisive defeat had been inflicted upon the enemy. He may also have feared that if he left his ships relatively unattended they would receive unwelcome and potentially disastrous attention from the English navy; William of Poitiers speaks of Harold preparing a fleet of up to 700 ships (other sources of fewer), and nothing is more likely than that there was an attempt to reactivate English vessels once William had landed.[76] During this waiting period the French ravaged the surrounding countryside (the Bayeux Tapestry shows the burning down of a house), partly to secure provisions (the *Carmen* says that they took all the cattle) and partly perhaps to provoke the English into action; certainly William of Poitiers claims that Harold hastened his march on that account, and the damage done to the surrounding area is evident in the statistics recorded by the Domesday commissioners twenty years later.[77] Probably the French also continued to train, as they waited for their scouts to report the approach of the enemy.

[72] Below, p.211.

[73] Note, for example, that at the siege of Falaise c.1043, WJ, *GND*, ii. 102–3.

[74] See, for example, Vegetius, *Epitome*, pp.23, 79–83.

[75] Above, p.37. Compare also the actions of the army which King Æthelstan defeated at *Brunanburh* in 937, and those of Swegen Forkbeard in 1013 and Cnut in 1015.

[76] *GG*, pp.124–5; the *Carmen*, l. 319, says 500 ships; OV, ii. 172–3, reduces the number to seventy.

[77] *Carmen*, l. 166; *GG*, pp.122–5; Palmer, 'The Conqueror's Footprints in Domesday Book', p.26: the rape of Hastings lost about three-quarters of its value after 1066, and its three coastal hundreds over 80%.

If the earliest French sources are to be believed, that approach was accompanied by exchanges of ambassadors. The *Carmen* says that Harold sent an eloquent monk to scout out William's camp and deliver the message that he must leave immediately, a request which was, of course, rejected. The following day William dispatched one of his monks to Harold: he urged the justice of his master's claim to the English throne and received the reply that on the day following God would make his own judgement; on his return to William he reported that Harold, who was at the head of a vast army, hoped to catch him unawares; as he listened, William was already deploying his men for battle.[78] William of Poitiers has a slightly different version of events: according to him, when William met the English envoy he received Harold's message while pretending to be his own steward, and then the following morning received it formally as part of an assembly of his followers. As he returned to his master with the duke's (negative) answer, the envoy was accompanied by a monk of Fécamp who had been instructed by William to lay out his claims to the throne and offer Harold single combat so that innocent men should not die in battle. Harold received this message as he was advancing and supposedly lifted his face to heaven and asked that God would that day decide what was just between himself and William; meanwhile, William's scouts reported the immediate approach of the enemy.[79] These extensive preliminaries allowed both authors to heighten their audiences' anticipation of their accounts of the battle itself, to remind them of the justice of the duke's cause and to put Harold in a bad light, but William of Poitiers specifically states that he had gone to some trouble to discover the content of William's message to the English king rather than confecting it himself, and it is not particularly easy to regard the monk of Fécamp as a complete invention; nor is it inherently unlikely that as Harold approached there should have been negotiations between two leaders who only about two years

[78] *Carmen*, ll. 203–334.
[79] GG, pp.116–23.

previously, during his visit to Normandy, had spent some time in each other's company, and ostensibly been on good terms.

Both the *Carmen* and the *Gesta Guillelmi* agree that Harold attempted to take William by surprise, and the same belief is also to be found in William of Jumièges' *Gesta Normannorum Ducum* and may well be implied by the *Anglo-Saxon Chronicle* E text's statement that he fought before all his army had come. Round was correct in commenting that the events immediately preceding the battle are 'doubtful and difficult to determine'.[80] William of Poitiers says that when his scouts reported the approach of the English William hastily assembled the men in his camps (which must surely mean Pevensey and Hastings rather than camps further north) as most had gone out foraging, took communion, hung around his neck the relics upon which Harold had sworn his oath, put on his mailcoat (at first reversed), made a speech to his men and then advanced into battle.[81] The implication of this, of course, is not only that the foragers took no part in the battle, but that those who did must have marched from the coast to Senlac before fighting began, although the source says nothing of any march.[82] Even if it stood alone this would not be a particularly convincing account of events, which in its emphasis on the French foragers, whom any competent commander would have called in once he knew the English were in the vicinity, may be thought to have been distorted by its author's desire to draw parallels between the Conqueror and Julius Caesar's battles with the Britons in 55 and 54 BC, in which Roman foragers figure rather prominently; at a later stage in his history, William of Poitiers used his familiarity with *The Gallic War* to stress at length how the Conqueror's achievements in England surpassed those of Caesar.[83] In any case, it is explicitly contradicted by William of Jumièges' statement that William ordered his men to

[80] Round, 'Wace and his Authorities', 683.

[81] *GG*, pp. 124–7.

[82] In the translation of *GG* in *The Norman Conquest*, ed. Brown, the editor (p. 32) footnoted the day upon which men were out foraging as Friday 13 October, the day before the battle. This would get out of the difficulty, but there is no warrant for it in WP's text.

[83] Above, pp. 99, 102.

stand to arms from dusk to dawn because of fear of a night attack, and that when dawn had broken he drew them up and advanced against the enemy. This gives the impression that the French had reached the vicinity of Senlac the day before, if not earlier, and camped there overnight; nor is this at all unlikely for other reasons. In 1066 the area which William's army had occupied probably formed a peninsula protected to the east by the estuary of the Brede and to the north by marshland through which the only viable route was the high ground which runs south through Battle to Telham and then on to Hastings.[84] Harold could no doubt have reached Pevensey by making a wide sweep to the west around Pevensey Bay via the South Downs, but William must by this stage have known that he was not doing so. To protect his fortifications and ships, and because he needed a decisive victory, it would there-fore have made sense for him to block the route along the high ground by advancing some way along it and offering battle in that area. If his army bivouacked in the vicinity of Blackhorse and Telham hills at a height of between 100 and 140 metres, and possi-bly in the area lying south of the present Powdermill Lane (the road from Battle to Catsfield), some of his troops may from the northern slopes (i.e. perhaps in the vicinity of the modern Starr's Green) have had a good view of the ground beyond, dominated by Caldbec Hill and the ridge to the south of it upon which Harold placed his standards.[85] It is also not inconceivable that if William's scouts had gained some idea of enemy numbers the duke was aware that they would have insufficient room to deploy in the ground before him without their lines being cramped for space.

[84] See the map reprinted by M&M, p.111; Tetlow, *The Enigma of Hastings*, p.135. Those travelling the Roman road which connected Hastings with Rochester in Kent must presumably have crossed the Brede estuary either by bridge or ferry. If there was a bridge (which seems very likely given the military role of the fortress at Hastings in King Alfred's time) William may have either held it in force or destroyed it.

[85] Burne, *The Battlefields of England*, p.45, and Lemmon, *The Field of Hastings*, p.47, noted that Harold's standard would not have been visible from the summit of Blackhorse Hill, but only from the lower slopes to the north (see the map, M&M, p.111). The names of the hills in this area are likely to cause confusion, as the eminence known as Telham Hill is some way to the west of Blackhorse Hill, to the north of which the village of Telham now stands. Some OS maps mark as Battle Hill the area between Starr's Green and the south side of the railway line.

6

THE BATTLE

The impossibility of giving any straightforward account of the battle of Hastings will have been evident from the discussion of the primary sources in earlier chapters. This one will therefore proceed by considering the various statements relevant to each stage of the proceedings, and then suggesting what seems to be the most plausible course of events. Nevertheless, it remains true that, rather like a jigsaw made up of a series of cubes which will produce six different pictures as their different faces are turned upwards, and endless jumbles if individual blocks get out of sequence, the impression one gets of the battle depends very much upon which elements of the evidence one chooses to stress. Thus, the views on offer include a large-scale engagement involving tens of thousands of men on each side deployed over a considerable area, or a small-scale one fought by perhaps less than ten thousand soldiers in total around no more than the crest of the Battle Abbey ridge; a fight which was largely decided, on the French side, by their cavalry and archers, or one which was mainly a conflict of dense bodies of infantry on both sides; one in which most attention is paid to the statements of contemporary sources like the *Carmen*, and the works of William of Jumièges and William of Poitiers, or one in which their accounts are significantly modified by evidence drawn from twelfth-century authors such as John of Worcester, William of Malmesbury, Henry of Huntingdon and Wace.

The prelude to the engagement, as we saw at the end of the last chapter, involved Harold marching rapidly into Sussex in an attempt to take the French by surprise and William advancing north from Pevensey and Hastings to offer battle in the vicinity of the place called Senlac. It is likely enough that negotiations of some sort preceded the actual conflict, but if so they were probably prior to the point at which the two armies came into sight of each other, a point which may have been rapidly followed by the first fighting. William of Jumièges, whose account of the timing of the opening of the battle is contemporary, more detailed and coherent than that of the *Carmen*, and more convincing than that of William of Poitiers, says that the duke ordered his men to stand by their weapons from dusk to dawn in case of a night attack, and that when dawn had broken he deployed them and advanced against the enemy, battle being joined at around the third hour; as for Harold, his forces had ridden through the night and appeared on the battlefield early in the morning.[1] Late on Friday 13 October a moon which had been full eight days earlier rose at Battle at about 22:14 GMT and in clear conditions would have provided a degree of illumination for the rest of the night. The following day, Saturday 14 October, the feast day of St Calixtus, there would have been some light in the sky, unless the weather was very overcast, by 5:30, and the sun appeared above the horizon at about 6:32.[2] If dawn is therefore reckoned as being around 6 o'clock, the third hour, at about the time the battle began, would have been about 9 o'clock.

The precise line of the English advance is not known. A Roman road ran down to Hastings from Rochester in Kent and the discovery

---

[1] WJ, *GND*, ii. 166–9. The use of the preposition *sub* in the phrase *sub hora diei tercia* may indicate a degree of vagueness about the exact time, the classical sense of the word being either 'immediately before', 'at the approach of', or 'in the course of', 'during'. The *Ab hora tamen diei tertia* of JW, ii. 604–5, 'from the beginning of the third hour', is less ambiguous; on WP, see above, p.196.

[2] The times of moonrise and sunrise have been computed using Focus Multimedia's program *Red Shift* 4. The moon was still high in the sky to the south-south-west at 6:32, and eventually set around 13:30.

in 1876 of a large coin hoard at Sedlescombe, a short distance to the west of it, has sometimes been taken as evidence that Harold's force utilised this route on its way to Battle.[3] Alternatively, it may have travelled down the Roman road connecting London and Lewes, subsequently taking local routes eastwards, for it is likely that there was a substantial roadway which connected Hastings and the London–Lewes road, and passed through the high ground upon

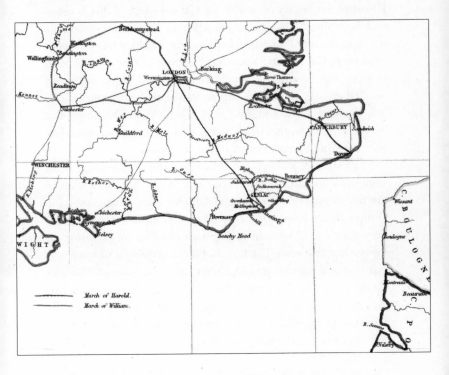

Detail from Freeman's map of 'The Voyage and Campaign of William', showing the modern rather than the medieval coastline of Sussex and a conjectural route taken by Harold to the battle of Hastings. *FNC*, iii. opp. 385.

[3] Lemmon, *The Field of Hastings*, pp.41–2. The hoard ends with the penultimate coin type of Edward the Confessor, and is not certainly connected with the events of 1066.

which the battle was fought.[4] It is possible, of course, that levies from the southern shires, who must have known that their services would be required immediately they heard of William's landing, in some instances joined him on the way or at an agreed rendezvous, and Caldbec Hill, immediately to the north of the Battle Abbey ridge, has occasionally been identified as both this spot and the location of the 'hoar apple tree' which according to the D text of the *Anglo-Saxon Chronicle* was where the battle took place.[5] However, for what it is worth the *Carmen* suggests that Harold's men were already fully assembled when the French saw spears glittering in the forest (presumably that of the Weald, whose southern edge lay in the vicinity), for this is then said to have poured forth units in dense formation which seized a hill, a valley, and rough untilled ground. William of Poitiers also speaks of the seizure of a hill, in dense formation, by forces which had come through a wood.[6] The assumption that Caldbec Hill was the rendezvous does not, therefore, have very much to recommend it.

The extent of the two armies' deployment is something of an open question, and it may be useful here to reiterate points made in the discussion of this problem in Chapter Four.[7] There are some grounds for thinking that it covered no very great area, and this has been the received wisdom among most historians of the battle for the last hundred years. The E text of the *Anglo-Saxon Chronicle* says that Harold fought before all his army had come; John of Worcester that his forces were only half as big as they might have been and that they took up position in a place so narrow that many withdrew from the ranks; William of Malmesbury that they contained few shire levies and were mainly composed of professional troops.[8] Such

---

[4] Lemmon, *The Field of Hastings*, pp.18–19, offered suggestions on the line this route took between Battle and the London–Lewes road.

[5] Lemmon, *The Field of Hastings*, pp.20, 40; Bradbury, *The Battle of Hastings*, pp.173–8, who suggests that the fighting was actually on Caldbec. In his 'The Campaign of 1066', pp.97–8, Lemmon assumed that Caldbec was the rendezvous and then criticised Harold for 'the strategic blunder of attempting to concentrate his forces within striking distance of the enemy'.

[6] *Carmen*, ll. 343–4, 363–8; GG, pp.126–9.

[7] Above, pp.138–54.

[8] *ASC* E, i. 198, JW, ii. 604–5; WM, *GR*, i. 422–3.

evidence, combined with the idea that the losses sustained against the Norwegians at Fulford and Stamford Bridge must have had their effect, and a firmly entrenched belief that medieval armies were nearly always small, led in the late nineteenth century to a scholarly consensus in favour of an English deployment extending over 600 to 800 yards rather than the much longer line which had been posited by Freeman in the 1860s. Furthermore, those who have relied on William of Poitiers' account of the prelude to the battle have taken him to mean what he does not actually say: that the French forces marched from Hastings to Battle in the early morning and deployed all before 9 o'clock,[9] something which seems impossible if they were of any great size, and may well have been so even if they were not. C.H. Lemmon followed William of Poitiers unquestioningly, but suggested that William had previously advanced to the area of Baldslow, north of Hastings (something which the *Gesta Guillelmi* specifically contradicts if, as seems certain, the camps from which he assembled his men were those at Pevensey and Hastings), and began his march at 6 a.m., dawn having been at 5:30. This desire to both reduce the length of the march and to allow it to begin as quickly as possible may indicate a degree of unease on Lemmon's part about the entire timescale,[10] and this is all the more reason to credit the more plausible evidence of William of Jumièges, which may well mean that the French were in the vicinity of Battle the previous evening. However, having disposed of the early morning march does not by itself disprove the idea that both English and French deployed over a small area, and there is in fact no way of proving that they did not. Nevertheless, there is a counter-case which falls short of proof, but provides good

[9] The same impression could also be derived from the Bayeux Tapestry, which shows the French cavalry leaving Hastings and then charging into battle; of course, a source which presents all events as a seamless sequence is poor evidence on such a point.

[10] Lemmon, 'The Campaign of Hastings', pp.95, 102–3. Burne, *The Battlefields of England*, pp.43–4, had already said of the battle's chronology that the 'chief difficulty is that so much seems to have happened in the 2½ hours between sunrise and the opening of the battle', eventually suggesting that the French march began at 6 a.m. and the fighting at 9:30. Another ex-soldier, Brigadier C.N. Barclay (*Battle 1066*, p.55), thought that 'the time it would take William's men to march six or seven miles' and then deploy would have meant that the battle did not begin 'before 9:30 or even 10 a.m.'.

reason to doubt whether the long-accepted view of the geographical extent of the battle is correct.

It can be stressed, for example, that both John of Worcester and William of Malmesbury show clear signs of wishing to diminish the impact of the English defeat, writing as they were in the first half of the twelfth century at a time when it was still a very sore point, and that the implications which their statements have for the size of the English army need not therefore be taken very seriously.[11] Moreover, even if the *Chronicle* E text's assertion that Harold fought before all his army had come is less easily explained away, our knowledge of the military capacities of late Anglo-Saxon government still renders it possible that he commanded tens of thousands of men, and there is the same possibility about the international army with which William had crossed the Channel in what may have been a very large number of ships.[12] To these general points can be added a more concrete argument. The Bayeux Tapestry has a scene (illus. 45-6) in which French cavalry are being brought down by what look like stakes in a body of water, and nearby is an eminence defended by what may be a specialist unit of English light infantry. The locality concerned cannot be identified beyond doubt, but those who have suggested that the eminence is the area of Horselodge Plantation, on the south-western edge of the Battle Abbey ridge, and the water the sandy stream to the south and south-west of it which may even have given the fight its name of Senlac, need not have erred; this may also fit Guy of Amiens' statement in the *Carmen* that William's enemies occupied not only a hill (*mons*), but also a valley (*vallis*). Moreover, this evidence that the English deployment extended to an area well away from the crest of the ridge raises the possibility that it also extended further still, and into the relatively flat country traversed by the watercourse as it runs down to the present Powdermill Lake, for if the depiction in the Tapestry is a reliable indication of the volume of

[11] Above, pp.60-70.
[12] Above, pp.176-186.

water involved (and of course it may not be) the area concerned could be that which today lies immediately to the north-east of that lake, the stream much further east perhaps being too narrow, even in the days before the construction of New Pond, to be represented in this way; however, given that the three Stew Ponds at the head of the valley, and almost due south of Harold's standard, had not been created in 1066 it is far from impossible that there were marshy pools not far from what would one day be their location.[13] As the more cautious commentators on the battle have stressed, the only certainty is the location of Harold's standard, and beyond that there is only speculation. It may be, as virtually all have believed, that his men principally faced south-east to meet an attack coming mainly from the direction of Blackhorse Hill and Starr's Green, and that his left flank rested somewhere in the vicinity of the former Battle primary school, where there was probably a steep gradient to the east,[14] and his right, as just suggested, on the marshy pools north-east of Powdermill. However, another possible line of deployment would be one in which the English army faced south-west to meet an attack coming mainly from the area of Powdermill. Wherever they stood, they must have been readily visible to their king, positioned on the highest point of the ridge behind them, alongside a dragon standard of a type probably used by English armies time out of mind, and his personal standard of the Fighting Man, sumptuously worked in gold.

An aspect of John of Worcester's account of the battle which seems to find confirmation elsewhere is his stress on the constricted nature of the English position, for the *Carmen*, William of Poitiers and other sources refer to the closely packed nature of their line.[15] This renders it virtually certain that many of Harold's troops were formed into one or possibly more shield-walls, and it may be that such formations sometimes fought not only line abreast but also one behind, and in support of, another. However,

[13] See above, p.152 and illus. 57–8.
[14] Above, pp.53–5 and illus. 63–4.
[15] *Carmen*, ll. 415, 417–21; GG, pp.128–9, 130–3.

there is no detail to be had upon such matters from the French sources which have most to say about the battle, English formations not being a matter which they found of any great interest, apart from the statement in the *Carmen* that the flanks were strengthened with noble men (*nobilibusque uiris* – perhaps a reference to the professional housecarls) and that having fixed his standard upon the crest of the ridge Harold ordered other banners to be joined to his (whatever that means); rather later, Baudri of Bourgeuil spoke of a rank of spears so dense that it looked like a forest and of the English pressing close together in a single wedge (*cuneum densatur in unum*), while Henry of Huntingdon believed that Harold had placed all his men in a single very close line, and William of Malmesbury that all the infantry possessed axes and formed an impenetrable mass (*impenetrabilem cuneum*) with a wall of shields to their front.[16] There must, however, have been rather more to his deployment than simply this, even if such references give no support to the idea of multiple densely packed formations. The presence on the Bayeux Tapestry (illus. 18) of a single archer in front of the shield-wall hints at lines of skirmishing missile troops,[17] and should the light infantry depicted in its hillock scene have been in occupation of it from the beginning of the battle they need to be taken into account too, as does the Tapestry's evidence that heavy infantry defended the line of the watercourse. Moreover, as this source is most unlikely to be a complete guide to the English dispositions, it follows that light infantry and mailed soldiers in loose order may also have been stationed elsewhere on the field. Furthermore, if the serrated shapes which it shows above the water are stakes, as seems likely, this suggests that some of the English occupied the prelude to the battle, which may mean much of the three hours or so after dawn, by creating field defences to obstruct the advance of the French, and especially that of their cavalry. Even a shallow ditch can act as a

---

[16] *Carmen*, ll. 373–6; *AC*, ll. 403–6; *HA*, pp.392–3. GR, i. 452–3. The *Carmen*, ll. 421, 428, 530, also refers to the English ranks as like a forest.

[17] See above, p.81, on the danger of arguing from this single figure that the English were short of archers.

major obstacle to horses, and it is not impossible that Harold's men went further than this by constructing concealed pits of the sort which Vikings had employed to bring about the demise of Margrave Henry of Neustria in 887.[18] Henry of Huntingdon, at least, reports that during the battle many of the French were laid low by a great ditch cunningly hidden (*foueam magnam dolose protectam*), while William of Malmesbury speaks of a ditch being filled to the brim with enemy bodies.[19] Wace went much further than this – saying at different points that Harold had the place examined and protected by a good fosse with an entrance on each of three sides; that the English had made a fosse which went across the field, guarding one side of their army; and that during the battle the Normans were forced back into a fosse which they had previously passed around the side of, that horses and men kicked helplessly, that many of the English fell there too, and that at no time in the day did as many Normans die as perished in the fosse, as those who saw the dead said.[20] How far such details may derive from authentic tradition, rather than being a muddled reflection of statements about ditches found in the earlier sources known to Wace, is difficult to say.

To sum up: it is possible, as has long been believed, that Harold's men occupied a position around no more than the crest of the ridge, with the flanks protected by vegetation and perhaps on the left by steep slopes to the north and east in the vicinity of the former primary school;[21] it is also possible, indeed more likely in the view of the present writer for reasons already stated, that their forces extended over much of a ridge one kilometre long, and also down into the valley to the south of it, with at least one watercourse being held in force against the enemy. The orientation of the English units was probably either to the south-east, facing Starr's Green with Blackhorse Hill beyond, or to the south-west, in the

---

[18] Above, p. 171.

[19] *HA*, pp. 392–3; *GR*, i. 454–5. If the ponds to the rear of Horselodge Plantation (above, p. 52 and illus. 29, 37) existed in 1066 it would have been very easy for unsuspecting French troops coming against this area from the north to have fallen into them.

[20] *RR*, ll. 6969–72, 7847–8, 8079–96.

[21] On this area, see above, pp. 53, 142 and illus. 62–4.

direction of Powdermill. There is no way of arriving at any satisfactory estimate of the numbers of men under Harold's command: it is likely to have been a figure between a few thousand and many (perhaps tens of) thousands; the same is true of Duke William's army.

Both the steep slopes to be found on parts of the ridge, and especially immediately to the south of the English king's own position, and what the *Carmen* calls the roughness of the uncultivated ground[22] rendered the area generally unsuitable for cavalry, as did the small streams which abound in the vicinity and the probably distinctly marshy drainage area which extended from east of the location of what is now New Pond down to that of what is today Powdermill Lake. Geography probably made the English position virtually impossible to outflank,[23] and what is known of the battle itself tends to confirm this belief. Wherever his flanks lay, Harold would have been aware of the danger of their being turned by the French horse, and there is no difficulty in believing that he stationed renowned men there, as the *Carmen* says, and rested them on significant obstacles. Otherwise, his troops consisted of a range of types, from those protected by a chain-mail byrnie, helmet and shield, and with spears, swords and axes as offensive weapons, to those with no defensive protection at all, and wielding only bows, clubs or spears. There is, of course, no way of knowing the relative proportions of the different types, or how the shire levies, some of whom were probably very well armed,[24] were deployed relative to each other and the professional housecarls, for the Bayeux Tapestry, which can reasonably be taken as valuable evidence on what English soldiers might look like, is of little help in answering questions such as these. However, shield-walls are likely to have been at least several and probably many ranks deep,[25] and if the D text of the *Anglo-Saxon Chronicle* is correct in stating that William

[22] *Carmen*, l. 366: *Et non cultus ager asperitate sui.*

[23] Lemmon, 'The Campaign of 1066', p.100, stressed the difficulties which the ground presented to cavalry, and suggested (like Burne, *The Battlefields of England*, p.23) that Harold had reconnoitred the ridge the previous summer.

[24] Above, pp.154–5

[25] Above, pp.165–8.

launched his attack before the English ranks were properly formed it looks as though the battle began before everything was in suitable order. As the French are said to have seen the enemy emerge from woodland and occupy the ridge in dense formation one cannot be sure that the process had necessarily taken all of the three hours or more which separated dawn from the beginning of the fighting; even so, the more time it took the greater any estimate of the numbers in this dense formation would be likely to be, and the time involved in their deployment seems to have been at least great enough for the construction of field defences elsewhere.

The sources have more to offer on the French deployment. The account of the opening stages of the battle in the *Carmen* is both rather incoherent and complicated by the insertion of the story of the heroic exploits of the juggler Taillefer, but prior to this Guy of Amiens speaks of archers and crossbowmen whom the duke had intended supporting with cavalry had the onset of the battle not prevented it, and then of infantry armed with arrows and quarrels (i.e. archers and crossbowmen) preceding him up the hill, together with helmeted men who rushed to crash shields against shields. The information on the missile troops is repeated again after the Taillefer story, as is the point that shields were of no avail against the bolts from crossbows. Then, Guy seems to say, the French attacked the left (of the English) and the Bretons the right, while the duke and the Normans occupied the centre. William of Poitiers' belief that Breton horsemen were on William's left and Robert of Beaumont on the right goes some way to support this,[26] just as his more coherent account of the French deployment is generally very similar to that of the *Carmen*. Here, too, infantry in the front rank were armed with bows and crossbows, while in the

---

[26] *Carmen*, ll. 335–42, 381–414; *GG*, pp. 128–31. The use in the *Carmen* of the verb *peto* creates difficulty here, as it can be translated either 'occupy' or (more plausibly) 'attack'. As Barlow points out (*Carmen*, p.lxxix, n.266) 'if the French "occupied" the left and the Bretons the right, their positions are clear enough. But if they attacked the English left and right wings... their position in the ducal army is reversed'. His translation (p.25) chooses the second option. On the possibilty that the Norman Robert of Beaumont was fighting on the right with the French, see above, p.174, n.2.

second line were steadier, armoured foot-soldiers (*pedites...
firmiores et loricatos*) and finally there were the squadrons of horsemen (*turmas equitum*) with the duke himself in their midst.[27] An
advance in three lines, but without further detail, is also reported
by William of Jumièges.[28] It had plenty of classical precedents, and
Caesar sometimes arranged his infantry thus,[29] but there is no
need to reject French statements as groundless fabrications on
this score, as the dispositions described are plausible enough.
However, a more obvious place for cavalry would have been on
the wings, where Vegetius was adamant that it should be placed,
and where King Henry I did place it in 1106 at the battle of
Tinchebrai, when a charge on the enemy flank decided the day.[30]
That William does not seem to have done this may mean that he
was deploying over a frontage which was rather restricted relative
to the number of his men, or that the English flanks were so
securely anchored that he could see that there was no possibility
of their being turned.

Stories, some of them fabrications, probably gathered around the
battle almost immediately, perhaps assisted by a demand for *chansons*
which celebrated the French victory. In this context, it is not surprising that the tale of Taillefer should have found its way into a
piece as early as the *Carmen* is now believed to be, as it did later into
the works of Henry of Huntingdon, Gaimar and Wace. It is not
necessarily completely fictitious, but even if one of William's men
did taunt the English by juggling with his sword and inflicting their
first casualty, it is not likely that many were deflected more than

---

[27] *GG*, pp.126–7; *turmas equitum* may be a conscious echo of the *equitum turmas* and *turmisque
equitum* to be found in Caesar's *The Gallic War*, iv. 33, vii. 88, pp.222, 506. On the use of crossbows
at Hastings, see M&M, pp.112–5, who suggested that of the four archers who appear in the main
register of the Bayeux Tapestry (illus. 17) the one wearing mail is a crossbowman. Baring, 'On the
Battle of Hastings', pp.226–7, used Wace's *Roman de Rou*, which 'no doubt followed a tradition
which in this matter was probably trustworthy', as evidence that 'the geographical principle was
carried out in detail, the various contingents being arranged from east to west according to the
position of the places they came from', and that 'individual lords with their followers were as a
rule arranged by the neighbourhood from which they came'.
[28] *GND*, ii. 168–9.
[29] Caesar, *The Gallic War*, i. 49, 51, pp.80–3.
[30] Vegetius, *Epitome*, pp.47, 98. On Tinchebrai, see further, below, pp.214–5.

momentarily from the serious business of making war. In this context the *Anglo-Saxon Chronicle* D text's claim that William attacked before his opponents were properly drawn up is particularly important, for this is of course not only what a skilled general might well have sought to do, but it is also the sort of stratagem the duke had employed successfully on at least one occasion in the past, when at Varaville in 1057 he caught and defeated his opponents by advancing swiftly as they were crossing the river Dives; he was to act similarly against northern English rebels in 1069.[31] Nor is it impossible that the apparently very constricted nature of the English lines was to an extent the result of this tactic. Yet even if this is so it can have given the French no very decisive advantage, as the sources are agreed that once joined the fighting went on for many hours.

Any attempt to chart the course and extent of the conflict in any detail over such a lengthy period is bound to fail given the inadequate nature of the evidence, and accordingly there will be no such attempt made here. Even so, the statements of the sources do at points coincide in ways which almost certainly reflect what might be termed real issues and events. One of these is the French use of missile troops. Archers who did not know how many they had killed and wounded were assigned their own penance by Norman bishops shortly after the battle,[32] and they and their confrères figure very prominently in the Bayeux Tapestry, even if they spend most of their time in the lower border, and rather less prominently (for they are quickly left behind) in the early written accounts. The *Carmen*, William of Poitiers and Baudri of Bourgeuil all comment on the French assault being preceded by discharges from archers and crossbowmen, the *Carmen* noting that shields were no defence against the latter, while Baudri suggests that the English had not faced the crossbow before. He also thought that the losses they sustained from this missile attack led them to abandon their dense

[31] Above, p.193; below, p.245. Note also, 'It is notable how often he appears to have surprised his opponents and caught them off balance either on the battlefield, as at Varaville, or at sieges such as Alençon or Arques', Bates, *William the Conqueror*, pp.42–3.
[32] *Penitential articles issued after the Battle of Hastings*, c. 6.

formation in pursuit of the enemy, and that the Normans then simulated flight and used their cavalry to surround and slaughter their
pursuers.[33] The *Carmen*, however, which also speaks of a feigned
flight after the missile attack, suggests that infantry fighting,
when spear was met with spear and sword with sword, intervened
between the two, and the same impression is also to be derived
from William of Poitiers, if it is assumed that the foot-soldiers
(*pedites*) who killed and wounded many during an exchange of
missiles with the English, and who eventually received cavalry support, included the armoured infantry mentioned by the same
author at an earlier stage; it can be noted that he also eventually
describes the flight of *pedites* and Breton horse and such auxiliaries
as were on the left wing.[34]

The sources do their best to obstruct those who would seek out
the role of French infantry in the battle. It is, to begin with,
extremely unlikely that they consisted solely of missile troops and
men in chain-mail, for it is probable that only a portion of the
duke's men could afford such an expensive form of protection. Yet
of unarmoured French infantry who were not missile men the
sources say nothing whatever. The designer of the Bayeux Tapestry
depicted at least 179 horses in the work's main register, and as
R.H.C. Davis commented, 'made it his business to show William's
army as an army of cavalry',[35] but if it is reasonable to suppose that
this reflected the interests of the militaristic and aristocratic audience for which the piece was made, it is far less so to conclude that
they and their mounts played as decisive a role in the fighting as the
Tapestry might lead one to think. The earlier depiction (illus. 9) of
the attack on Dinan during the campaign in Brittany is significant
here. Horsemen bearing spears and shields gallop towards the fortification, while two of the defenders stand outside the wall ready to
hurl spears in response. Below the walls two men attempt to set fire

[33] *Carmen*, ll. 337–40, 381–2, 409–12; *GG*, pp.126–9; *AC*, ll. 409–21. I follow M&M, p.115, who
made sense of an otherwise curious passage in Baudri by suggesting that his 'arrow which they
had not known' was the crossbow bolt.
[34] *Carmen*, ll. 383–4, 416; *GG*, pp.126–9.
[35] Davis, 'The Warhorses of the Normans', 68.

to the structure, and then the keys are handed over in token of surrender. Of course, this is the sketchiest of representations of an
attack on a fortified site (although not necessarily much more
sketchy than the Tapestry's account of the battle of Hastings), but
the impression that men on horseback played any significant role in
assaulting the walls must be misleading, and even when it comes to
operations on foot these are performed by what look like dismounted horsemen rather than the somewhat less glamorous
infantry who must surely have been responsible for such activities
in reality. In the light of this, it is reasonable to question the reliability of the Tapestry's depiction of horsemen with spears at the ready
charging the English shield-wall at Hastings, and it is worth noting
that according to William of Poitiers when they came up in support of the infantry they used their swords. Nevertheless, such is
the power of the Tapestry that some historians have concluded that
the battle represented a victory of cavalry and archers over infantry.
In his 1884 Lothian Prize Essay, for example, the young Charles
Oman compared the trials of the English array with that of the
British squares at Waterloo: 'incessant charges by a gallant cavalry
were alternated with a destructive fire of missiles'. Eventually,
unable to 'bear the rain of arrows' many of the English followed the
retiring cavalry down the hill and were surrounded and cut to
pieces. The remainder fought on for another three hours, but the
day was lost: the 'tactics of the phalanx of axemen had been deci-
sively beaten by William's combination of archers and cavalry'.[36]
Not much later, J.H. Round went so far as to suggest that the
French army consisted only of horsemen and armoured and unarmoured missile troops.[37]

[36] Oman, *The Art of War in the Middle Ages A.D.378–1515*, pp.25–6. In his expanded 1898 treatment
(*A History of the Art of War*, pp.149–64) Oman provided a much more elaborate account of the
battle but re-stated his basic conclusion, and while acknowledging the presence of French
armoured infantry judged the mailed knights 'the really important section of the army'.

[37] Round, *Feudal England*, pp.368–70, drawing on his 1893 *Quarterly Review* article, 75–6, and
upon an interpretation of WP's words (*GG*, pp.126–7) that was unreasonable, as Kate Norgate
observed, 'The Battle of Hastings', 42–3; it was also a shift from the position of his *Quarterly
Review* article of 1892, 17, where he spoke of the English being 'first riddled by Norman arrows
and then attacked by Norman infantry'.

Yet as far as cavalry goes, one can acknowledge that possession of it gave William tactical options not available to Harold, and that at points in the battle it may have been of great importance, without concluding that it was inevitable that its actions would prove decisive. Its effectiveness on the rough ground over which the battle was fought would have been influenced by the location of the English position. If they occupied no more than the crest of the ridge, this would have yielded a flattish area to the west[38] upon which horsemen could perhaps have galloped in the way that the Tapestry suggests, but if they were stationed on something like the whole of it there would have been many gradients for the horses to face. In this case, and while it would be foolish to be dogmatic given our ignorance of the precise nature of the terrain, the ground as it now exists provides good reason to wonder whether effective charges could have been made over many of the southern slopes of the ridge, even allowing that horses can climb very steep gradients indeed. It might also be stressed that it is doubtful how useful horsemen would have been against densely packed, steady infantry even in more favourable conditions,[39] that the massed charge in which riders in close order couched heavy lances beneath their arms had probably not been developed in 1066,[40] that there is no way of knowing what proportion of the French forces the cavalry formed, that their steeds had no armour to protect them from English missiles, and that even well-bred stallions carrying men in chain-mail must have tired as the day advanced (assuming, of course, that they found much employment).

All this raises the question of whether Hastings was much more of an infantry conflict than has sometimes been realised.[41] At

---

[38] That is, that running from the western edge of the abbey terrace to the location of the OS height marker of 69 metres, some 500 metres further west, above, p. 51, and see illus. 52, 54.

[39] See the comments of Verbruggen, *The Art of Warfare*, pp.46–7; Morillo, *Warfare under the Anglo-Norman Kings*, pp.155–6; Strickland, 'Military Technology and Conquest', 360–1; and especially Bennett, 'The Myth of the Military Supremacy of Knightly Cavalry', pp.309–12, and his conclusion (p.316) that 'knightly cavalry were generally as impotent before well-trained foot as the French cavalry against British infantry squares at Waterloo'. Vegetius, *Epitome*, p.84, states that the strength of an army depends mainly on its infantry.

[40] See France, *Victory in the East*, p.71.

[41] The likely importance of the French infantry was stressed by Brown, 'The Battle of Hastings', 11; similarly, Morillo, *Warfare under the Anglo-Norman Kings*, p.164, n.98.

Tinchebrai in 1106, fought between William's sons Duke Robert of Normandy and King Henry I of England, Orderic Vitalis reports that the latter's iron-clad lines (which included Englishmen) were drawn up and then advanced in a disciplined fashion in close order, with the first of the three under the command of Ralph of Bayeux, while Robert's front line was led by William, count of Mortain, and his rear by Robert of Bellême. When the opposing ranks met, however, they were so crowded together that it was impossible from them to use their weapons properly, and the conflict was decided when Henry's cavalry charged the enemy's flank and Robert of Bellême took to flight. According to the priest of Fécamp, the fighting had then lasted an hour.[42] There are two points of interest about this. The use of dense lines of infantry by both sides may have owed something to Norman experience of facing the English at Hastings, or it may be that their infantry had fought in this fashion in the past, including at Hastings itself; and in the latter case, the length of time that the closely massed foot-soldiers struggled without result at Tinchebrai could have implications for Hastings, for in a situation where a flank attack by cavalry seems not to have been a possibility it is not hard to see how a battle of this type could have gone on for many hours.

Dr Morillo has commented that it is 'difficult to find more than a handful of ancient and medieval battles that lasted more than an hour or two',[43] but in fact there are a number of engagements involving the Anglo-Saxons of which one can be tolerably certain that this is true. Even leaving aside John of Worcester's assertion that Sherston, fought by Edmund Ironside against Cnut in 1016, took up two days, Alfred's defeat of the Vikings at Ashdown in 871 is said to have lasted until nightfall, while his fights against the same enemy in the same year at *Meretun* and Wilton apparently both went on for much of the day. Similarly, the poem on his grandson Æthelstan's victory at *Brunanburh* in 937 speaks of the slaughter

---

[42] *HÆ*, vi. 88–91; Priest of Fécamp, *Letter on the Battle of Tinchebrai*; HH, *HA*, pp.452–5. On Tinchebrai, see also David, *Robert Curthose*, pp.245–8.
[43] Morillo, 'Hastings: An Unusual Battle', p.220.

extending from morning until sunset, and of the West Saxons pursuing the enemy all day long, while Stamford Bridge in 1066 saw fighting until late in the day.[44] All these conflicts are likely to have seen shield-wall pitted against shield-wall, a formation used by the Vikings as well as the English, and perhaps involved considerable numbers of men. Could it be, despite the prominence given by the Bayeux Tapestry to the French cavalry, that Hastings was so long and hard fought because much of the day was taken up by struggles between dense bodies of infantry on both sides of a type with which the Anglo-Saxons had long been familiar, and because the Normans had retained their Scandinavian ancestors' practice of deploying their foot-soldiers in this fashion too?

Yet even if this were the case, the sources suggest that the battle had other significant features. One was a French retirement which almost turned into a rout, another the use of the feigned retreat. William of Poitiers says that after a period of fighting in which the English were greatly helped by their numbers, the density of their formation, their use of weapons which easily penetrated shields and other defences, and the advantage of occupying higher ground, the foot-soldiers, Breton cavalry and auxiliaries on William's left wing turned away, and almost all his line began to give ground, for the Normans believed that the duke himself had been killed. However, William dealt with this crisis by removing his helmet to prove that he was still alive, urging his men on to victory, and leading a charge which surrounded thousands of the pursuers and annihilated them to a man. Subsequently, further heavy fighting was followed by two feigned flights which drew forward and destroyed more of the English forces.[45] Guy of Amiens' *Carmen* has a slightly different version of events, claiming that the French would not have been able to penetrate the dense English formation had it not been for their skill in war, as they deliberately simulated flight and then turned on their pursuers, while their two wings attacked an enemy now more

[44] JW, ii. 486–9; *ASC*, A text, i. 70, 72, 106, 108; C, i. 198. As Harold travelled some miles to reach Stamford Bridge the battle cannot have begun early in the day.
[45] *GG*, pp. 128–33, followed in its essential details by OV, *HÆ*, ii. 174–5.

dispersed than formerly. Ten thousand of the English were killed at this stage, but the rest fought on effectively enough to force the Normans into a real flight, which William halted by removing his helmet (there is no mention here of any belief that he had been killed), making a speech and leading his forces in a renewed attack in which he performed great feats of arms, killing Harold's brother Gyrth who had unhorsed him with a spear cast, forcing a trooper from Maine to yield up his steed and then being unhorsed a second time, but once again wreaking vengeance on the man responsible, the 'son of Helloc'. The duke is then said to have received a third mount from Count Eustace of Boulogne, with whom he cleared the field of English soldiers, and from here the *Carmen* moves to the role of both men in the killing of Harold.[46]

The authors of other sources, too, knew of the simulated flight. According to Baudri of Bourgueil, the English broke ranks because the torment caused by the opening French missile attack apparently coincided with a feigned Norman withdrawal; they were intercepted by cavalry and slaughtered, but further attacks upon the English front resulted in a real withdrawal fuelled by the rumour that the duke had been killed. He responded to this by removing his helmet, making a speech similar in tenor to those reported by William of Poitiers and the *Carmen*, and leading his men in a further assault in which he surpassed the deeds of Hector and Achilles; these deeds are followed by the report of Harold being killed by an arrow.[47] The Battle Abbey *Brevis Relatio* says nothing of difficulties experienced by the French in the early stages of the battle, only that not long after William had opened it by killing one of the English a unit of almost 1,000 Norman horsemen rushed upon the enemy line, but fled in apparent fear once they reached it; as a result some of the English followed, wishing to kill them if possible, but the Normans, who were more wary in war than their enemies, soon returned, interposed themselves between their pursuers and

[46] *Carmen*, ll. 421–530.
[47] *AC*, ll. 409–63.

the main English line, and quickly killed all of them.[48] William of
Malmesbury and Henry of Huntingdon connect the simulated
French withdrawal with fighting around a ditch (see below), while
Wace does not mention it until after describing Harold being
wounded by an arrow,[49] and the Bayeux Tapestry does not show it
at all; however, it does show Bishop Odo of Bayeux comforting the
boys and William removing his helmet (illus. 20-1), presumably to
prove that he is still alive.

Of course, none of these sources is in complete agreement with
any of the others, the most similar being the *Carmen* and Baudri of
Bourgeuil, who both place the real French flight after a simulated
one, in contrast to William of Poitiers' assertions that the latter preceded the former, and that there were two simulated withdrawals,
not one. It is impossible to make any definite choice between these
different versions of events, for while William of Poitiers as a
Norman with close contacts in the ducal court[50] ought to have been
the most well informed there is a perhaps suspicious neatness about
his claim that the French learnt from the advantage they had reaped
from the outcome of the real flight. There are also the problems, discussed in Chapter Three, about how far the elements common to
these sources may be the result of direct borrowing from one to the
other, or how far they may instead or in addition reflect traditions
about the battle which were widely known at the time and accordingly found their way in different forms into different works. Unless
one is to take what seems the unreasonable view that the *Carmen*
was the only source ultimately behind William of Poitiers', Baudri
of Bourgeuil's and later sources' knowledge of these events,[51] the
second conclusion appears much the most likely basic explanation
of the similarities and dissimilarities of their statements about the
real and feigned French withdrawals. Indeed, it would not be at all
surprising if those who survived the conflict came away with

---

[48] *BR*, p.32.
[49] *RR*, ll. 8175–252.
[50] Above, pp.95–6.
[51] For other comment on this, see above, p.122, n.102.

confused impressions and memories of what had happened, and if their reports were further distorted by constant repetition and the passage of time to yield the inconsistent picture which is all that now remains. Yet while this may not provide any very clear narrative of the course of events, nor is it completely useless. It looks as though in the years following the battle it was said that there was a point at which Duke William managed to stem the rout of significant numbers of his men only with difficulty and by disproving the rumour that he had been killed by removing his helmet, and that at another stage or stages the French managed to reduce the impenetrability of the English lines by engaging in feigned retreats in which their cavalry could to an extent come into its own.

While this takes us some way in establishing what happened during the battle it is possible to get further still by turning to other sources which describe elements of the fighting to which the contemporary and near-contemporary French writers make no reference. The Bayeux Tapestry, as has been mentioned several times already,[52] shows (illus. 45-6) what appear to be English light infantry defending a hillock near a watercourse in which stakes seem to have been fixed to impede the French horse, and with considerable success, judging by the legend 'Here the English and the French fell at the same time in the battle' and the depiction of two horses which have been brought down and of a third lying dead in the lower border to their right. It is clear that the Tapestry's designer, and presumably the patrons for whom the work was being done, saw this as a significant stage of the conflict, and nothing could sound a more effective warning of the limitations of sources such as the *Carmen*, William of Poitiers' *Gesta Guillelmi* and Baudri of Bourgeuil's *Adelae Comitissae* than the fact that they are silent on these events, either through ignorance or because they did not wish to stress elements of the fighting which reflected little credit on Duke William and his men. Others are not silent. Whatever reservations one might have about William of

[52] Above, pp. 149-54, 164, 172, 204-5.

Malmesbury's account of the battle,[53] he does speak of a feigned retreat which broke up the English formation, and of how some of the troops who were put to flight by this stratagem seized a hillock from which they threw down the Normans into a valley, and by throwing spears and rolling down stones upon them routed them to a man. Also, he says, making their way around a deep ditch by a short cut known to them, the English killed so many of the enemy that their corpses filled it to the brim.[54] Henry of Huntingdon was another Anglo-Norman author of the first half of the twelfth century who had heard about events involving a ditch. When Duke William ordered his men to simulate flight, he states, they came to a cunningly hidden large ditch as they fled where a great number fell and were crushed, but as the English continued their pursuit beyond it they saw the main Norman line break through their own centre, and the greater part of them fell around the same ditch as they retired.[55] Wace's several statements about ditches, like those of William of Malmesbury and Henry of Huntingdon, were noted earlier,[56] but the final one is worth repeating: that the Normans were forced back on a ditch into which horses and men were thrown, that many of the English were killed there too, and that at no time in the day did as many Normans die as in that ditch, as those who saw the dead said.

Of course, these sources may not be completely independent of each other, for Wace probably used the works of both William of Malmesbury and Henry of Huntingdon (though they were not known to each other) and it is not inconceivable that William derived some of his knowledge directly or indirectly from the Tapestry.[57] However, he did not draw his comments on the throwing of missiles and rolling down of stones from the hillock, or that on the ditch being filled level to the brim with bodies, from that

[53] Above, pp.64–70.
[54] GR, i. 454–5.
[55] HA, pp.392–5.
[56] Above, p.207.
[57] Brown, 'The Battle of Hastings', 20, was in little doubt that WM had seen the Tapestry, but B&W, 27–8, were more cautious; there is no convincing reason to believe so.

source, and nor did Wace owe his statement on the recollections of those who saw the dead to any authority that has survived. Hence, it is most likely that the way in which these stories about fighting around ditches and hillocks both resemble and do not resemble each other is attributable to the same sort of reason mentioned above with reference to the French flights and feigned flights: that there was a firm tradition that events of this kind had taken place, but that with the passage of time this reached different authors in different forms. It is a corollary of this, of course, that again as with the feigned flights it is not possible to come to any definite conclusions about the truth of what happened. It is the belief of the present writer, as expressed earlier,[58] that the Tapestry's details are strong evidence that hillock and watercourse were occupied by the English at the start of the battle. It is difficult to say whether the statements of William of Malmesbury, Henry of Huntingdon and Wace are to be taken as closely related to events depicted in the Tapestry's hillock scene, or whether they may also reflect other activity at different times and/or different places. However, it would not be difficult to believe that the English both defended the stream which flows west from New Pond (if this is the Tapestry's watercourse) at the beginning of the battle, were eventually pushed back from it, and then fought around it again when pursuing the enemy at a later stage. If so, Wace's assertion that more of the Normans fell there than elsewhere would be perfectly credible.

If the French sources, and especially William of Poitiers, are to be believed, the English were greatly weakened by the fact that many of them abandoned their strong position to pursue a retiring enemy who then used his cavalry to take advantage of breaks in their formation by enveloping their flanks and destroying them. Were this so, there is no denying that it may reflect indiscipline on the part of some of Harold's troops. Still, there are other possibilities. The reports that at one point William's men almost routed must be taken seriously, and it would not be surprising if the

[58] Above, pp.150–1.

English commanders decided that this was something which had to be exploited in order to gain a decisive victory; this might also fit Adam of Bremen's almost contemporary report that the English were at first victors but then were defeated by the Normans.[59] Harold may or may not have been aware of Vegetius' warning that heavy infantry should not follow a retiring enemy because of the danger that they may become disordered and thus vulnerable to counter-attack, and that pursuit is the role of light troops and cavalry.[60] If he was, and if the heavily armed housecarls, thegns and shire-levies left the task to light-armed men who were more mobile and intended for use in such circumstances, then one could not necessarily take their pursuit as a gross tactical blunder. Nevertheless, it may have been so, for it allowed the French horse to come into its own, and points up the limitations imposed upon the English by the fact that they were not employing cavalry themselves. As Harold had apparently decided to stand on the defensive, as Edward III would later do at Crécy in 1346, his son the Black Prince at Poitiers ten years later and Henry V at Agincourt in 1415,[61] it would seem that this is a strategy he should have persisted in, and one might discern here the same haste that led him to fight the battle when all his army had not yet come.

Beyond the damage caused to the English by the French retirements, the sources have little more to offer in determining why they lost the battle. The Bayeux Tapestry, whose designer did not, of course, intend it as an analysis or explanation of this problem, shows the deaths of Harold's brothers Leofwine and Gyrth before the scene depicting fighting around the watercourse and hillock, and Bishop Odo rallying the boys and Duke William proving he is still alive after it; then French horsemen fight mailed infantry

[59] Adam of Bremen, *Gesta*, ed. Schmeidler, p.197. Morillo, 'Hastings: An Unusual Battle', p.224, suggests that WP's statement (*GG*, pp.130–1) that 'a great part' of the English line moved forward is evidence of a deliberate counter-attack.

[60] Vegetius, *Epitome*, p.50.

[61] At Poitiers, as James Campbell has reminded me, the Black Prince ordered his men to mount their horses to deliver their final attack on the French.

described as 'those who were with Harold' (perhaps a reference to his bodyguard), a mailed Frenchman on foot beheads an unarmed and unarmoured enemy, and many French archers occupy the lower border and the stripping of the dead begins as Harold is killed in the main register (see below). One might guess that there were stories about the deaths of his brothers which were familiar enough for the designer of the Tapestry to think or know that its patrons would have wished them included, but he seems to have been unaware of Guy of Amiens' statement in the *Carmen* that Gyrth was killed by none other than Duke William himself; Wace, who has a great deal to say about Gyrth at an earlier stage, also reports that he was felled by a blow delivered by the duke, but more or less concurrently with the death of his brother Harold.[62] One might suspect that both he and Leofwine commanded significant bodies of men in parts of the field distant from their brother (although William of Poitiers says that their corpses were found near his), but even so it is doubtful whether the way in which the Tapestry illustrates their deaths is of much significance in terms of the battle's outcome.[63] Nor is it impossible that the neatness of the way in which it shows them dying together is itself rather suspect, and reflective more of its audience's desire to see their fall rather than of the precise historical circumstances in which these events occurred.

William of Poitiers suggests that there was plenty of hard fighting even after the destruction of those of the English who pursued the French retirement which almost became a rout; still William's men faced an enemy who were closely massed,

---

[62] *Carmen*, ll. 471–80; *RR*, ll. 8819–28.

[63] *GG*, pp.138–41. See above, p.165 and illus. 19, for the possibility that they were with heavy infantry fighting in loose order. Morillo ('Hastings: An Unusual Battle', p.224) suggests that Harold may have ordered them to lead the counter-attack and that their fall was one reason why it failed, but his claim that the 'placement of their deaths in the Bayeux Tapestry is consistent with such an interpretation' only convinces if every scene from this point to that of William rallying his troops belongs to the same sequence of events; however, because the stakes (if such they are) in the watercourse and hillock scene must have been in position when the battle began, and the scene thus probably shows another distinct stage in the fighting (as, on this view, do probably all those under discussion here) this seems to me unlikely.

although inroads were made into their lines by the weapons of the strongest soldiers.[64] Moreover, despite the success of the subsequent two (according to him) feigned retreats, the English ranks are still said to have been so dense that the lightly wounded could not escape and were crushed to death by the mass of their companions. From this he moves to a list of the more notable of the duke's followers who took part in the battle and then to a paean, complete with classical parallels, of the deeds of the duke himself, who is reported to have had three horses killed beneath him. Only after this are we told that as the day declined the English army knew that they could stand against the Normans no longer, and that one of the reasons for this was that their king had been killed.

The omission of the details of Harold's death is not a feature of the *Gesta Guillelmi* shared by other sources. The only information given by William of Poitiers on the matter which is at all relevant is that the corpse, which lacked all adornment, could not be recognised from the face but only by certain marks.[65] This is in itself perfectly plausible, and there is something of a parallel to it in William of Malmesbury's report that after Stamford Bridge Tostig's remains were recognised by a wart between the shoulder blades, and in the discovery at Riccall Landing of bodies perhaps connected with the events of 1066 which bore the marks of so many edged weapons as to suggest that they had been struck repeatedly.

---

[64] *fortissimorum militum ferro.* Some (for example, Davis and Chibnall's recent edition, p.131, and *The Norman Conquest*, ed. Brown, p.33) have translated *miles* here as 'knight', thus increasing the apparent importance of such men in the fighting. However, the *guerriers* of Professor Foreville's edition (p.193), 'soldiers' of *EHD2*, p.241, and 'fighters' of *The Battle of Hastings*, ed. Morillo, p.13, are preferable. WP's vocabulary is classical and as he accordingly tends to employ the terms *pedites, equites* and *milites* in their classical sense, the latter probably usually means soldiers of any type. It is true that in some cases it seems to denote people of higher status (see, for example, the reference to Baldwin V of Flanders as *Romani imperii miles, GG*, p.30) or specifically horsemen (for example, on p.16, where Duke William captures seven *milites* after fighting fifteen men who gloried in their horses and arms), but note also the implications of *milites uero mediae nobilitatis atque gregarios* (translated by Davis and Chibnall as 'knights of middling rank and the common soldiers', *GG*, pp.158–9), and when WP reports (p.102) that the duke had 50,000 *milites* at Dives the word is clearly being used in its more general sense; the same seems likely to be true of the comment about those who cut inroads into the English line. See further the important study by Morillo, '*Milites,* Knights and Samurai', pp.175–7.

[65] *Ipse carens omni decore, quibusdam signis, nequaquam facie, recognitus est, GG,* p.140.

Similarly, one of the men exhumed in 1996 from a mass grave connected with the Wars of the Roses battle of Towton in 1461 received a blade wound which bisected his face when he was probably already dead.[66] Presumably it was not unusual for battles such as these to result in a sort of fighting fury in which the dead might be savagely disfigured as well, of course, as later (but sometimes before the conflict was fully over, if the Tapestry is anything to go by) being stripped of items of value. Nevertheless, if William of Poitiers has nothing to offer on the way in which Harold died this is likely to reflect a reluctance on his part to broach the subject, for whatever reason, rather than any shortage of information upon it, for in the years immediately after Hastings it is probable that it was a matter upon which many tales were told.

One of them apparently reached Bishop Guy of Amiens and was inserted into the *Carmen*. According to this, Harold was cut down by Duke William himself, accompanied by Count Eustace of Boulogne, Hugh the noble heir of Ponthieu and Gilfard, known by his father's surname. The first speared the king through shield and chest, the second beheaded him, the third pierced his belly with a lance and the fourth cut off his thigh and removed it some distance.[67] The *Carmen* agrees with the Tapestry that the dead were already being stripped at this stage, but otherwise its details have found little credence with historians, some of whom have judged that they are evidence that the poem is not a contemporary work.[68] Certainly they are not convincing, even if the statement about the thigh may reflect material also found in other sources. If true, it would be remarkable that Harold happened to be killed by two of the leading men on the French side – Duke William and Count Eustace – together with the nephew, Hugh of Ponthieu, of the author of the *Carmen* itself. It would also be difficult to see why such a renowned event has not found its way into the work of other authors, for as R.A. Brown said,

---

[66] Above, p.40. *Blood Red Roses*, ed. Fiorato, p.100.

[67] *Carmen*, ll. 533–50.

[68] Above, p.91.

'the feat of arms would have been bruited abroad in every court and *chanson* in Latin Christendom'.[69] This being the case it can be rejected with some confidence, being perhaps evidence not so much of a real occurrence as of the kind of legend to which events such as Hastings can quickly give rise, possibly in this case with the assistance of a degree of mendacity on the part of Hugh of Ponthieu and/or his uncle Guy of Amiens. It might also be remembered in this connection that the reasons which led Guy to write the *Carmen*, whatever they were, may also have caused him to wish to flatter William by attributing to him the death of the usurper king; that William would have known it to be literally untrue may have mattered less than one might think to a man whom William of Poitiers judged prepared to be likened to the greatest heroes of antiquity.

Determining the actual way in which Harold died is not easy. In one of its most famous scenes, which has undergone much restoration, and accompanied by the words *Hic Harold rex interfectus est* ('*Here King Harold has been killed*'), the Bayeux Tapestry shows a French horseman approaching several Englishmen – first of all a dead standard-bearer lying on the ground with the pole of his dragon standard beneath him, then a man with a shield and a spear held overarm who stands next to a figure carrying a round shield and holding a dragon standard; next to the standard-bearer, and directly beneath the word *Harold*, is a soldier wearing a scabbard whose left hand holds a shield and spear and whose right hand grasps (as the present form of the Tapestry has it) an arrow which has evidently entered his skull somewhere in the vicinity of the right eye, the nasal of his helmet masking the precise area concerned. To the right of this individual, beneath the words *rex interfectus est*, a horseman has evidently just struck with his sword a man with an axe and scabbard but no shield who is shown as either falling or lying on the

---

[69] Brown, 'The Battle of Hastings', 18. The problem could, of course, be avoided if this difficult passage in the *Carmen* were read in such a way as to exclude the duke from the quartet, see above, p.90, n.9.

ground (perhaps the former, given that the horse's left foreleg may be interposed between the legs of the stricken figure),[70] the lower part of the Frenchman's weapon apparently coming to rest just above the victim's right knee; further right still, a group of Englishmen is resisting an assault by horsemen coming from the right.

Exactly what this scene is supposed to represent has been the subject of much debate. Whether the figure grasping the arrow and the differently equipped one cut down to the right both represent Harold or whether only one of them does so, and if so which one, has long seemed a major problem. At the end of an exhaustive investigation of this matter, which suggests that both the dead standard-bearer and the dead men near to Harold's brothers Gyrth and Leofwine in the scene depicting their demise are duplicates of their standing counterparts, Brooks and Walker concluded that both the standing and the fallen figure beneath the words *Harold rex interfectus est* are intended to be the king, and that the Tapestry is accordingly good evidence of the belief that he was hit in the eye by an arrow.[71] Since then, Bernstein has pointed out that a series of seventeen stitch holes fully visible only on the back of the Tapestry raise the possibility that the second figure was originally depicted with an arrow lodged in his skull. However, the nineteenth-century restorers of the Tapestry muddied the water sufficiently for this to be extremely doubtful (for the earlier pictorialisations of the scene do not show these holes), and in any case the fact that this second figure carries equipment markedly different to that of his supposed counterpart might alone raise

---

[70] Benoît's drawing of 1729 (see illus. 74 and the Appendix) is not easily interpreted at this point and differs slightly from the Tapestry as subsequently restored; this shows the foreleg entirely behind the figure.

[71] B&W, 23–34, with comment on the probable accuracy of the essential elements of the nineteenth-century restoration of the Tapestry. Their argument is judged 'almost certainly right' by Wilson, *BT*, p.194. Gibbs-Smith had previously contended (*The Bayeux Tapestry*, p.15) that the first figure has been hit by an arrow but is not Harold; this was followed (among others) by Brown, *The Normans and the Norman Conquest*, p.173, n.154. In 1966 Gibbs-Smith ('What the Bayeux Tapestry does not show') suggested that the designer originally intended this man to be throwing a spear but substituted an arrow when the raised arm had already been embroidered because 'he did not want any more horizontal lines crossing his composition'. I owe this reference to Barlow, *The Godwins*, p.107.

serious doubts as to whether they are really intended to be the same person.[72]

Moreover, all this assumes that the first figure has indeed been hit by an arrow, when it seems almost certain from an examination of the oldest representation of this part of the Tapestry that in fact he has not. Shortly before the publication of the second volume of his *Les Monumens de la Monarchie Françoise* in 1730, the great French scholar Bernard de Montfaucon sent the draughtsman Antoine Benoît to Bayeux to draw the Tapestry as accurately as possible; from these drawings, which still survive in the Bibliothèque Nationale in Paris, the engraved plates in the second volume of *Les Monumens* were made, and shortly afterwards they were also used to create a different set of engravings to accompany a paper delivered to the French Academie Royale des Inscriptions et Belles-Lettres by the historian Antoine Lancelot. The latter assured his audience that his illustrations were a very accurate copy of Benoît's work, but in fact this was not really true either of them or of the engravings done for Montfaucon, and on the figure supposedly struck by an arrow they differ significantly. Montfaucon's engraver (illus. 75) showed an individual holding in his right hand a missile (represented as a continuous line) which extends to the lower edge of his helmet, while Lancelot's (illus. 76) depicted it as a broken line which does not touch the helmet and extends well to the left of the hand in which it is held. In the latter case, then, this soldier appears to be a figure possessed not of an arrow which has just hit him, but

---

[72] Some of the holes are visible in the plate in *BT*. Bernstein, pp.148–52, with illustrations of both the front and rear of the Tapestry, considers the possibility that they may be the subsequently removed work of a restorer. Wilson (*BT*, pp.194–5) notes their absence from early reproductions of the Tapestry and comments that 'as there is no place where they are more obvious, they are presumably a fabrication of the last century'. The different weaponry of the second figure is not dealt with by B&W, but their discussion of parallels in manuscript depictions of biblical scenes and other supposed duplicates within the Tapestry itself leans heavily on the argument that the figures (for example, the standard-bearer) are the same person because they look the same; this is clearly not the case with the two figures in question. Bernstein (pp.144–7, and 218, n.9) provides examples where, as (allegedly) here, the hose of different figures intended to represent the same person changes colour, but weaponry is arguably another matter, and a context in which the military-minded audience of the Tapestry may have viewed inconsistency with some surprise; see below for a probable solution of this problem, and the Appendix for a more detailed treatment of what follows.

of a spear which he is about to use against the enemy. Moreover, this conclusion is substantially confirmed by the drawing (illus. 74) from which the engravings were made. Here, the missile reaches to the lower edge of the helmet (as in Montfaucon) but also extends as a broken line further to the left of the hand than Montfaucon's engraver indicated, if not quite as far as Lancelot's did. It is both considerably longer than the arrows sticking in the shield of the same figure and unlike them it has no flights. Thus, it is probably not an arrow, but all that Benoît could make out of a spear, in a scene that had clearly been damaged. The soldier who holds it flanks the standard bearer on the one side and is apparently a close companion of the very similar figure, who also holds a spear in his raised right hand, on the other. Together the three may well represent the English king's bodyguard. Thus, there is no very strong reason to suppose that the Bayeux Tapestry is part of the corpus of evidence that Harold was hit by an arrow, and the only one of its figures which can plausibly be taken as representing the king is the one struck by the French horseman; this, of course, is why this man's equipment is different to that of the right-hand member of the trio.[73] Benoît's drawing also suggests the possibility that the inscription did not originally read *Hic Harold rex interfectus est* but perhaps *Hic Harold rex in terra iactus est* ('Here King Harold has been struck to the ground'); if so, this was a precise description of the figure who has just received the horseman's blow.

Yet if the apparent evidence of the present form of the Bayeux Tapestry that Harold was struck by an arrow is very likely to be the work of those who drew and restored it in the nineteenth century, an arrow really is mentioned in connection with his demise in two sources more or less contemporary with the Tapestry. Baudri of Bourgeuil says that he was killed by an arrow without specifying

[73] David Hill generously sent me his photograph of the Benoît drawing of this part of the Tapestry, one of a number of Benoît's work taken in the Bibliothèque Nationale for himself and John McSween. Although it has fallen to me to be the first to publish the results of their work, they had already arrived at the conclusion outlined above. It will be obvious that the publication of a full set of photographs of the Benoît drawings is much to be desired.

where it struck him, while Amatus of Montecassino wrote *c.*1080 that he was hit by an arrow in the eye.[74] These statements may represent a belief about Harold's death that was fairly widespread, and which some years later also reached William of Malmesbury and Henry of Huntingdon, for the first says that Harold was killed by an arrow which entered his brain, the second that he was hit in the eye by one of the missiles fired by a group of archers which had been ordered by William to shoot into the air in order to blind the enemy; he then sank to the ground and was dispatched along with his brothers Gyrth and Leofwine by a group of horsemen, and at much the same time twenty of their companions broke through the English line and carried off the standard, although it cost some their lives.[75]

William of Malmesbury thus agrees with Baudri in suggesting that the arrow was the sole cause of Harold's demise, and this is plausible enough, for if a missile had entered the midbrain through an eye socket, which would not have been difficult, death would have been almost instantaneous.[76] On the other hand it is also possible that it would simply have caused a grievous wound, and that he might then have had to be cut down in the way that Henry of Huntingdon describes. William of Malmesbury says that a soldier hacked at his thigh with a sword as he lay on the ground, for which disgraceful act William expelled him from the ducal forces. Our earlier examination of the *Gesta Regum* established that William of Malmesbury, while generally condemnatory of English morals, regarded the Conquest as a disaster for his country and may have manufactured or adapted from *chansons* details which allowed him to present Harold's fighting prowess as matching that of William.[77] This being so, one might wonder whether he would have been inclined to report all that he may have heard about what happened

[74] *AC*, l. 463; on Amatus, see above, p.109.
[75] *GR*, i. 454–7; *HA*, pp.394–5. Greenway (*HA*, p.xxxv) says that it is 'not obvious' that HH was acquainted directly with Baudri's poetry.
[76] I am grateful to Dr George Brown for discussion of this matter.
[77] Above, pp.67–69.

to Harold after he was hit by the arrow, the detail about the soldier who struck at his thigh and was disgraced as a result possibly being a relic of more extensive material which, had it been transmitted, would have contradicted the belief that the courageous English king died very quickly. Baudri of Bourgeuil, on the other hand, whose account of the battle is not a particularly detailed one except in recording the exploits of Duke William, the father of the lady to whom his poem was addressed, may not have thought that Harold's death merited any more space than he gave it; alternatively, it is possible that both he and William of Poitiers had heard gory accounts of Harold's last moments and felt that it was not to William's credit or advantage to repeat them.

It may be then that Henry of Huntingdon and possibly the *Carmen*, if there is any truth at all behind its account, are together enough to suggest that the English king was wounded by an arrow and then cut down later, his corpse eventually being so badly damaged that it became almost unrecognisable.[78] Whether even the French soldiers responsible knew the identity of their victim and therefore the significance of their action is perhaps not certain, although it is not unlikely that in after times some were willing to put forward spurious claims about these matters. If so, none seems to have become universally accepted by posterity. Neither his extensive reading in the documentary sources nor oral tradition seem to have given Wace any clue as to who was really involved. He first reports that Harold was wounded by an arrow which struck him on the right eye and put it out before he speaks of the French

---

[78] Shortly before 1820 Sir Godfrey Webster commissioned the artist Frank Wilkin to produce a painting of the battle to hang in the Great Hall of Battle Abbey. The work originally measured 31 by 17 feet and depicts the Conqueror (Sir Godfrey apparently sat for the figure himself) at the head of his men being shown Harold's body and offered his crown; the corpse exhibits scant sign of injury, but behind it a French soldier holds up an arrow. It was subsequently given to Hastings Corporation, which in 1979 presented it to English Heritage; it has recently been returned to its original location following restoration. Sir Godfrey, who also built New Pond, evidently paid 2,000 guineas for the picture, and later sold the medieval archives of the abbey (they are today in the USA) for a far smaller sum; the nineteenth-century estate archive in the East Sussex Record Office contains much evidence of the anguish of local tradesmen at his reluctance to meet the bills incurred during his extensive restoration of his seat. I am grateful to Victoria Williams, Curator of Hastings Museum, for information on Wilkin's *Battle of Hastings*.

feigned flight and of fighting involving a great many of their lords. Only, he says, when they eventually penetrated to the English standard did they find the wounded king still standing there, and one of the soldiers struck him on the helmet and beat him to the ground; as he tried to recover he was struck again by a blow which pierced his thigh to the bone; eventually there was such a press of men around him seeking his death that, says Wace, 'I know not who it was that slew him', and, 'I do not tell, and I do not indeed know, for I was not there to see, and have not heard say, who it was that smote down king Harold'.[79]

The way in which the Tapestry shows these events can be taken to mean that the king, with his own men to either side of him, was standing within the shield-wall when he was struck down,[80] and if so it is by no means impossible that he was wounded some time before being killed, or simply killed outright by an arrow with no further French intervention. Despite the fact that William of Jumièges is one of our earliest sources it is very difficult to accept the apparent statement that he perished in the first onset,[81] and the Tapestry and *Carmen* together speak fairly strongly for the view that he died in the final stages of the conflict.[82] It would not be surprising if news of this event precipitated the final English rout, as the *Carmen* and William of Malmesbury claim, and was thus the final turning point in the battle.[83] William of Poitiers, however, attributes it to a variety of reasons: as the day was ending, he says, the English army understood that it could stand against the Normans no longer, for they knew that they had lost many men and that these included the king and his two brothers with no small number of magnates; furthermore, those who remained were virtually exhausted and they could expect no reinforcement, while they

---

[79] *RR*, ll. 8161–4, 8803–18, 8829–34, 8851–6. I have quoted from Edgar Taylor's translation, pp.254–5. It is probable that elements of Wace's account were drawn from sources such as WP, WM, HH and perhaps the Tapestry (see above, p.114).

[80] *BT*, p.194.

[81] Above, pp.94–5.

[82] Above, p.225.

[83] *Carmen*, ll. 551–4; WM, *GR*, i. 454–5;

saw that their enemies were not much weakened by their casualties and that the duke's ardour was such that he would accept nothing less than victory; hence, they turned to flight, some on horses they had taken, others on foot.[84] The sun set at Battle on the afternoon of Saturday 14 October 1066 at about 16:54 GMT; it would have been fairly dark by 17:54 and completely so by 18:24, while the moon did not rise until 23:12. William of Jumièges says that the English turned tail at nightfall and John of Worcester agrees that fighting lasted until dusk, when Harold himself fell.[85] A last stand by his housecarls tends to feature in re-enactments of the battle and doubtless will continue to do so; it is a pity that the sources provide no grounds for believing that any such thing occurred.[86]

Probably, then, much of the pursuit took place in the dark, and the *Carmen* says specifically that night was falling as God made the duke the victor, and that only darkness and flight through the thickets of the dense forest saved the defeated English, as William rested on the battlefield among the dead and awaited the return of daylight; however, Guy of Amiens also asserts that his own nephew Hugh of Ponthieu spent the night hunting down the enemy,[87] and it is probable that the French now reaped the maximum benefit from their cavalry, who may have killed as many of the English in this final phase of the battle as at any earlier time.[88] William of Poitiers reports that many left their bodies in dense woods and that the Normans, although ignorant of the area, pursued them zealously. Harold's own forces had harried the Norwegians all the way to their ships after the battle of Stamford Bridge, and Duke

[84] GG, pp.136–7.

[85] GND, ii. 168–9; JW, ii. 604–5.

[86] Freeman (FNC, iii. 500–1) did his best to argue otherwise, but there is no evidence for his 'quarter was neither given nor asked; not a man of the *comitatus* fled; not a man was taken captive'.

[87] *Carmen*, ll. 557–66. I accept here Barlow's identification of Hugh of Ponthieu as the *Hectorides* of the *Carmen*.

[88] The presence of the Weald to their rear would not have facilitated the English withdrawal, and one might compare events after the battle of Towton in 1461, when the Lancastrian rout was hindered by a stream in spate and they suffered heavy casualties during a pursuit which extended for ten miles to the gates of York, *Blood Red Roses*, ed. Fiorato, p.23.

William was evidently no less aware that an effective pursuit would render his victory all the more decisive. However, his enemies made a stand when they came to a broken rampart and a series of ditches; just as Count Eustace of Boulogne was preparing to retire with fifty men the duke came upon the scene, and although he thought the English newly arrived reinforcements ignored Eustace's advice that he should withdraw; then he charged and dispersed his opponents. Even so, Eustace himself received a blow which caused the blood to gush from his nose and mouth and some of the more noble Normans were killed there. Orderic Vitalis' additions to William of Jumièges assert that the pursuit lasted throughout the night and that high grass concealed a rampart which caused the Norman horsemen to fall one upon the other so that they were crushed. It was said that almost 15,000 fell there (whether the word 'there' refers to events around the rampart or, as seems more likely,[89] the battle as a whole, is not completely clear). In his later *Historia Æcclesiastica* Orderic fused his earlier story with that of William of Poitiers by claiming that it was the French disaster at the rampart that caused the English to rally around this earthwork and the series of ditches, where they inflicted heavy losses on the Normans. There, he says (and again this may refer to the battle as a whole), Engenulf of Laigle and many others fell, and those who were present said that 15,000 Normans were killed. The roles of Count Eustace and the duke in this final stage of the conflict, as reported by William of Poitiers, Orderic decided to omit.[90] There is a third account of a disaster to the French in the closing stages of the battle in the late twelfth-century Battle Abbey *Chronicle*, which says that near the battlefield was a great ditch concealed by brambles which engulfed large numbers, especially of Normans, and that it is called *Malfosse* to this day as a result. One might well, however, wonder whether this account, which says nothing of any English involvement, and those

[89] Similarly, Brown, 'The Battle of Hastings', 19.
[90] *GG*, pp.138–9; *GND*, ii. 168–9; *HÆ*, ii. 176–7.

of William of Poitiers and Orderic Vitalis, do necessarily all refer to events at the same location.[91]

The following morning, says the *Carmen*, the duke took up and buried his own dead, while leaving the bodies of the English as carrion for birds and beasts. Harold's lacerated corpse he wrapped in purple linen and took with him when he returned to his camp on the coast, where he subsequently rejected a request that it be handed over for interment to the dead king's mother, despite being offered its weight in gold in return. Later, a man of part-Norman and part-English descent, who was also connected to Harold, carried out the duke's order that it be placed on the top of a cliff, and it was laid beneath a tombstone which read:

> By command of the duke, you repose here, King Harold, so that you may remain guardian of the shore and the ocean.[92]

That the corpses of the rest of the English were left as carrion is credible enough, for it seems to have been the practice of the period not to bury the enemy dead, as evidence on the battle of

---

[91] *Chronicle of Battle Abbey*, ed. Searle, pp. 38–9. Stevenson, 'Senlac and the Malfossé', 302–3, noted that Laigle is only a few miles from OV's monastery of St Évroul and suggested that he had discussed matters with members of Engenulf's family or their men; similarly, Brown, 'The Battle of Hastings', 19, who also commented on the awkward way in which he later combined the story with that of WP. There have been various attempts to locate the site of this incident or incidents, whose historicity Brown clearly doubted (along with the accounts of deaths in ditches during the battle). Freeman (*FNC*, iii. 502–3, 750, and map) thought the ditch one of the drainage channels on the north-eastern slope of the Battle Abbey ridge; Baring ('On the Battle of Hastings', pp. 229–30) opted for a channel to the west of the ridge later known as Manser's Shaw, a name which in his opinion derived from *Malfosse*; similarly, Burne, *The Battlefields of England*, pp. 25, 43, although he followed Stevenson in rejecting Baring's derivation of the later name. Chevallier, 'Where was Malfosse?', argued for a location over a mile to the north of the battlefield at Oakwood Gill. This was accepted by Lemmon, *The Field of Hastings*, pp. 33–5 and 'The Campaign of 1066', pp. 111–13, who thought the site the fruit of deliberate 'reconnaissance and occupation by order of some unknown Saxon leader', and supplied a number of details of his own devising, such as the statement that Eustace of Boulogne 'was struck down by a battle-axe, presumably wielded by some Housecarl who had contrived to creep up unobserved'. Bradbury, *The Battle of Hastings*, p. 210, describes Chevallier's location as reasonably certain; see also Clephane-Cameron *et al.*, *The 1066 Malfosse Walk*.

[92] *Carmen*, ll. 567–92. The meaning in this context of *compater*, the word used to indicate the man's relationship to Harold, is uncertain. M&M, p. 39, translated 'comrade', Barlow 'relative'.

Stamford Bridge and other material indicates.[93] William of Poitiers states that the battlefield was covered far and wide with the flower of the English nobility and youth, that Harold's two brothers were found near him and (as noted earlier) that he could only be recognised by certain signs; refusing the mother's offer of their weight in gold for the remains after they were carried into his camp, Duke William allowed them to be laid to rest by William Malet, considering it unseemly to accept gold in such circumstances and to fall in with the mother's wishes when many men lay unburied as a result of her son's greed; it was said jokingly that he should be buried as custodian of the shore and ocean which he had previously, in his madness, occupied in arms, and accordingly he was put in a tumulus on the seashore.[94] William of Malmesbury chose to reject this part of the *Gesta Guillelmi*, stating that the Conqueror sent Harold's mother the corpse without payment, although she had offered much, and that she had it buried at the church of Holy Cross at Waltham in Essex, a church which he had built himself and filled with canons.[95] Later, Waltham claimed that two members of their community accompanied him to the battle and sought his body from William after it in exchange for ten marks of gold;[96] the gold the duke is said to have rejected, while

[93] Above, p.39. Note, for example, the way in which poetry tends to speak of the bodies of the defeated serving as food for birds and beasts, for example in the piece on the battle of *Brunanburh* in 937 (*ASC*, i. 109) and in Ottar the Black's celebration of the victories of King Cnut in his *Knútsdrápa* (*EHD1*, pp.335–6); also, according to *EE*, pp.28–9, after the battle of *Assandun* in 1016 the victors buried their own dead while stripping the enemy and leaving them as carrion. WP's claim (*GG*, pp.142–3) that the duke allowed those who wished to collect the English dead for burial to do so may indicate unease at such practices. However, if the mass burial found at Riccall Landing (above, p.40) contains the bodies of Scandinavians who fell in 1066 it is not impossible that they were buried by the English. There is a valuable treatment of a range of evidence on Anglo-Saxon battlefield burial practices in J. Hooper, 'The "Rows of the Battle Swan": The Aftermath of Battle in Anglo-Saxon Art'.

[94] *GG*, pp.138–41; on the possible ultimate derivation from the *Iliad* of the statement in the *Carmen* and *GG* that William was offered the body's weight in gold, see above, p.104. Davis and Chibnall (141, n.5) note Pompey's burial in a tumulus on the seashore in Lucan's *Pharsalia*, although the corpse, which had no head, had first been cremated. WP's account of these events is very close to that of the *Carmen*, but clearly (as he is able to give the name of William Malet) not solely dependent upon it, if dependent at all.

[95] *GR*, i. 460–1.

[96] Note the ten talents of gold which formed part of the ransom given to Achilles for Hector's body, *Iliad*, xxiv, l. 232.

granting their request for the remains, which were buried at Waltham with great honour. Their late twelfth-century chronicle, from which these details are drawn, may here be almost entirely fictional, but we owe to it the story that the corpse could not be recognised until one of the pair returned home and brought back with him Edith Swanneck, Harold's handfast wife, who because of her intimacy with the king could recognise the secret marks upon it better than others.[97]

The numbers who fell in the battle are no clearer than those of the totals engaged. In commenting on the entire campaign the annalist of Nieder-Altaich on the Danube reports French casualties as 12,000, while we have just seen that Orderic Vitalis is perhaps to be taken as meaning that 15,000 (upon whether simply Normans or French as a whole he is inconsistent) were killed at the battle of Hastings itself.[98] Orderic's Engenulf of Laigle is the only Norman known to have died there, but there is a slightly longer list available from Domesday Book and other records of the named English dead, in addition to Harold and his two brothers. Breme and Edric the Deacon, who both held land in Suffolk, are known from William's great survey to have been among them, along with Ælfric, a man of some note who held sixteen hides in Huntingdonshire from the abbot of Ramsey. The twelfth-century chronicle of the monastery of Abingdon adds Godric, sheriff of Berkshire, and the local landowner Thurkill, while the name of Abbot Ælfwig of New Minster, Winchester is contributed by the records of his own house, and (anonymous) dead of the men of the abbey of Bury St Edmunds are mentioned in a writ addressed to Abbot Baldwin early in the Conqueror's reign.[99]

[97] *The Waltham Chronicle*, ed. Watkiss and Chibnall, pp. 50–7. The author of this work wrote shortly after 1177, and naturally rejects tales that Harold lived in a cave at Canterbury after the battle and was eventually buried at Chester. The notion that he survived the conflict could, of course, be paralleled in the histories of other leaders whose deaths have had ill consequences for their people. On Edith Swan-neck, whose connection with Harold may have been of long standing and produced many children, see *FNC*, iii. 763–5; Barlow, *The Godwins*, pp. 55–6, 120–1.

[98] Above, pp. 36, 233–4.

[99] DB, ii. 409b, 449a; i. 207a–208a; *Chronicon Monasterii de Abingdon*, ed. Stevenson, i. 484–5, 490–1; *Heads of Religious Houses*, ed. Knowles, p. 81; *Regesta Regum Anglo-Normannorum*, ed. Bates, No. 37, p. 198 (trans. *EHD2*, No. 238). See also above, pp. 156–7, for unnamed English dead mentioned in Domesday, and *FNC*, iii. 425–7, 730–1, although Freeman's belief that Abbot Ælfwig was Harold's uncle now seems mistaken. A twelfth-century addition to the E text of the *Anglo-Saxon Chronicle*, i. 198, says that Abbot Leofric of Peterborough returned home sick and died on 31 October.

The English defeat in 1066 can be attributed to many factors. The fact that they had to prepare for two invasions rather than one, and that both arrived much later in the year than might reasonably have been expected, obviously tested the defenders' resources to the limit. When the provisions of the forces which Harold had stationed on the south coast ran out on 8 September this probably does not represent a failure in the workings of the late Anglo-Saxon administrative system so much as the fact that the system itself was not designed to cope with such unusual circumstances. If William brought this about through deliberately delaying his arrival until he knew his opponents had dispersed then he had played a clever and risky game with an iron nerve; if, as the French sources say, he had just been held in port by contrary winds he was simply extremely lucky. The reasons for the outcome of the battle itself are naturally not easy to determine considering that we know neither the absolute nor the relative size of the two armies and are ill-informed on their composition and deployment on the battlefield; nor, of course, can much be had in the way of detail about the course of fighting which lasted (if the pursuit is included) well over eight hours. Nevertheless, the sheer length of the conflict must reveal something, for neither side can have had an overwhelming superiority of numbers or of military technique. It is a commonplace about Hastings that Harold fought before he should have done and that had he waited his men would have been both more numerous and better rested after their exertions on the Stamford Bridge campaign. It is also easy to believe that the earls Edwin of Mercia and his brother Morcar of Northumbria were either not present or withdrew earlier than they should have done, either because of their losses at Fulford or because the force of old rivalries between their family and Harold's reappeared in October 1066; once their enemy Tostig was dead they were perhaps as ready to do a deal with Duke William as with King Harold.[100] One

---

[100] The only source to offer information on their behaviour is JW, ii. 604–5, whose words (*Cuius morte audita, comites Eduuinus et Morkarus, qui se cum suis certamini substraxere, Lundoniam venere...*) are not without ambiguity. They mean either that Edwin and Morcar were not present at the battle with their men and went to London when they heard of Harold's death, or that they withdrew from it during its course and went to London once they knew that Harold had been killed. Freeman (*FNC*, iii. 421–2) had no doubt that the former meaning is correct, and suggested that they hoped to divide the kingdom with William, themselves taking Mercia and Northumbria and leaving to him Wessex and East Anglia.

should probably also allow a role (if a completely unquantifiable one) in reducing support for Harold to his broken oath, the appearance of Halley's Comet as a perceived harbinger of disaster and the duke's possession of a papal banner, carried into battle at the head of his army. Yet while the significance of all these points can be acknowledged, it is not obvious that he was short of men in the battle itself, or that those he had were incapable of fighting with great determination and vigour. It is quite unclear what proportion of his force had been at Stamford Bridge, and those who had may well have travelled to and from Yorkshire on horseback, for both the *Carmen* and William of Poitiers say that the English dismounted from their horses before fighting William.[101] Certainly, repeated statements about the density of their lines suggest that Harold's army was more than large enough to cover the frontage on which it fought, and nor does its morale seem to have been a problem until after news spread that the king had been killed. It may be, however, that shire levies of the less well-equipped type formed a greater proportion of it than would have been the case if Stamford Bridge had never been fought, or if Harold had waited longer for his army to gather. Yet even on the timing of the battle it is impossible to be sure that he erred, for according to the D text of the *Anglo-Saxon Chronicle* William received reinforcements from oversea shortly after the battle, and Harold may have both known that this was a possibility and acted with it in mind.[102]

Indeed, as far as one can see the really critical events (and flaws in the English king's leadership, if such there were) took place not before the conflict, but during it. Thus, while it may have been common in this period for infantry to fight in very close order indeed, and this was perhaps often very advantageous, it may be that he did deploy in an area too narrow to satisfactorily accommodate the numbers at his disposal, and that (following the *Anglo-Saxon Chronicle* D text) William reaped the maximum advantage

---

[101] *Carmen*, l. 377; *GG*, pp.126–9. See above (pp.125, 140 n.63, 157) on the earlier use of forces on horseback by the English and note also the men fleeing on horses in the final much-restored scene of the Tapestry, although these mounts may, of course, have been plundered from the French.
[102] *ASC* D, i. 200.

from this by attacking before they were properly arrayed. Even so, the English lines proved very difficult to break down, and their tenure of a watercourse, which may well have been that running west in the valley to the south, also gave the French considerable trouble, for here the progress of their cavalry may have been hindered by sharpened stakes planted in the bed of the stream, and specialist English light infantry and perhaps heavy infantry too also fought in this area.[103] Such features of the English conduct of the battle are a reminder that their army was the product of a formidably organised state with an impressive past record in gearing its people for war, led by a commander who was well aware that the French and their cavalry needed to be taken seriously.[104] In this, he was not mistaken. Duke William had more experience of leading his men in war than his counterpart, and the troops who had gathered under his command had everything to gain by victory and everything to lose in defeat. All are likely to have been reasonably well-equipped, and while they may not have had the possibly years of training given to its levies by the late Anglo-Saxon state, they had been under the duke's control for months and probably done as much preparation in terms of manoeuvring and fighting together as the time available allowed. The fighting capacities of this *ad hoc* force need occasion no surprise: just over thirty years later an army of a similarly confederate nature assembled as the result of the preaching of the First Crusade and then proceeded to win the astonishing series of victories over the Muslims which eventually delivered the city of Jerusalem into its possession.

As already noted, the length of the battle strongly suggests that the two forces were fairly equally matched, and had the English been content to stand on the defensive all day it is doubtful whether they could have been defeated. In this context their pursuit of an enemy who was retiring, whether in a real or a simulated flight, is critical. The pursuers, who were on foot, left their flanks exposed

[103] Above, pp. 149–54.
[104] Above, pp. 127–37.

and were immediately vulnerable to cavalry attacks which may have inflicted heavy losses upon them. Whether the pursuit was a deliberate counter-attack by commanders who ought to have stood their ground or the result of indiscipline on the part of their troops is not clear, but the English fighting methods were not at this point the equal of those of the French, and it looks as though this played a major role in giving victory to their opponents. Contrary to the views of some earlier historians of the battle, it was not their lack of cavalry which proved decisive, but their failure or inability to persist in the defensive strategy which may well have led to the eventual failure of the French assaults launched against them. Had the day ended in a stalemate Harold would still have been king of England and William's credibility may have been seriously damaged. It is a possible criticism of Harold, or of his subordinate commanders and his troops, that they were too impatient to secure a decisive victory, when the way in which the French had made repeated attacks on a strong defensive position might have told them that William needed such a victory just as much and probably more than they did.

William's army may not have been better than that of the English, but as a commander he was probably Harold's superior.[105] Establishing a bridge-head on the English coast and remaining there until his enemy came to him was the act of a cautious commander and perhaps also of a very shrewd one. It is questionable whether he could have maintained himself in the Hastings area for much longer than he did, especially if English naval forces had been sent to cut off his links with Normandy as some sources say that they were;[106] it may also be indicative of the state of his men that when they eventually reached Dover some ate fresh meat and drank water, with the result that many died of dysentery.[107] However, he had everything to gain by staying where he was providing there was a good chance that Harold eventually came to

---

[105] Note Morillo's comment ('Hastings: An Unusual Battle', p.227) that 'Given essentially equal armies, William simply outgeneraled Harold and had a bit more luck'.

[106] Above, p.194.

[107] WP, *GG*, pp.144–5.

him, and that William was willing to play this game may have stemmed from the knowledge of his adversary's character gained during the months the latter had spent in Normandy not long before, months which may have told William more about Harold than Harold learnt about William.

Once the appearance of the English army presented him with his great opportunity he took it, advancing to prevent the enemy attacking his camp and ships, moving against them on the morning of the conflict before their lines were properly formed, repeatedly carrying the battle to them during a long day's fighting, putting both his archers and cavalry to good use, and ensuring that there was a relentless pursuit as night fell and his foes fled the field. Although William of Poitiers claims[108] that he directed everything by voice and gesture it may well be that during the fighting much was owed to the skills of subordinate commanders, but the duke can still be credited with halting the rout which almost cost him the day and with the personal military prowess which is unlikely to be a complete invention of the French sources. Of course, that there is much less evidence on Harold's role in the battle makes any detailed comparison of the two men impossible. Even so, if William had been lucky in being able to land on the English coast when his enemy was in Yorkshire, he may also have had considerable luck in the battle itself, passing unscathed through the fighting while Harold, who may never have fought hand-to-hand at all,[109] was either seriously injured or killed outright by an arrow shot from a distance. This particular stroke of good fortune may have finally turned the battle in the duke's favour, but if so it can hardly be said to have been undeserved, considering his skills as a strategist, tactician and fighter; and married to them was the iron will which would be evident again during his reign as king of England.

[108] GG, pp.126–7.
[109] WM's evidence to the contrary is unsafe, see above, p.69.

7

EPILOGUE

Although it might readily be thought that William conquered England by fighting only one battle, in the months following Hastings he would not appear to have been of that opinion himself. It looks very much as if he feared that another army might be brought against him, and after returning to his camp,[1] and according to the D text of the *Anglo-Saxon Chronicle* receiving reinforcements from oversea, he marched eastwards to deal with Romney, the scene of a conflict in which those of his followers who had landed there by mistake had been routed. From there he moved to Dover, where the defences were surrendered despite the large number of Englishmen present, and shortly afterwards the men of Canterbury too submitted. William then made a circuit to the south and west of London, crossing the Thames at Wallingford and ravaging as he went until he reached Berkhamsted, where he was met by Archbishop Ealdred of York, Edgar the Ætheling, the earls Edwin and Morcar and the leading citizens of London; they gave hostages and swore oaths of fealty, whereupon he promised them that he would be a good lord. This submission was no foregone conclusion.

[1] The *Carmen*, l. 597, says that he stayed at Hastings a fortnight.

It is known from the *Chronicle* D text and John of Worcester that there had been a proposal that Edgar should be made king, and that Edwin and Morcar had undertaken to fight for him, although according to John they withdrew their forces as many others were preparing for battle.[2] If so, they may by this time have been attempting to balance the risks of opposing William against the possible benefits of coming to terms with him, and when they opted for the latter course the duke, who cannot have relished the prospect of further fighting, was no doubt willing to appear conciliatory. Orderic Vitalis says that when he made peace with Edwin he granted him authority over both his brother Morcar and almost a third of England.[3] If so, this was not a promise which he necessarily intended keeping, or which subordinates eager to taste the full fruits of victory would have been happy for him to keep.

The submission at Berkhamsted was eventually followed by William's coronation by Archbishop Ealdred in Westminster Abbey on Christmas Day. Early the following year he returned to Normandy, taking care that the remaining English leaders accompanied him, and his new kingdom did not see him again until December 1067. There had, however, been trouble while he was away, when his half-brother Odo of Bayeux and Hugh of Montfort were beyond the Thames with the greater part of their men. Count Eustace of Boulogne, who was presumably disappointed with whatever share of the spoils he had received for his exploits at Hastings, and perhaps mindful that he might be able to claim the throne as the husband of Edward the Confessor's (dead) sister, accepted the invitation of the English to launch an attack upon the castle at Dover. This failed, but as an event it marked the beginning of several years of

---

[2] WP, *GG*, pp.142–9; *ASC*, D, i. 199–200; JW, ii. 604–7. The latter lists the shires ravaged by the French as Sussex, Kent, Hampshire, Middlesex and Hertfordshire. The *Carmen*, ll. 597–752, differs in having William send to Winchester to secure the submission of Queen Edith and in suggesting that a siege of London was necessary before its citizens accepted him, abandoning Edgar, whom they had made king; WJ, *GND*, ii. 170–1, also mentions fighting against the Londoners, and recently discovered archaeological finds have been claimed as evidence of it (*Carmen*, pp.lxxxvii–viii). WP, *GG*, pp.146–7, agrees that Edgar had been chosen king; similarly, WM, *GR*, i. 416–7.

[3] OV, *HÆ*, ii. 214–5. This may have been taken from the part of WP's *GG* which is now lost.

struggle for the Normans as they attempted to completely sudue the country over which William now ruled. In 1068, and with an army said to have included Englishmen, he marched against Exeter, which was refusing to accept him as king, and after a siege of eighteen days it prudently submitted. He built a castle within its walls and subsequently moved into the midlands and north, erecting further castles in Nottingham, York (illus. 40) and Lincoln. Yet these measures did not prevent a major rebellion north of the Humber in 1069, almost certainly co-ordinated with risings in the south-west and on the Welsh border, and eventually assisted by the arrival of a fleet from Denmark. A force which included Edgar the Ætheling attacked the castle at York but William came upon them swiftly and dispersed them after what may have been virtually a pitched battle.[4] He then built a second castle in the city[5] before going to deal with events elsewhere, but the subsequent appearance of forces sent by King Swegen Estrithson of Denmark brought another crisis, and both the castles in York fell to them and their English allies. When William marched for York for the third time he was determined that he would never need to do so again; delayed for three weeks because of the difficulty of crossing the Aire near Pontefract against opposition, when he eventually reached the city he found that the Danes had fled, and then began the process of extensive devastation now known as the Harrying of the North. Nowhere else, says Orderic Vitalis, had he shown such cruelty, commanding that the region should be stripped of all sustenance, with the consequence that more than 100,000 people died of famine; the figure may or may not be exaggerated, but the effects of his action on the countryside were still visible when his commissioners carried out the Domesday survey in 1086 and were obliged to record many villages as 'waste'; a recent examination of this evidence has suggested that 'Yorkshire could well have been a desert in 1070'.[6]

---

[4] OV, HÆ, ii. 222–3; similarly, ASC D, i. 203, which says that William came upon them unexpectedly and many hundreds were killed.

[5] I follow OV on this; ASC D, i. 202, says that he had built both the York castles in 1068.

[6] OV, HÆ, ii. 230–3; Darby, Domesday England, pp.248–52. More than half of those in the North Riding and over a third in both the West and East Ridings were either wholly or partly waste. The quotation is from Palmer, 'War and Domesday Waste' p.274, who rejects recent suggestions that the harrying was a relatively minor affair.

The Harrying of the North was intended to put an end to English opposition and largely did so. The following spring the Danes returned home probably after being bought off. In 1071 William received the surrender of English rebels who included Earl Morcar at Ely, and the next year campaigned in Scotland, where King Malcolm submitted. The Danes were a threat again in 1075 and in 1085, in the former year in conjunction with a plot against the king of which the ringleaders were the last surviving native earl, Waltheof (the son of Edward the Confessor's earl Siward of Northumbria) and Earl Ralph of East Anglia, son of a Breton of the same name who had also served the Confessor, together with the Norman earl of Hereford, Roger. This was easily suppressed in the king's absence, with Ralf escaping abroad, Roger suffering imprisonment and Waltheof being beheaded. In 1085 King Cnut of Denmark, son of Swegen Estrithson, intended leading an expedition against England which in fact never sailed, although William made extensive preparations to deal with it. Few kings of this period were free of trouble for long and the Conqueror was no exception, but it must have been evident to most people that if the consequences of the events of 1066–70 were to be overturned it was not after the latter date likely to be solely by Englishmen.

With the benefit of hindsight Hastings probably tends to look more decisive today than it did to contemporaries. William did not destroy the territory north of the Humber because he felt that English opposition was of no account, and the willingness of his opponents to keep fighting shows that they and their resources had not been broken by the three battles of 1066. However, they had no leader worthy of them, and their call for Danish assistance in 1069 suggests an awareness that the odds were not in their favour. That the Danes were not willing to face the king on a major battlefield when they arrived probably owed something to his reputation for indefatigability, won over a long period, and as evident in his ruthless suppression of the rebels as it had been in his youthful struggle to assert his control over Normandy and on the field of Hastings. The outcome of that battle itself must have discouraged some, and while it is true that it had not ended all opposition it is also true that it was an opposition in which large parts of the country were never involved. It did, therefore, play a major role in winning England for William, and to this extent its reputation as one of the most decisive events in the nation's history is not ill-deserved.

As such it will retain its fascination in the future, as it always has in the past, assisted by the complexities which inevitably arise when dealing with sources about which there will never be complete agreement, and by the never-ending attractions of the Bayeux Tapestry. The study of Hastings must ultimately be a study of the characteristics and the strengths and weaknesses of those sources, and of what interpretations of the battle they seem to render most plausible. Moreover, this source criticism must necessarily be an elaborate process, and is not one ever likely to yield definite conclusions. Nevertheless, it has been one of the primary purposes of this book to question the validity of the scholarly consensus upon the scale of the battle which was established in the years around 1900 and has acted as a straitjacket upon interpretations of it ever since. If the idea that it was contested by about 7,000 men on each side simply around the crest of the Battle Abbey ridge cannot be proved to be wrong, nor can it be proved to be right, and indeed no very convincing evidence was ever produced in its favour. Yet, if in this sense less is known about the battle than previously seemed the case, what has been gained in compensation is that the possibilities about its nature have been extended, and that those possibilities include a large-scale conflict fought over a large area by well-trained and resourceful troops on both sides, the English army being the product of a powerfully organised state with a long history of administrative competence behind it, and that of the French being an international force under a great captain.

The tendency of writers like Spatz and Baring to minimise not only the scale of the battle but also the military competence of its captains and soldiers found its most startling expression in Spatz's refusal to allow the English use of a formation as complex as the shield-wall, and was ultimately grounded in a reluctance to grant to

medieval political and military systems any great degree of competence in these areas, or others. This desire to simplify matters by
denying the complexity and power of early societies persists to this
day, despite compelling evidence that it can be mistaken. If such
worlds did not have access to modern technology, they had need of
powerful systems of human organisation precisely on that account.
Just how remarkably effective such systems could be can be widely
illustrated, from the pyramids to the buildings of the Inca empire,
and from Stonehenge to Offa's Dyke. Tangible physical remains such
as these are inevitably, and to an extent rightly, more persuasive than
mere references to administrative organisation in written sources,
but they are also an indication that such references should not simply be swept aside when there is no physical evidence to support
them. Moreover, in the late Anglo-Saxon period the witness of the
coinage is a powerful indicator of the ambitions and effectiveness of
the state, and the physical remains of Alfred's burhs together with the
document known as the Burghal Hidage[7] proof that the same gov-
ernmental competence was also to be found in the organisation of
its military systems. These systems may or may not have demanded
more of the English people in martial terms than at any subsequent
date prior to 1914, but at least they committed three armies to battle
in a period of twenty-five days in the autumn of 1066, in the process
annihilating a Norwegian army under a famous commander and
holding the French for almost the whole of a long day nearly three
weeks later. While it may be true that the 'organisation and the
economy of a state are largely reflected in and determined by its
organisation for war',[8] it is very questionable how far defeat on the
battlefield can be taken as evidence of administrative incompetence.
War brings many chances, not least those of personality and circumstance, and the defeat of 14 October 1066 is scarcely a more plausible
witness to the ineffectiveness of the late Anglo-Saxon military system than the conquest of South America by small numbers of

[7] Above, pp.131–2.
[8] Campbell, 'Some Agents and Agencies', p.201.

Spanish is of administrative failings in the Inca empire, which despite lacking writing and the wheel is known to have been one of the most impressive of ancient civilisations in terms of its ability to organise public works. Hastings was decided by a narrow margin, in a world hardly less rich and complex than our own.

Yet if the battle has to be left there for the time being, and the complexities of the written sources are unlikely ever to be resolved, that is not to say that there is no possibility of making further progress. Fortunately, much of the battlefield was purchased for the nation when finally sold by the Webster family in 1976, and is there to be investigated. William of Jumièges says that William buried his men after despoiling the English corpses, the *Carmen* that he took up the bodies of his own dead and buried them in the earth while leaving his enemies as carrion, William of Poitiers simply that he buried his own men and allowed those of the English who wished to inter their fellow countrymen.[9] It is not unlikely that some bodies were taken to local churches to be placed in consecrated ground, and that this was at least a not unknown practice with men of high social standing is suggested by William of Malmesbury's statement that King Harold's brother Tostig was buried in York after the battle of Stamford Bridge. It is also possible that skeletons bearing marks of weapons injuries excavated at the church of St Andrew, Fishergate in York, may be some of the fallen from the battle of Fulford.[10] Nevertheless, while none of the sources specifically say so, it seems very probable that most of the French rank and file were laid to rest no great distance from where they fell. Thus, somewhere upon or near the battlefield there may be grave pits containing their remains, and if those pits are ever located they could have evidence to offer on many things, and not least on the question of the extent of the fighting.

It has been suggested above that the English may have deployed and fought around the stream which flows west from New Pond, and it is worth noting that for about 250 metres west of the Pond,

---

[9] WJ, *GND*, ii. 170–1; *Carmen*, ll. 567–72; WP, *GG*, pp. 142–3.
[10] Above, p.40; Daniell, 'Battle and Trial'.

mostly on the south bank but then for a brief stretch on the northern one, lies a series of rather prominent mounds (illus. 65-69), the
easternmost (that is, east of the little bridge which crosses the
stream) being pierced by mature oak trees. It may well be the case
that these features, which need not all be the result of activity of the
same period, are of relatively recent origin, some of it connected
with management of the stream for the benefit of the Battle gunpowder mills,[11] but there is no way of being certain of this until we
know what, if anything, lies beneath them. Moreover, even if they
do not contain burials, it is worth noting Wace's comment on the
numbers of William's men who fell around a ditch, and the possibility that this ditch, the watercourse shown in the Bayeux Tapestry,
the 'sandy stream' after which the battle may have been named and
the sandy stream visible today are all one and the same; if so, inves-
tigative surveys in this area might be well worth the trouble, and
even a negative result would at least tell us more than is known at
present. It is perhaps worth noting that there are also (illus. 71) what
look like artificial hummocks on the extreme south-western side of
the Battle Abbey ridge, along the eastern fringe of Saxon Wood.
Whatever phenomena they represent, it seems unlikely to be the
dredging of the Saxon Wood stream, which is some distance away.[12]

Wace also comments on the digging of ditches by the English
as defensive works. This may, of course, be completely erroneous,
but it is not inherently improbable, and such activity, like the
interment of the dead, could well have left traces which are there
to be found. The recent English Heritage survey of the battlefield
has drawn attention to a linear feature which it maps as Feature J
and describes as 'a prominent east-west scarp'. It is clearly visible
on the slope below the abbey ruins (illus. 70), but much less so
where it seems to reappear (illus. 72) not far from the western
shoulder of the ridge, just to the north of Horselodge Plantation.[13]

---

[11] Above, pp.54-6.
[12] It is possible, however, that at least some of these features are nothing more than the remains of
the root mantles of fallen trees.
[13] *Survey*, p.9 and opposite.

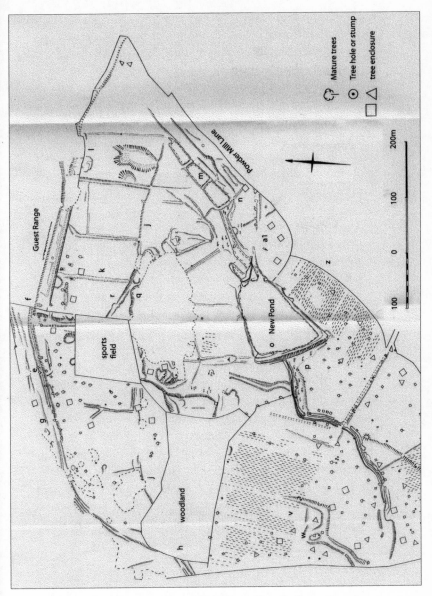

The English Heritage survey of the battlefield, *Survey*, Fig. 5. On Feature J, see also illustrations 70, 72.

Just over a hundred years ago debate raged over whether Freeman had been right to take Wace to mean that the English had constructed a palisade to their front, and the result of that debate was that it largely disappeared from historians' accounts of the battle. Like other aspects of Freeman's treatment, it may one day have to be reinstated, for it is not impossible that Feature J is nothing less than the remnants of a fieldwork used during the battle and extending over a considerable frontage. Moreover, immediately to the north of its easternmost surviving section are two depressions in the ground which have been interpreted by the surveyors as the remains of quarries:

> The eastern depression, which measures up to 1.5m in depth, is substantially larger than the other, with access routes to the south and north-east. The western depression is cut along its western side by one of the close boundary ditches. The form of these depressions, and the access points, suggests that they were probably former quarries, perhaps for clay, dating before the 18th century, that have later been 'landscaped' within the parkland setting.[14]

Quarries they may very well have been, but their location immediately south of the abbey buildings must also raise the possibility that they do in fact represent the burials of at least some of the French dead. Of course, it may seem ridiculous to suggest that the remains of William's men are marked at one point by mounds above ground level and at another by depressions below it. Nevertheless, future archaeological investigations of the battlefield, which should include an attempt to locate graves over a very wide area, could hardly ignore either. Upon the fight of Senlac, whose renown has always been so great, the last word should not be yet.

[14] Ibid., p.10, and fig. 5.

APPENDIX

GENEALOGIES

THE LANCELOT ENGRAVINGS
OF THE BAYEUX TAPESTRY

SELECT BIBLIOGRAPHY

ILLUSTRATION LIST

INDEX

APPENDIX

THE DEATH OF HAROLD AND THE AUTHORITY OF THE PRESENT FORM OF THE BAYEUX TAPESTRY

The earliest surviving drawing of the Bayeux Tapestry, which is coloured but covers only the first thirty feet, was found among the collections of N.J. Foucault, governor of Normandy between 1689 and 1704, following his death in 1721. It is now in the Bibliothèque Nationale in Paris and may be the work of his daughter Anne, who was born in 1687 and is known to have been possessed of some skill in drawing.[1] It was brought to the attention of the French historian Antoine Lancelot, who presented a paper upon it, and the visit of Earl Harold to Normandy which obviously formed its subject, to the French Académie Royale des Inscriptions et Belles-Lettres on 21 July 1724; this was published in the sixth volume of their *Mémoires* in 1729, along with an engraving of the drawing. Lancelot introduced it to his fellow academicians because he believed it to be contemporary with the Conqueror himself, but acknowledged that he had been unable to discover the nature and whereabouts of the original from which it had been taken, the requests for information he had sent to Caen not having been favoured with a reply;

[1] For what follows, see Huard, 'Quelques Lettres'; Janssen, 'La redécouverte de la Tapisserie de Bayeux'; and Brown, *The Bayeux Tapestry*, pp.4–22.

however, he suggested that it perhaps represented part of the tomb of William the Conqueror, which had been located in the church of St Stephen, Caen and was destroyed by the Huguenots in 1562.[2] At this point the famous French classical scholar Bernard de Montfaucon intervened. Being then engaged in assembling for publication a collection of artistic and archaeological sources for the history of medieval France, he wrote to Dom Romain de La Londe, prior of St Stephen's, in the hope of discovering the original upon which the Foucault drawing was based. La Londe knew of nothing like it within the abbey, but was advised by the oldest of his monks to make enquiries in Bayeux, and accordingly passed Montfaucon's letter to Dom Mathurin L'Archer, prior of the monastery of St Vigor. On 22 September 1728 L'Archer replied that the item in question was a tapestry which belonged to the cathedral of Bayeux and which tradition reported to be the work of the Conqueror's wife Matilda; he had himself seen it displayed there, but not being aware that it concerned the deeds of Duke William had never examined it at close quarters. Eventually, on 11 February 1729, after a delay which he said was not his responsibility, La Londe sent Montfaucon readings of the Tapestry's inscriptions made by L'Archer. Montfaucon published engravings based on the Foucault drawing in the first volume of his *Les Monumens de la Monarchie Françoise* the same year, but when he knew of the Tapestry's location sent the draughtsman Antoine Benoît to Bayeux to produce an accurate copy of the rest of the hanging.[3] Benoît's drawings, which were engraved for publication in Montfaucon's second volume, survive today in the Cabinet des Estampes of the Bibliothèque Nationale.

At much the same time as Montfaucon's second volume appeared Lancelot returned to the scene. On 9 May 1730 he presented to the Académie a further paper, accompanied by engravings which were also based on Benoît's drawings, but which differ from those done for

[2] Lancelot, 'Explication d'un monument', 739–40.
[3] Benoît's work was complete by mid-July 1729, by which time he was in Bec and short of the funds necessary to return to Paris; Huard, 'Quelques Lettres', 370–2.

Montfaucon in significant respects. They were published in England in Ducarel's *Anglo-Norman Antiquities* in 1767, but have attracted little attention for many years. This is surprising, because they have some notable evidence to offer on the scene dealing with the death of Harold, and specifically on the figure which many have thought to represent the king immediately after he has been struck by an arrow. Montfaucon's engraving (illus. 75) shows this individual holding a missile represented by a continuous line which extends to the lower rim of his helmet. However, that missile hardly looks like an arrow, for it does not have the flights which feature so prominently on what are clearly arrows elsewhere (including the three sticking in the same soldier's shield) and it is also distinctly longer. Lancelot's engraving (illus. 76) shows something both similar and at the same time dramatically different. Here the missile is again without flights and is depicted as a series of dashes (suggesting that the wool had to an extent disappeared), extends well to the left of the Montfaucon line and ends to the left of the figure's helmet without touching it. Now neither of these engravings is a completely accurate copy of the drawing they were supposed to represent, for examination of that drawing indicates (illus. 74) that Montfaucon's engraver was more correct in showing the missile extending to the rim of the helmet, while Lancelot's was more accurate in having it extend well to the left of the hand in which it is grasped, although he actually pushed it rather further than Benoît's drawing warrants. The crucial point, however, is that the Benoît drawing tends to confirm the impression given by the Lancelot version of it: that this is not an Englishman holding an arrow which has struck him in the head so much as an Englishman who is about to use a spear against the enemy. Thus, this figure to the right of the standard-bearer is a very close companion of the very similar one to the left, both holding spears in their raised right arms, and probably intended by the Tapestry's designer to represent, together with the standard-bearer himself, Harold's bodyguard.

Of course, it may be objected that on the contrary the identity of this individual is powerfully suggested by the way in which he stands directly beneath the word *Harold* with his head separating the letters *o* and *l*, and that this argument is strengthened by other scenes where names have apparently deliberately been placed in close proximity to the figures to which they refer: Bishop Odo, for example, rides in battle beneath the words *Odo* and *ep(iscopu)s*, which are separated by his raised staff, while to his right the duke raises his helmet to prove that he is still alive in very close proximity to the word *Wilel(mus)*; in the scene which shows William and his half-brothers seated together after their landing in England the three are all positioned beneath their names, and the duke's head separates the first *l* of *Willelm* from the second, while shortly afterwards he receives news of the imminent arrival of the English army with his head touching the letter *e* of the same word. These examples could be multiplied, but there are also others which clearly demonstrate that the designer of the Tapestry followed no single rule in such matters. In the section which represents Count Guy of Ponthieu handing Harold over to William in 1064 the word *Haroldum* is above its subject, but *Wilgelmum* is above Guy's head, which separates the *m* and the *u*, while Guy's own name, *Wido*, appears well to the left, above the second rank of the cavalry escort. In a lengthy sequence involving five ranks of horses (more, if one adds William's escort) and with a lengthy inscription, it was neither possible nor necessary to place names in close proximity to the figures they represented, whose identity was clear enough. There is a very similar example as the duke and his men set out for Brittany beneath the words *Hic Willem dux et exercitus eius venerunt ad monte(m) Michaelis* ('Here Duke William and his army came to Mont St Michel'). Here the fact that the inscription begins well to the left of the figure who is leading the column means that William is positioned beneath the word *monte(m)* while the *e* and *m* of *Willem* are separated by a spear carried by the rearmost trooper. There is, however, no possibility of mistaking that trooper for William or the figure of the duke for a common soldier. In this context there seems no reason to come to any very different conclusion on the significance of the wording of the Harold death scene. The *Hic* of *Hic Harold rex interfectus est* is well to the left of the trio which includes the standard-bearer and if *Harold* is above the right-hand man of that trio this would have caused no confusion if originally it was obvious that this individual was a soldier using a spear rather than the king holding an arrow, for it would have been clear enough that the word *Harold* could only refer to the man struck by the French horseman.

Their separate identities also, of course, explain the distinctly different equipment of the two figures. The much-favoured theory that both represent the king, first being hit by an arrow and then being cut down, is for all these reasons unlikely to be correct. In so far as we can judge from the Benoît drawing, the Tapestry as it existed in 1729 did not show the first figure holding an arrow at all. It is therefore hardly surprising that neither Montfaucon nor Lancelot, who must both have seen Benoît's work, took the soldier to the right of the standard-bearer to be anything other than one of Harold's men, despite the fact that Lancelot knew and mentioned Wace's evidence that the English king had earlier been wounded in the eye by an arrow and elsewhere cited William of Malmesbury, who speaks of an arrow in the brain causing his death, while Montfaucon also knew evidence on the arrow and no more thought that he was looking at a figure holding such an item than did Lancelot.[4]

If the present form of the Tapestry shows something different this may be largely the responsibility of Charles Stothard, who went to Bayeux to draw it for the Society of Antiquaries shortly after the end of the Napoleonic Wars. Stothard may or may not have seen the stitch holes visible in Benoît's time, but he mentions the Montfaucon engraving of Benoit's work in a way that indicates his familiarity with it,[5] and perhaps decided that the missile being held by the individual concerned would benefit from having flights

---

[4] Lancelot (ibid. 668) suggested that the trio which includes the standard-bearer were members of Harold's bodyguard; Montfaucon, *Monumens*, ii. 29, thought the figure being struck by the French horseman represented a Harold who had fallen from his own horse, and that the Tapestry here confirms WM's story that he was struck on the thigh as he lay on the ground.

[5] Stothard, 'Observations on the Bayeux Tapestry', 185.

attached to its left end. Alternatively, it is not impossible that the flights had been added during a restoration prior to his time but subsequent to that of Benoît. At any rate, the engraving produced from Stothard's drawing is fairly close to that of Montfaucon, but the figure's head is inclined back a little more to the right, thus decreasing the angle between the shaft of the missile and nasal of the helmet and increasing the impression that the head has been tilted in order to facilitate the extraction of the 'arrow'. It would not be surprising if Stothard or earlier restorers were misled on this by Montfaucon's engraving, which had itself decreased the angle between the missile and the nasal shown in Benoît's drawing, and by their familiarity with sources which speak of the king being hit by an arrow.[6] At any rate, by Stothard's time it was perfectly possible to interpret this figure as King Harold being struck by an arrow, and this Stothard's wife duly did in her *Letters written during a tour through Normandy*, commenting that the Tapestry agrees closely with the documentary evidence on the battle, and that 'Harold is represented receiving the arrow in his eye, he falls to the ground; a soldier pierces him in the thigh, with a sword'.[7] If the work thus far had nevertheless stopped short of representing the 'arrow' as embedded in the figure's face, this was to be remedied by the restorers who followed; accordingly the visitor to Bayeux today sees the 'arrow' terminating in the vicinity of the right eye (illus. 78). Of course, it is open to anyone to argue that Benoît misrepresented the length of the shaft held by this figure and also missed stitch holes which indicated that it had borne flights, although these were visible to Stothard almost ninety years later. This would restore the confidence of modern visitors to the Tapestry in the basic authenticity of the present stitchwork, but hardly seems to be the most plausible interpretation of the evidence.

At the time it first became known beyond the confines of Normandy parts of the Tapestry were already seriously damaged, showing that it had been subjected to hard usage at a period in its

---

[6] I deduce Stothard's familiarity with these sources from that of his wife; see the following note.
[7] Mrs Stothard, *Letters*, p.131. As far as I know this is the earliest expression of the idea that both figures represent the king.

history which is now completely obscure. There was a great tear near the beginning,[8] what is today the end was in a very poor state and some of the inscriptions elsewhere were difficult to read, a clear indication that other wool too had been degraded or had disappeared altogether. Montfaucon published the engravings in his *Monumens* along with his own commentary and a list of the Tapestry's inscriptions, this being partly derived from the list produced by Mathurin L'Archer and sent to him by La Londe.[9] However, these readings do not always accord with what Benoît drew. L'Archer, for example, had not been able to make out much of the inscription which accompanied the depiction of Halley's Comet, managing only the word *isti* and the comment 'il y a environ une ligne effacée', while Montfaucon offered *ISTI MIRANTVR STELLAM* ('These marvel at the star') and the engraving in the *Monumens* taken from Benoît's drawing showed *ISTI MIRANT S——A*, but with traces of the missing letters which might easily be reconstructed (as they have been) as *TELL*.[10] The final inscription recorded by L'Archer was *Hic Harold rex interfectus est* and Montfaucon followed this, although the plate which he published from Benoît's drawing goes only as far as the *R* of *INTER(FECTUS)*, which is followed not by the *F* one might expect but by a *P* partly in dotted lines; in the register below, and also in rather faint dotted lines, can be seen *IVS* (the *I*, however, being possibly the remains of a *T* or some other letter). Finally, there is a colon and further marks which are difficult to make much of at all. The engraving was here a reasonable representation of Benoît's drawing except in dealing with these marks, to whose significance we shall return. While preparing the paper which he presented to the Académie in 1730, Lancelot wrote to the bishop of Bayeux asking for a further close examination of the inscriptions,

---

[8] The patch which eventually replaced the material lost beneath the first occurrence of the word *Harold* is obvious in modern reproductions.

[9] There is a facsimile of the letter in Hill and McSween, *The Bayeux Tapestry*; Huard, 'Quelques Lettres', 369, published the address but not the list of inscriptions.

[10] I have not seen the Benoît drawing of this part of the Tapestry.

and the prelate entrusted the task to a competent man who carried it out, according to Lancelot, 'avec une attention aussi exacte qu'on pouvait le souhaiter'.[11] This may be so, for while L'Archer had written that 'Il y a encore deux ou trois lignes auplus entièrement effacées au bout de la tapisserie' (implying, of course, that there was something to be seen there) the bishop's man not only confirmed the reading *Hic Harold rex interfectus est* but added *et fuga verterunt Angli* ('And the English turned in flight').[12]

Although both the prior of St Vigor and the man employed by the bishop of Bayeux agreed on the reading *Hic Harold rex interfectus est*, we should perhaps not be too hasty in following them. The wording was obviously damaged, or Benoît would have concurred in showing it, and the part of it which he does show could be expanded rather differently. The *P* which he read after the *R* of *INTER...* is not easily turned into Latin, but this would not be the case if it were in fact the truncated remains of a second *R*. Indeed, if this were so one might guess that the reading was not *interfectus* but *in terra*, and that the whole inscription read something like *Hic Harold rex in terra iactus est* ('Here King Harold has been struck to the ground'), or, if *iactus* was a participle and the sentence continued further, perhaps *Hic Harold rex in terra iactus et fuga verterunt Angli* ('Here King Harold struck to the ground and the English turned in flight'). In either case, of course, it would have precisely fitted the figure falling beneath the horseman's blow.[13] As presently restored the *F* and *E* of *interfectus* are very close together, and it is conceivable that if much of the *E* except the upper part of the ascender had disappeared Benoît could have produced *P* by reading them together; also, the difference between *interfectus* and *in terra iactus* is not great, but it would require space for an extra *i* and *a*, and the fabric in this area does not today exhibit the slightest trace

[11] Lancelot, 'Suite de l'explication', 602. Huard, 'Quelques Lettres', 348, names him as Louis Rustaing de Saint-Jory, an *écuyer* of the bishop; he was admitted as a member of the Académie de Caen in 1731.

[12] Lancelot, ibid., 668, noted the poor Latinity of this phrase (the verb *verto* should be in the passive) and the same usage in the earlier *Conan fuga vertit*.

[13] I am grateful to John Davie for discussion of possible Latin wording at this point.

of the stitch holes which might suggest that these letters ever stood there. However, this may well be much less significant than one might care to think. There is in fact plenty of space in which these letters could once have stood, if one were to assume that the restored *E* and *C* are not in their original positions, and that the fabric of the Tapestry may once have exhibited stitch holes which have since disappeared.

There is good reason to believe that the latter is almost certainly the case. The missile held by the soldier to the right of the standard-bearer is clearly shown by Benoît as extending to the rim of the helmet and it seems likely that originally it also passed behind it and went on into the lettering beyond; Stothard (if he did not simply copy the Montfaucon engraving of Benoît) concurred on the line between the figure's hand and the helmet rim, yet there are no stitch holes to be seen on this line today, at least on the front of the Tapestry. There is also the question of the marks which Benoît drew after the colon following the word usually read as *interfectus*. It is very difficult to believe that they are the remains of work of a single period, for the lettering (assuming that it is lettering) looks as though it has been revisited more than once, and thus that what Benoît saw was a feature which had already been restored and then suffered further serious damage before 1729. Naturally, it can be argued that his drawing need not always have been accurate, but this would not be an easy position to sustain in this particular case, for the tendency would surely be to simplify a feature like this to make it intelligible rather than to record it faithfully in all its confusion, yet the latter is what Benoît seems to have done. It would also be necessary to completely reject the features he drew if one were seeking to avoid the conclusion that the Tapestry once bore stitch holes which are no longer to be seen, for around the reconstructed word *EST* there is today no trace of the marks which he saw there nearly three hundred years ago. One might wonder how many other tell-tale signs the fabric once bore which have since been wiped away forever. The effect of washing seems a likely explanation for the disappearance of stitch holes, and it has recently been acknowledged that the Tapestry was washed with soap before it was restored in the nineteenth century.[14]

We have just seen evidence that the Tapestry may have undergone changes before 1729 as a result of the lack of care with which it had evidently been treated at a time in its history which is now unknown, and that it is not impossible that before that date parts of it had been damaged and restored more than once. However, this was not to be the end of its vicissitudes. During the French Revolution it narrowly escaped destruction twice, and was exhibited in Paris when Napoleon was preparing to invade England and then returned to Bayeux. In 1814 it was seen by the Englishman Hudson Gurney:

> It was coiled round a machine, like that which lets down the buckets to a Well; and I had the opportunity of drawing it out at leisure, over a table.[15]

Shortly afterwards it received a visit from Dawson Turner, who confirmed Gurney's evidence on the way in which it was exhibited:

> The tapestry is coiled round a cylinder, which is turned by a winch and wheel; and it is rolled and unrolled with so little attention, that if it continues under such management as the present, it will be wholly ruined in the course of half a century. It is injured at the beginning: towards the end it becomes very ragged, and several of the figures have completely disappeared. The worsted is unravelling too in many of the intermediate portions. As yet, however, it is still in good preservation, considering its great age, though, as I have just observed, it will not long continue so.[16]

[14] Information supplied to John McSween by Mlle Sylvette Lemagnen, Curator of the Bayeux Tapestry. If reproductions of the Benoît drawings are ever published it may be that detailed comparison of them and the present fabric will eventually throw much light on the history of the hanging and the features it bears, and that this will modify some of the thoughts offered here. The results of scientific examinations of the Tapestry carried out in the early 1980s were presented to a conference at Cerisy-la-Salle in 1999; when this book went to press the proceedings of this conference had not been published.

[15] Gurney, 'Observations on the Bayeux Tapestry', 459.

[16] Turner, *Account of a Tour in Normandy*, ii. 242.

It was also in these years that the Society of Antiquaries sent Charles Stothard to Bayeux to produce accurate drawings from which hand-coloured engravings were eventually produced. He reported that the work in some parts of the Tapestry was destroyed, especially towards the end, which was a mass of rags, and that comparison with Montfaucon's engraving suggested that there had here been 'much injury even since his time'. However, he also said that he had been able to recreate much of what was missing by identifying minute particles of coloured wool in the stitch holes; where there were no such particles he simply recorded the holes:

> The restorations that I have made commence on the lower border with the first of the archers. Of these figures I found scarcely one whose colours of any kind remained perfect. In the upper border and historical part, the restorations begin a little after, with the Saxons, under the word '*ceciderunt*'. From the circumstance of the border being worked down the side at the commencement of the Tapestry, it is evident that no part of the subject is wanting; but the work in many places is defaced, and these parts have been restored in the same manner as at the end.[17]

As this gives no very precise guide to the amount he had recreated, we shall never know just how much was readily visible to those who saw the hanging at this date, just as the same is true of its state in Benoît's time. However, Thomas Dibdin, who described it soon after Stothard, commented that:

> The first portion of the needle-work, representing the embassy of Harold, from Edward the Confessor to William Duke of Normandy, is comparatively much defaced – that is to say, the stitches are worn away, and little more than the ground, of fine close linen cloth, remains… About the last five feet of this extraordinary roll are in a yet more decayed and imperfect state than the first portion.[18]

[17] Stothard, 'Some Observations on the Bayeux Tapestry', 184–5.
[18] Dibdin, *A Bibliographical Antiquarian and Picturesque Tour*, i. 378–9. For Dibdin's illustration of the drum upon which the Tapestry was stored, see illus. 79.

Not long after Dibdin's time it was restored into more or less its present condition. The Bayeux Tapestry is a historical monument of immense interest and value, and it seems inconceivable that in its essentials it differs significantly today from the piece which passed out of the workshops in the late eleventh century; even so, attempts to interpret its scenes and inscriptions need always to be preceded by doubts about how far they are now as they once were.

GENEALOGIES

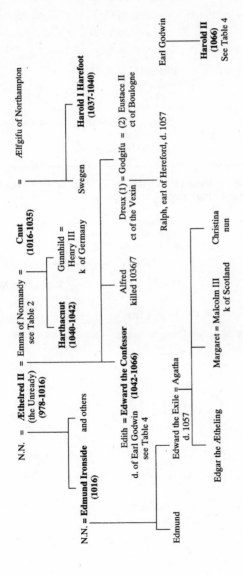

Genealogical Table 1.

Kings of England: Aethelred II to Harold II. Kings are in bold; dates are regnal years. Between 1035 and 1037 the throne was disputed between Harold Harefoot and Harthacnut.

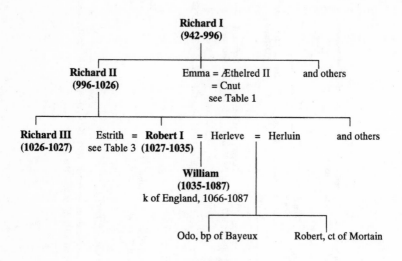

Genealogical Table 2.

The Norman ducal dynasty. Dukes are in bold; the dates are ducal years.

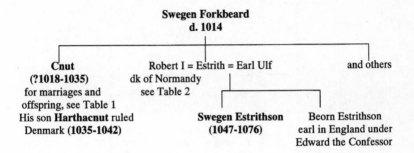

Swegen Forkbeard
d. 1014

Cnut	Robert I = Estrith = Earl Ulf	and others
(?1018-1035)	dk of Normandy	
for marriages and	see Table 2	
offspring, see Table 1		
His son **Harthacnut** ruled	**Swegen Estrithson**	Beorn Estrithson
Denmark **(1035-1042)**	**(1047-1076)**	earl in England under
		Edward the Confessor

Genealogical Table 3.

The Danish royal family. Kings are in bold; the dates are regnal years. Between 1042
and 1047 the Danish throne was disputed between Swegen Estrithson and King
Magnus of Norway.

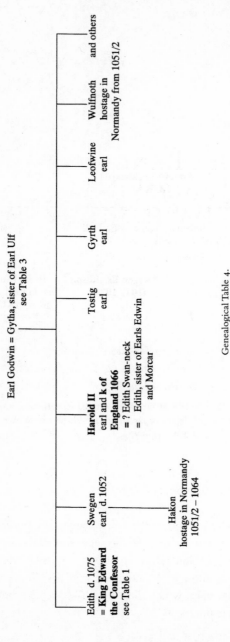

Genealogical Table 4.

The House of Godwin. Kings of England are in bold. Tostig was killed at the battle of Stamford Bridge on 25 September 1066; his brothers Harold, Gyrth and Leofwine at Hastings on 14 October.

The Lancelot
Engravings
of the Bayeux Tapestry

In a sense, there is no 'authentic' version of the Bayeux Tapestry, given that even the fabric now hanging in Bayeux is known to differ in certain respects from that displayed there early in the eighteenth century. Of the plates which follow, the first is an engraving of the Foucault drawing of the first thirty feet of the Tapestry, and was published by Antoine Lancelot in 1729; the remainder, published by Lancelot in 1733, were modelled upon the drawings of the rest of the Tapestry made by Antoine Benoît for Bernard de Montfaucon, and differ from those published by Montfaucon himself. Lancelot's engravings omit the wavy line used to indicate the ground in the battle scenes, the figures are rather freely drawn and the inscriptions seem sometimes to stray from their proper positions. Even so, they are in other respects more accurate than those of Montfaucon, and have some value while the drawings upon which they were based remain unpublished. See the Appendix.

PLATE I

Lancelot's version of the Foucault drawing, published in 1729. King Edward the Confessor with two figures, one of whom is probably Earl Harold; Harold and his soldiers go to the church of Bosham (Sussex), eat and drink in a hall and then sail to the land of Count Guy (of Ponthieu)...

...where Harold is apprehended by Guy and taken to Beaurain; Harold and Guy talk, and messengers of Duke William arrive. The word *Edward*, which today stands above and to the left of the two figures who are with the king in the first scene, does not appear here, and is clearly a later addition; there was a great tear in the fabric to the right of the king.

The following plates, based on the drawings of Antoine Benoît, were published by Lancelot in 1733.

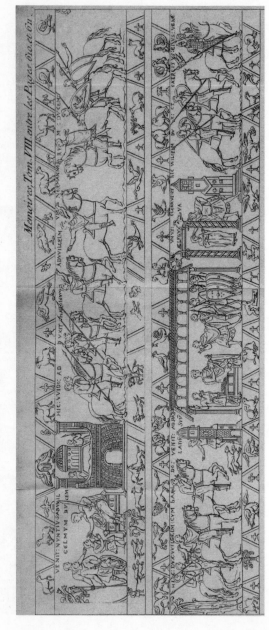

PLATE 2

A messenger comes to Duke William and Guy brings Harold to him; William comes with Harold to his palace, where there is a cleric and Ælfgyva. Duke William and his army...

...come to Mont St Michel; Harold rescues men from the sands of the river Couesnon and they come to Dol; Conan turns in flight and William's soldiers fight against the men of Dinan; Conan surrenders the keys; William gives arms to Harold.

PLATE 3

William comes to Bayeux where Harold swears an oath to him; Harold returns to England and comes to King Edward; the body of Edward is carried to the church of St Peter (Westminster Abbey)...

...(after he) talks to his faithful followers and dies; they give the king's crown to Harold and he sits enthroned with Archbishop Stigand by his side; men marvel at the star (Halley's Comet) and an English ship comes to the land of Duke William; William orders ships to be built and the work begins.

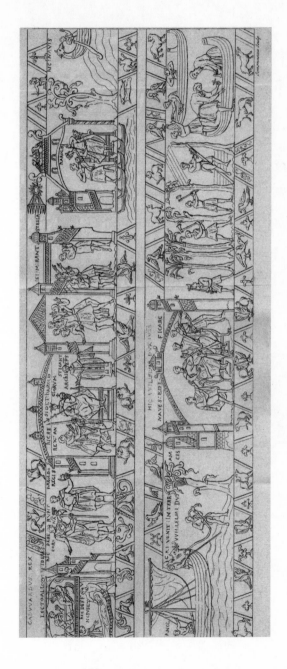

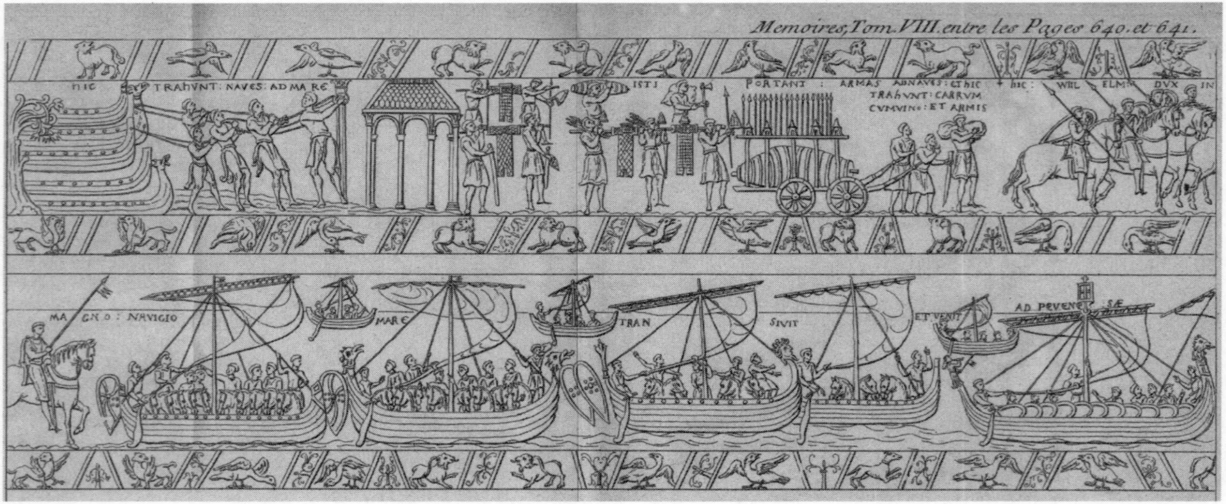

PLATE 4

The ships are dragged to the sea and arms and wine are carried down to them; Duke William in a great ship crosses the sea to Pevensey...

...the horses disembark from the ships and the soldiers hurry to Hastings to seize food; here is Wadard; the meat is cooked and served and they make a meal, as the bishop blesses the food and drink; Bishop Odo sits with...

Memoires, Tom. VIII. entre les Pages 650. et 651.

PLATE 5

...Duke William and Robert (of Mortain); a castle is built at Hastings and news is brought to William about Harold; a house is burnt; the soldiers leave Hastings and come to the battle against King Harold...

...Duke William asks Vital if he has seen Harold's army and Harold is informed about William's army; here Duke William exhorts his soldiers to prepare themselves manfully and wisely for the battle, and cavalry and archers (possibly including a crossbowman) move forward.

281

Memoires, Tom. VIII entre les Pages 66 4 et 665.

PLATE 6

The cavalry attack the English shield-wall from left and right; Gyrth and Leofwine, the brothers of King Harold, are killed; the English and the French fall at the same time in the battle around a watercourse...

...and a hillock defended by English light infantry; Bishop Odo holding a staff comforts the boys and William removes his helmet; here the French fight and those who are with Harold are killed.

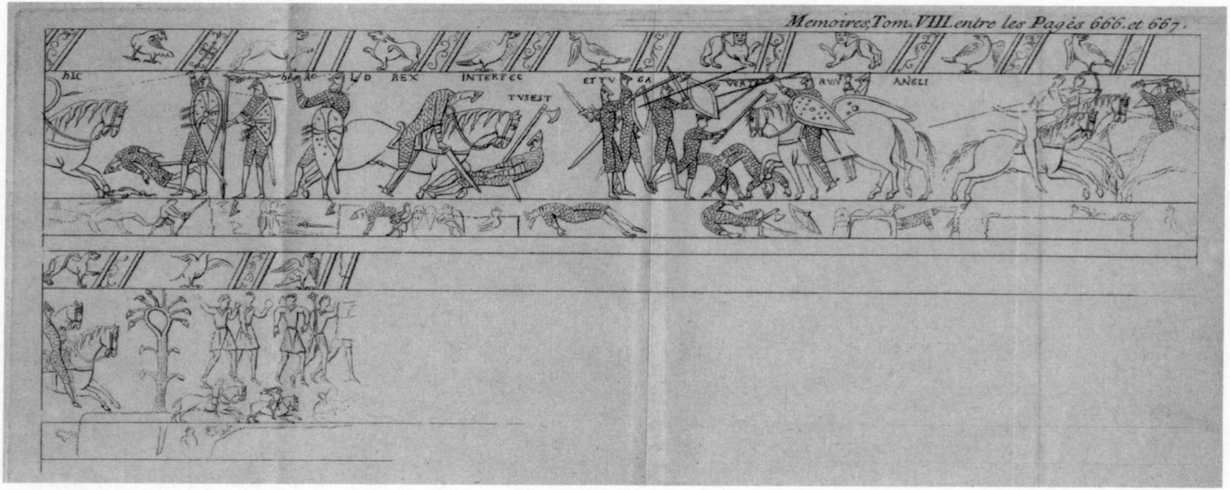
Memoires, Tom. VIII. entre les Pagès 666. et 667.
REX
INTERFEC
TVSEST
ANGLI

PLATE 7

King Harold is killed and the English turn in flight.

SELECT BIBLIOGRAPHY

MANUSCRIPT SOURCES

East Sussex Record Office.

BAT 4421, Nos 6/7. Surveys by Richard Budgen of the eastern part of the town of Battle and of the part of the estate south-west of the abbey, 1724.

BAT 4435. Plans of the Several Farms Constituting the Estates of Sir Godfrey Webster Bart. in Sussex according to Mr Willock's Survey, 1811. No. 1: The Abbey Park.

TD/E 158 (Tithe Map of Battle). Plan of the Parish of Battle, Sussex, surveyed by J.W. Cole, 1859.

PRIMARY SOURCES

Adam of Bremen, *Gesta Hammaburgensis Ecclesiae Pontificum*, ed. B. Schmeidler (3rd edn, Hannover, 1917); trans. F.J. Tschan, *History of the Archbishops of Hamburg-Bremen* (New York, 1959).

Æthelweard, *Chronicle*, ed. A. Campbell (London, 1962).

Alfred the Great: Asser's Life of King Alfred and other contemporary sources, ed. S.D. Keynes and M. Lapidge (Harmondsworth, 1983).

Amatus of Montecassino, *Storia de' normanni*, ed. V. de Bartholomaeis (Rome, 1935).

Anglo-Saxon Chronicle, in *Two of the Saxon Chronicles Parallel*, ed. C. Plummer (2 vols, Oxford, 1892–9); the 'D' text is also in *The Anglo-Saxon Chronicle: a collaborative edition. Volume 6. MS D*, ed. G.P. Cubbin (Cambridge, 1996); there is a facsimile of E, *The Peterborough Chronicle*, ed. D. Whitelock (Early English Manuscripts in Facsimile IV, Copenhagen, 1954); the best translation of the *Chronicle* is in *EHD1*, No. 1 and *EHD2*, No. 1 (the entries for 1066 are reprinted *The Battle of Hastings*, ed. Morillo, pp.22–7; *TNE*, pp.133–42; they are reprinted and abridged in *The Norman Conquest*, ed. Brown, pp.69–72); also trans. in full in *The Anglo-Saxon Chronicle*, ed. M.J. Swanton (London, 1996). References here are to Plummer's edition.

An Anglo-Saxon Dictionary, ed. J. Bosworth and T.N. Toller (Oxford, 1898) and *Supplement*.

Anglo-Saxon Writs, ed. and trans. F.E. Harmer (2nd edn, Stamford, 1989).

Annals of Nieder-Altaich. The Latin text of the entry for 1066 is given and trans. by van Houts, 'The Norman Conquest through European Eyes', 841, n.3; the trans. is reprinted, *TNE*, p.131.

Asser, *Life of King Alfred*, ed. W.H. Stevenson (Oxford, 1904); trans. *Alfred the Great*, ed. Keynes and Lapidge, pp.67–110.

The Battle of Maldon, ed. and trans. D. Scragg, in *The Battle of Maldon AD991*, ed. Scragg, pp.18–31; also trans. *EHD1*, No. 10 (reprinted, *The Norman Conquest*, ed. Brown, pp.94–8).

Baudri of Bourgueil, *Adelae Comitissae*, in *Baldricus Burgulianus: Carmina*, ed. K. Hilbert (Heidelberg, 1979), No. 134; *Les Oeuvres Poétiques de Baudri de Bourgueil (1046–1130)*, ed. P. Abrahams (Paris, 1926), No. CXCVI; trans. of ll. 207–572 of the Hilbert text (which is superior to that of Abrahams) by M.W. Herren in Brown, *The Bayeux Tapestry: History and Bibliography*, Appendix III, pp.167–77; extracts reprinted, *TNE*, pp.125–8.

The Bayeux Tapestry. There are a number of important early reproductions and treatments of the Tapestry. They are:

Lancelot, 'Explication d'un monument de Guillaume le Conquérant', *Memoires... de L'Academie Royale des Inscriptions et Belles Lettres*, vi (1729), 739–55.

Lancelot, 'Suite de l'explication d'un Monument de Guillaume le Conquérant', *Memoires... de L'Academie Royale des Inscriptions et Belles Lettres*, viii (1733), 602–68.

Montfaucon, B. de, *Les Monumens de la Monarchie Françoise*, i–ii (Paris, 1729–30), i. plate xxxv, ii. plates i–ix.

Ducarel, A.C., *Anglo-Norman Antiquities considered in a tour through part of Normandy* (London, 1767). Reproduces the Lancelot engravings of 1733.

Stothard, C.A., 'The Bayeux Tapestry', *Vetusta Monumenta*, vi (London, 1819–23), plates 1–17.

La Tapisserie de Bayeux... édition variorum... texte par Achille Jubinal... dessins et gravures par Victor Sansonetti (Paris, 1838).

Hill, D. and McSween, J., *The Bayeux Tapestry: The Establishment of a Text* (forthcoming). This volume will publish some of the early reproductions in parallel.

The Bayeux Tapestry, ed. F.M. Stenton (London, 1957).

The Bayeux Tapestry, ed. D.M. Wilson (London, 1985).

Brevis Relatio de Guillelmo nobilissimo comite Normannorum, ed. E.M.C. van Houts, in *Chronology, Conquest and Conflict in Medieval England*, Camden Miscellany XXXIV, Camden Fifth Series vol. 10 (Cambridge, 1997); reprinted and trans. E.M.C. van Houts, *History and Family Traditions in England and the Continent, 1000–1200* (Aldershot, 1999), pp. 1–48.

The Burghal Hidage, ed. and trans. in *The Defence of Wessex*, ed. Hill and Rumble, pp. 24–35; trans. *Alfred the Great*, ed. Keynes and Lapidge, pp. 193–4.

Caesar, J., *The Gallic War*, trans. H.J. Edwards (London, 1917).

Capitularia regum Francorum, i, ed. A. Boretius (Hanover, 1883).

Carmen de Hastingae Proelio, ed. and trans. C. Morton and H. Muntz (Oxford, 1972); abridged reprint of the translation, *The Battle of Hastings*, ed. Morillo, pp. 46–52; *TNE*, p. 129.

Carmen de Hastingae Proelio, ed. and trans. F. Barlow (Oxford, 1999).

Charlemagne: translated sources, trans. P.D. King (Kendal, 1987).

The Chronicle of Battle Abbey, ed. and trans. E. Searle (Oxford, 1980); trans. extract, *The Norman Conquest*, ed. Brown, p. 121.

Chronicon Monasterii de Abingdon, ed. J. Stevenson (Rolls Series, 2, 1858).

Chronicon Monasterii de Hida, in *Liber Monasterii de Hyda*, ed. E. Edwards (Rolls Series, 45, 1866), pp. 283–321.

Chronicon Roskildense, in *Scriptores Minores*, ed. Gertz, i. 3–33.

La Chronique de Saint-Maixent 751–1140, ed. and trans. J. Verdon (Paris, 1979).

Domesday Book, ed. A. Farley and H. Ellis (London, 1783–1816); also published by the Phillimore Press in county volumes, with translations.

Dudo of St Quentin, *History of the Normans*, trans. E. Christiansen (Woodbridge, 1998).

Eadmer, *Historia Novorum in Anglia*, ed. M. Rule (Rolls Series, 81, 1884); trans. G. Bosanquet, *Eadmer's History of Recent Events in England* (London, 1964); trans. extracts, *TNE*, pp. 146–50.

Encomium Emmae Reginae, ed. and trans. A. Campbell, with a supplementary introduction by Simon Keynes (Cambridge, 1998). First published as Camden Third Series, lxxii, 1949.

English Historical Documents Volume 1: c.500–1042, ed. D. Whitelock (2nd edn, London, 1979).

English Historical Documents Volume 2: 1042–1189, ed. D.C. Douglas and G.W. Greenaway (2nd edn, London, 1981).

Ermold the Black, *In honorem Hludovici Pii*, ed. and trans. in part by P. Godman, *Poetry of the Carolingian Renaissance* (London, 1985), pp.250–5.

Etienne de Rouen, see Stephen of Rouen.

Florence of Worcester, see John of Worcester.

Fulcoius of Beauvais, *Jephthah*, trans. *TNE*, pp.132–3.

Gaimar, G., *L'Estoire des Engleis*, ed. A. Bell (Oxford, 1960); ed. and trans. Sir T.D. Hardy and C.T. Martin (Rolls Series, 91, 1888–9).

Die Gesetze der Angelsachsen, ed. F. Liebermann (Halle, 1898–1916).

Guy, bishop of Amiens, see *Carmen de Hastingae Proelio*.

Henry of Huntingdon, *Historia Anglorum*, ed. and trans. D. Greenway (Oxford, 1996); partial reprint of the translation, *TNE*, pp.150–6.

Herman the Archdeacon, *Liber de Miraculis Sancti Eadmundi*, in *Memorials of St Edmund's Abbey*, ed. T. Arnold, vol. i (Rolls Series, 96, London, 1890), 26–92.

John of Worcester, *The Chronicle of John of Worcester. Volume II. The Annals from 450 to 1066*, ed. and trans. R.R. Darlington and P. McGurk (Oxford, 1995); partial reprint of the translation, *TNE*, pp.142–6. The entry for 1066 is translated under the name Florence of Worcester, in *EHD2*, No. 2; trans. extracts also in *The Norman Conquest*, ed. Brown, pp.58, 68, 72–3, 78.

The Laws of the Earliest English Kings, ed. F.L. Attenborough (Cambridge, 1922).

Liber Eliensis, ed. E.O. Blake (Camden Third Series, xcii, 1962).

The Life of King Edward who rests at Westminster, attributed to a monk of Saint-Bertin, ed. and trans. F. Barlow (2nd edn, Oxford, 1992); partial reprint of the translation of the first edition, *The Norman Conquest*, ed. Brown, pp.82–93.

The Norman Conquest, ed. R.A. Brown (London, 1984). A collection of translated sources.

The Normans in Europe, ed. and trans. E.M.C. van Houts (Manchester, 2000).

Orderic Vitalis, *Historia Æcclesiastica*, ed. and trans. M. Chibnall (6 vols, Oxford, 1969–80); partial reprint of the translation, *The Norman Conquest*, ed. Brown, pp.100–14.

Penitential articles issued after the Battle of Hastings, in *Councils & Synods with other Documents Relating to the English Church. I. A.D.871–1204. Part II 1066–1204*, ed. D.Whitelock et al. (Oxford, 1981), 581–4; trans., *The Norman Conquest*, ed. Brown, pp.156–7; *EHD2*, No. 81.

Priest of Fécamp, *Letter on the Battle of Tinchebrai*; Latin text, *EHR*, xxv (1910), 296; trans. *EHD2*, No. 9. This translation omits the following words on the size of Robert of Normandy's forces, *Comes uero ad vi milia habuit, equites septingentos*.

Regesta Regum Anglo-Normannorum. The Acta of William I (1066–1087), ed. D. Bates (Oxford, 1998).

The Reign of Charlemagne: Documents on Carolingian Government and Administration, trans. H.R. Loyn and J. Percival (London, 1975).

Saxo Grammaticus, *Danorum Regum Heroumque Historia Books X–XVI*, ed. and trans. E. Christiansen (British Archaeological Reports, International Series, vols 84, 118, 1980–1).

Scriptores Minores Historiæ Danicæ Medii Ævi, ed. M. Cl. Gertz (Copenhagen, 1917–22).

Ship List of William the Conqueror, ed. E.M.C. van Houts, in 'The Ship List of William the Conqueror', *ANS*, X (1987), 175–6; trans. *TNE*, pp.130–1.

Snorri Sturluson, *King Harald's Saga*, trans. M. Magnusson and H. Pálsson (London, 1966).

Stephen of Rouen, *Draco Normannicus*, ed. R. Howlett, *Chronicles of the Reigns of Stephen, Henry II and Richard I* (Rolls Series, 82, 1884–9), ii. 589–781.

Sven Aggesen, *Lex Castrensis*, in *Scriptores Minores* ed. Gertz, i. 64–92; trans. E. Christiansen, *The Works of Sven Aggesen* (London, 1992), pp.31–43.

Symeon of Durham, *Historia Regum*, in *Symeonis Monachi Opera Omnium*, ed. T. Arnold (Rolls Series, 75, 1882–5).

Thietmar of Merseburg, *Chronicon*, ed. R. Holtzmann (2nd edn, Berlin, 1955); trans. extract *EHD1*, pp.347–50.

Vegetius, *Epitome of Military Science*, trans. N.P. Milner (Liverpool, 2nd edn, 1996).

Wace, *Roman de Rou*, ed. A.J. Holden (3 vols, Société des Anciens Textes Francais, Paris, 1970–3); the section on William the Conqueror is trans. E. Taylor, *Master Wace, His Chronicle of the Norman Conquest from the Roman de Rou* (London, 1837); Holden's text is reprinted and trans. in full by G.S. Burgess, *Wace. The Roman de Rou* (St Helier, 2002).

The Waltham Chronicle, ed. and trans. L. Watkiss and M. Chibnall (Oxford, 1994); partial reprint of the translation, *TNE*, pp.156–9.

William of Jumièges, *Gesta Normannorum Ducum*, ed. and trans. E.M.C. van Houts

(Oxford, 1992–5); partial reprint of the translation, *TNE*, pp. 113–7; translations of the passage on Hastings in *EHD2*, No. 3; (reprinted *The Battle of Hastings*, ed. Morillo, pp. 18–19); trans. extracts, *The Norman Conquest*, ed. Brown, pp. 3–15.

William of Malmesbury, *Gesta Regum Anglorum: The History of the English Kings*, ed. and trans. R.A.B. Mynors, R.M. Thomson and M. Winterbottom (Oxford, 1998–9); partial translations, *TNE*, pp. 161–70; *The Norman Conquest*, ed. Brown, pp. 115–7.

William of Malmesbury, *De Gestis Pontificum Anglorum Libri Quinque*, ed. N.E.S.A. Hamilton (Rolls Series, 52, 1870).

William of Malmesbury, *Vita Wulfstani*, ed. R.R. Darlington (Camden Society, Third Series, xl, 1928); trans. M. Swanton, *Three Lives of the Last Englishmen* (London, 1984); partial reprint of the translation, *TNE*, pp. 159–61.

William of Poitiers, *Gesta Guillelmi*, ed. and trans. R.H.C. Davis and M. Chibnall (Oxford, 1998); partial reprint of the translation, *TNE*, pp. 118–25; full translation of the passage on Hastings in *The Battle of Hastings*, ed. Morillo, pp. 12–15; abridged translations in *EHD2*, No. 4; *The Norman Conquest*, ed. Brown, pp. 32–5; full Latin text with French translation, *Histoire de Guillaume le Conquérant*, ed. R. Foreville (Paris, 1952).

Xenophon, *Spartan Society*, trans. R.J.A. Talbert, *Plutarch on Sparta* (London, 1988).

SECONDARY SOURCES

Abels, R.P., *Lordship and Military Obligation in Anglo-Saxon England* (Berkeley, 1988).

Abels, R.P., 'English Tactics, Strategy and Military Organization in the Late Tenth Century', *The Battle of Maldon*, ed. Scragg, pp. 143–55.

Abels, R.P., 'From Alfred to Harold II: The Military Failure of the Late Anglo-Saxon State', *The Normans and Their Adversaries at War*, ed. Abels and Bachrach, pp. 15–30.

Albu, E., *The Normans in their Histories: Propaganda, Myth and Subversion* (Woodbridge, 2001).

Anglo-Norman Warfare: Studies in Late Anglo-Saxon and Anglo-Norman Military Organization and Warfare, ed. M. Strickland (Woodbridge, 1992).

Archer, T.A., 'Mr Freeman and the "Quarterly Review"', *Contemporary Review*, March 1893, 335–55.

Archer, T.A., 'The Battle of Hastings. Part I', *EHR*, ix (1894), 1–41, 602–08.

Armies, Chivalry and Warfare in Medieval Britain and France: Proceedings of the 1995 Harlaxton Symposium, ed. M. Strickland (Stamford, 1998).

Bachrach, B.S., 'Some Observations on the Military Administration of the Norman Conquest', *ANS*, VIII (1985), 1–25.

Bachrach, B.S., 'On the Origins of William the Conqueror's Horse Transports', *Technology and Culture*, 26 (1985), 505–31.

Bachrach, B.S., 'The Feigned Retreat at Hastings', *Medieval Studies*, 33 (1971), 344–7; reprinted *The Battle of Hastings*, ed. Morillo, pp. 190–3. References here are to the reprint.

Bachrach, B.S., 'William Rufus' Plan for the Invasion of Aquitaine', *The Normans and Their Adversaries at War*, ed. Abels and Bachrach, pp. 31–63.

Ballard, A., *The Domesday Boroughs* (Oxford, 1904).

Barclay, C.N., *Battle 1066* (London, 1966).

Baring, F.H., 'The Conqueror's Footprints in Domesday', *EHR*, xiii (1898), 17–25; reprinted with additions and alterations as Appendix A of his *Domesday Tables*, pp. 207–16.

Baring, F.H., 'The Battle Field of Hastings', *EHR*, xx (1905), 65–70; reprinted with additions as Appendix B, 'On the Battle of Hastings', of his *Domesday Tables*, pp. 217–32.

Baring, F.H., 'The Malfosse at the Battle of Hastings', *EHR*, xxii (1907), 69–72.

Baring, F.H., *Domesday Tables* (London, 1909).

Barlow, F., 'Edward the Confessor and the Norman Conquest', Barlow, *The Norman Conquest and Beyond*, pp. 99–111.

Barlow, F., 'The *Carmen de Hastingae Proelio*', *Studies in International History Presented to W. Norton Medlicott*, ed. K. Bourne and D.C. Watt (London, 1967), pp. 36–67; reprinted Barlow, *The Norman Conquest and Beyond*, pp. 189–222. References here are to the reprint.

Barlow, F., *Edward the Confessor* (London, 1970).

Barlow, F., *The Norman Conquest and Beyond* (London, 1983).

Barlow, F., *The Godwins: The Rise and Fall of a Noble Dynasty* (Harlow, 2002).

Bates, D., 'The Character and Career of Odo, Bishop of Bayeux (1049/50–1097)', *Speculum*, l (1975), 1–20.

Bates, D., *Normandy before 1066* (London, 1982).

Bates, D., *William the Conqueror* (London, 1989).

The Battle of Hastings: Sources and Interpretations, ed. S. Morillo (Woodbridge, 1996).

The Battle of Maldon AD 991, ed. D. Scragg (Oxford, 1991).

Beech, G., 'The Participation of Aquitanians in the Conquest of England 1066–1100', *ANS*, IX (1986), 1–24.

Beeler, J., 'The Composition of Anglo-Norman Armies', *Speculum*, 40 (1965), 398–414.

Beeler, J., *Warfare in England 1066–1189* (New York, 1966).

Behrens, L.B., *Battle Abbey under Thirty-Nine Kings* (London, 1937).

Bennett, M., 'Poetry as History? The "*Roman de Rou*" of Wace as a source for the Norman conquest', *ANS*, V (1982), 21–39.

Bennett, M., 'Wace and Warfare', *ANS*, XI (1988), 37–57.

Bennett, M., 'The Myth of the Military Supremacy of Knightly Cavalry', *Armies, Chivalry and Warfare*, ed. Strickland, pp. 304–16.

Bennett, M., *Campaigns of the Norman Conquest* (Botley, 2001).

Bernstein, D.J., *The Mystery of the Bayeux Tapestry* (London, 1986).

Blacker, J., *The Faces of Time: Portrayal of the Past in Old French and Latin Historical Narrative of the Anglo-Norman Regnum* (Austin, 1994).

Blackman, H., 'The Story of the old gunpowder works at Battle', *Sussex Archæological Collections*, lxiv (1923), 109–22.

Blood Red Roses: The archaeology of a mass grave from the Battle of Towton AD 1461, ed. V. Fiorato *et al.* (Oxford, 2000).

Bond, G., '"Iocus Amoris": The Poetry of Baudri of Bourgueil and the Formation of the Ovidian Subculture', *Traditio*, 42 (1986), 143–93.

Boüard, M. de, *Guillaume le Conquérant* (Paris, 1984).

Bouet, P., 'La *Felicitas* de Guillaume le Conquérant dans les *Gesta Guillelmi* de Guillaume de Poitiers', *ANS*, IV (1981), 37–52, 174–81.

Bradbury, J., 'Battles in England and Normandy, 1066–1154', *ANS*, VI (1983), 1–12; reprinted in *Anglo-Norman Warfare*, ed. Strickland, pp. 182–93.

Bradbury, J., *The Battle of Hastings* (Stroud, 1998).

Brandon, P., *The Sussex Landscape* (London, 1974).

Brilliant, R., 'The Bayeux Tapestry: a stripped narrative for their eyes and ears', *Word and Image*, 7 (1991), 93–125; reprinted *The Study of the Bayeux Tapestry*, ed. Gameson, pp. 111–37. References here are to the reprint.

British Geological Survey, 1:50,000 Series, Sheet 320/321, *Hastings and Dungeness*.

Brooks, F.W., *The Battle of Stamford Bridge* (York, 1956).

Brooks, N.P., 'Arms, Status and Warfare in Late-Saxon England', *Ethelred the Unready: Papers from the Millenary Conference*, ed. D. Hill (Oxford, 1978), pp. 81–103.

Brooks, N.P., 'Weapons and Armour', *The Battle of Maldon*, ed. Scragg, pp.208–19.

Brooks, N.P. and Walker, H.E., 'The Authority and Interpretation of the Bayeux Tapestry', *ANS*, I (1978), 1–34, 191–9; reprinted *The Study of the Bayeux Tapestry*, ed. Gameson, pp.63–92. References here are to the original.

Brown, R.A., *The Normans and the Norman Conquest* (London, 1969).

Brown, R.A., *Origins of English Feudalism* (London, 1973).

Brown, R.A., 'The Battle of Hastings', *ANS*, III (1980), 1–21, 197–201; reprinted *Anglo-Norman Warfare*, ed. Strickland, pp.161–81, 273–7; *The Battle of Hastings*, ed. Morillo, pp.196–218. References here are to the original.

Brown, S.A., *The Bayeux Tapestry: History and Bibliography* (Woodbridge, 1988).

Brown, S.A., 'The Bayeux Tapestry: Why Eustace, Odo and William?', *ANS*, XII (1989), 7–28.

Brown, S.A. and Herren, M.W., 'The *Adelae Comitissae* of Baudri of Bourgeuil and the Bayeux Tapestry', *ANS*, XVI (1993), 55–73; reprinted *The Study of the Bayeux Tapestry*, ed. Gameson, pp.139–55. References here are to the original.

Bryce, J., 'Edward Augustus Freeman', *EHR*, vii (1892), 497–509.

Budny, M., 'The Byrhtnoth Tapestry or Embroidery', *The Battle of Maldon*, ed. Scragg, pp.263–78.

Bullough, D., '*Europae Pater*: Charlemagne and his achievement in the light of recent scholarship', *EHR*, lxxxv (1970), 59–105.

Burne, A.H., *The Battlefields of England* (London, 1950).

Campbell, J., 'Observations on English Government from the Tenth to the Twelfth Century', *TRHS*, Fifth Series, xxv (1975), 39–54; reprinted Campbell, *Essays in Anglo-Saxon History*, pp.155–70. References here are to the reprint.

Campbell, J., 'England, France, Flanders and Germany in the Reign of Ethelred II: Some Comparisons and Connections', *Ethelred the Unready: Papers from the Millenary Conference*, ed. D. Hill (Oxford, 1978), pp.255–70; reprinted Campbell, *Essays in Anglo-Saxon History*, pp.191–207. References here are to the reprint.

Campbell, J., 'The Significance of the Anglo-Norman State in the Administrative History of Western Europe', *Histoire Comparée de l'Administration (IVe–XVIIIe Siècles)*, Beihefte der Francia, IX (Munich, 1980), 117–34; reprinted Campbell, *Essays in Anglo-Saxon History*, pp.171–89. References here are to the reprint.

Campbell, J., 'Some Twelfth-Century Views of the Anglo-Saxon Past', *Peritia*, 3 (1984), 131–50; reprinted Campbell, *Essays in Anglo-Saxon History*, pp.209–28. References here are to the reprint.

Campbell, J., 'Asser's *Life of Alfred*', *The Inheritance of Historiography, 350–900*, ed. C. Holdsworth and T.P. Wiseman (Exeter, 1986), pp. 115–35; reprinted Campbell, *The Anglo-Saxon State*, pp. 129–55. References here are to the reprint.

Campbell, J., *Essays in Anglo-Saxon History* (London, 1986).

Campbell, J., 'Some Agents and Agencies of the Late Anglo-Saxon State', *Domesday Studies*, ed. Holt, pp. 201–18; reprinted Campbell, *The Anglo-Saxon State*, pp. 201–25. References here are to the reprint.

Campbell, J., 'Was it Infancy in England? Some Questions of Comparison', *England and her Neighbours, 1066–1453: Essays in Honour of Pierre Chaplais*, ed. M. Jones and M. Vale (London, 1989), pp. 1–17; reprinted Campbell, *The Anglo-Saxon State*, pp. 179–99. References here are to the reprint.

Campbell, J., 'The Late Anglo-Saxon State: A Maximum View', *Proceedings of the British Academy*, 87 (1994), 39–65; reprinted Campbell, *The Anglo-Saxon State*, pp. 1–30. References here are to the reprint.

Campbell, J., 'Stenton's *Anglo-Saxon England*', *Stenton's 'Anglo-Saxon England' Fifty Years On*, ed. D. Matthew (Reading, 1994), pp. 49–59; reprinted Campbell, *The Anglo-Saxon State*, pp. 269–80. References here are to the reprint.

Campbell, J., *The Anglo-Saxon State* (London, 2000).

Campbell, J., 'What is not known about the reign of Edward the Elder', *Edward the Elder*, ed. Higham and Hill, pp. 12–24.

Chevallier, C.T., 'Where was Malfosse? The End of the Battle of Hastings', *Sussex Archæological Collections*, ci (1963), 1–13.

Chibnall, M., 'Military Service in Normandy before 1066', *ANS*, V (1982), 65–77; reprinted, *The Battle of Hastings*, ed. Morillo, pp. 80–92. References here are to the reprint.

Clephane-Cameron, N. *et al.*, *The 1066 Malfosse Walk* (Battle, 2000).

Cleveland, Duchess of (published anonymously), *History of Battle Abbey* (London, 1877).

C.L.W.C., *A Guide to Battle Abbey* (Battle and Hastings, n.d.).

Coates, R., 'On the Alleged Frankish Origin of the Hastings Tribe', *Sussex Archæological Collections*, 117 (1979), 263–4.

Connolly, P., *Greece and Rome at War* (London, 1981).

Contamine, P., *War in the Middle Ages*, trans. M. Jones (Oxford, 1984).

Coupland, S., 'Carolingian Arms and Armor in the Ninth Century', *Viator*, xx (1989), 29–50.

Cowdrey, H.E.J., 'Bishop Ermenfrid of Sion and the Penitential Ordinance following the Battle of Hastings', *Journal of Ecclesiastical History*, xx (1969), 225–42.

Cowdrey, H.E.J., 'The Anglo-Norman *Laudes Regiae*', *Viator*, xii (1981), 37–78.

Cowdrey, H.E.J., 'Towards an Interpretation of the Bayeux Tapestry', *ANS*, X (1987), 49–65; reprinted *The Study of the Bayeux Tapestry*, ed. Gameson, pp.93–110. References here are to the reprint.

Daniell, C., 'Battle and Trial: Weapon Injury Burials of St Andrew's Church, Fishergate, York', *Medieval Archeology*, xlv (2001), 220–6.

Darby, H.C., *Domesday England* (Cambridge, 1977).

David, C.W., *Robert Curthose* (Cambridge, 1920).

Davis, R.H.C., 'Alfred the Great: Propaganda and Truth', *History*, lvi (1971), 169–82; reprinted Davis, *From Alfred the Great to Stephen*, pp.33–46. References here are to the reprint.

Davis, R.H.C., 'The *Carmen de Hastingae Proelio*', *EHR*, xciii (1978), 241–61; reprinted Davis, *From Alfred the Great to Stephen*, pp.79–100. References here are to the reprint.

Davis, R.H.C., 'William of Poitiers and his History of William the Conqueror', *The Writing of History in the Middle Ages*, ed. R.H.C. Davis and J.M. Wallace-Hadrill (Oxford, 1981), pp.71–100; reprinted Davis, *From Alfred the Great to Stephen*, pp.101–30. References here are to the reprint.

Davis, R.H.C., 'The Warhorses of the Normans', *ANS*, X (1987), 67–82; reprinted Davis, *From Alfred the Great to Stephen*, pp.63–78. References here are to the original.

Davis, R.H.C., *The Medieval Warhorse* (London, 1989).

Davis, R.H.C., Engels, L.J., *et al.*, 'The *Carmen de Hastingae Proelio*: a discussion', *ANS*, II (1979), 1–20, 165–7.

Davis, R.H.C., *From Alfred the Great to Stephen* (London, 1991).

Dawson, C., *The "Restorations" of the Bayeux Tapestry* (London, 1907).

Dawson, C., 'The Bayeux Tapestry in the hands of the Restorers', *The Antiquary*, xlv (1909), 470.

The Defence of Wessex: the Burghal Hidage and Anglo-Saxon Fortifications, ed. D. Hill and A.R. Rumble (Manchester, 1996).

Delbrück, H., *Geschichte der Kriegskunst im Rahmen der politischen Geschichte*, iii (Berlin, 1923). *Dritter Teil. Das Mittelalter.* (Berlin, 1907); trans. by W.J. Renfroe Jnr, *History of the Art of War Within the Framework of Political History. Volume III. The Middle Ages* (London, 1982). References here are to the translation.

DeVries, K., *The Norwegian Invasion of England* (Woodbridge, 1999).

DeVries, K., 'Harold Godwinson in Wales: Military Legitimacy in Late Anglo-Saxon England', *The Normans and Their Adversaries at War*, ed. Abels and Bachrach, pp.65–85.

Dibdin, T.F., *A Bibliographical Antiquarian and Picturesque Tour in France and Germany* (3 vols, London, 1821).

Dodwell, C.R., 'The Bayeux Tapestry and the French Secular Epic', *Burlington Magazine*, cviii (1966), 549–60; reprinted *The Study of the Bayeux Tapestry*, ed. Gameson, pp.47–62. References here are to the reprint.

Dodwell, C.R., *Anglo-Saxon Art: A new perspective* (Manchester, 1982).

Domesday Studies, ed. J.C. Holt (Woodbridge, 1987).

Douglas, D.C., 'Companions of the Conqueror', *History*, xxviii (1943), 129–47.

Douglas, D.C., 'Edward the Confessor, Duke William of Normandy, and the English Succession', *EHR*, lxviii (1953), 526–45.

Douglas, D.C. *William the Conqueror: the Norman impact upon England* (London, 1964).

Ducarel, A.C., see Bayeux Tapestry under Primary Sources.

Dumville, D., 'Some aspects of annalistic writing at Canterbury in the eleventh and early twelfth centuries', *Peritia*, 2 (1983), 23–57.

Dumville, D., 'The Tribal Hidage: an introduction to its texts and their history', *The Origins of Anglo-Saxon Kingdoms*, ed. S. Bassett (Leicester, 1989), pp.225–30.

Edward the Elder 899–924, ed. N.J. Higham and D.H. Hill (London, 2001).

Ekwall, E., *The Concise Oxford Dictionary of English Place-Names* (4th edn, Oxford, 1960).

Eley, P. and Bennett, P.E., 'The Battle of Hastings according to Gaimar, Wace and Benoît: rhetoric and politics', *Nottingham Medieval Studies*, xliii (1999), 47–78.

Engels, L.J., 'Once more: the *Carmen de Hastingae Proelio*', *ANS*, II (1979), 3–18, 165–7.

English Heritage, *An Earthwork Survey and Investigation of the Parkland at Battle Abbey, East Sussex* (Archaeological Investigation Report Series AI/13/2002, Swindon, 2002).

Focus Multimedia Ltd, *Red Shift 4* (Rugely, 2000).

France, J., *Victory in the East: a military history of the First Crusade* (Cambridge, 1994).

Freeman, E.A., *The History of the Norman Conquest of England* (2nd edn, 6 vols, Oxford, 1870–9). Reprint of part of vol. iii, *The Battle of Hastings*, ed. Morillo, pp.150–64.

Fuller, J.F.C., *The Decisive Battles of the Western World and their influence upon history* (3 vols, London, 1954–6).

Gameson, R., 'The Origin, Art, and Message of the Bayeux Tapestry', *The Study of the Bayeux Tapestry*, ed. Gameson, pp.157–211.

Garnett, G., 'Coronation and Propaganda: some Implications of the Norman claim to the throne of England in 1066', *TRHS*, Fifth Series 36, 1986, 91–116.

Garnett, G., 'Conquered England, 1066–1215', *The Oxford Illustrated History of Medieval England*, ed. N. Saul (Oxford, 1997), pp.61–101.

Gautier Dalché, P. and Tilliette, J.-Y., 'Un nouveau document sur la tradition du poème de Baudri de Bourgeuil à la comtesse Adèle', *Bibliothèque de l'école des chartes*, 144 (1986), 241–57.

George, R.H., 'The Contribution of Flanders to the Conquest of England', *Revue belge de philologie et d'histoire*, v (1926), 81–97.

Gibbs-Smith, C.H., 'What the Bayeux Tapestry does not show', *The Times*, 8 October 1966, p.9.

Gibbs-Smith, C.H., *The Bayeux Tapestry* (London, 1973).

Gillingham, J., 'William the Bastard at War', *Studies in Medieval History presented to R. Allen Brown*, ed. Harper-Bill, pp.141–58; reprinted *Anglo-Norman Warfare*, ed. Strickland, pp.143–60; *The Battle of Hastings*, ed. Morillo, pp.96–112. References here are to the original.

Gillingham, J., 'Henry of Huntingdon and the Twelfth-Century Revival of the English Nation', *Concepts of National Identity in the Middle Ages*, ed. S. Forde, L. Johnson and A.V. Murray (Leeds, 1995), pp.75–101.

Gillmor, M., 'Naval Logistics of the Cross-Channel Operation, 1066', *ANS*, VII, 105–31; reprinted *The Battle of Hastings*, ed. Morillo, pp.114–28. References here are to the original.

Glover, R., 'English Warfare in 1066', *EHR*, lxvii (1952), 1–18; reprinted *The Battle of Hastings*, ed. Morillo, pp.174–88. References here are to the original.

Godman, P., *Poetry of the Carolingian Renaissance*, see Ermold the Black under Primary Sources.

Grainge, C. and G., 'The Pevensey Expedition: Brilliantly Executed Plan or Near Disaster?', *The Mariner's Mirror*, 79 (1993), 261–73; reprinted *The Battle of Hastings*, ed. Morillo, pp.130–42. References here are to the reprint.

Gransden, A., *Historical Writing in England c.550 to c.1307* (London, 1974).

Grape, W., *The Bayeux Tapestry: Monument to a Norman Triumph* (Munich, 1994).

Grassi, J.L., 'The Lands and Revenues of Edward the Confessor', *EHR*, cxvii (2002), 251–83.

Gravett, C., *Hastings 1066: the fall of Saxon England* (London, 1992).

Greenway, D., 'Authority, Convention and Observation in Henry of Huntingdon's *Historia Anglorum*', *ANS*, XVIII (1995), 105–21.

Grierson, P., 'A Visit of Earl Harold to Flanders in 1056', *EHR*, li (1936), 90–7.

Grierson, P., 'The relations between England and Flanders before the Norman Conquest', *TRHS*, Fourth Series, xxiii (1941), 71–112.

Gurney, H., 'Observations on the Bayeux Tapestry', *Archaeologia*, xviii (1817), 359–70.

Hare, J.N., 'The buildings of Battle Abbey: a preliminary survey', *ANS*, III (1980), 78–95, 212–3.

Hare, J.N., *Battle Abbey: the eastern range and the excavations of 1978–80* (Historic Buildings and Monuments Commission for England, London, 1985).

Hart, C., 'The Canterbury Contribution to the Bayeux Tapestry', *Art and Symbolism in Medieval Europe: Papers of the 'Medieval Europe Brugge 1997' Conference*, V (1997), 7–15.

Hart, C., 'The Bayeux Tapestry and Schools of Illumination at Canterbury', *ANS*, XXII (1999), 117–67.

The Heads of Religious Houses England and Wales 940–1216, ed. D. Knowles, *et al.* (Cambridge, 1972).

Higham, N.J., *The Death of Anglo-Saxon England* (Stroud, 1997).

Hill, D., 'Offa's Dyke: Pattern and Purpose', *The Antiquaries Journal*, 80 (2000), 195–206.

Hill, D. and McSween, J. – see the Bayeux Tapestry under Primary Sources.

Hollister, C.W., *Anglo-Saxon Military Institutions on the Eve of the Norman Conquest* (Oxford, 1962).

Hollister, C.W., 'The Greater Domesday Tenants-in-Chief', *Domesday Studies*, ed. Holt, pp. 219–48.

Hooper, J., 'The "Rows of the Battle-Swan": The Aftermath of Battle in Anglo-Saxon Art', *Armies, Chivalry and Warfare*, ed. Strickland, pp. 82–99.

Hooper, N., 'The Housecarls in England in the Eleventh Century', *ANS*, VII (1984), 161–76.

Hooper, N., 'Some Observations on the Navy in Late Anglo-Saxon England', *Studies in Medieval History presented to R. Allen Brown*, ed. Harper-Bill, pp. 203–13.

Hooper, N., 'Edgar the Ætheling: Anglo-Saxon prince, rebel and crusader', *Anglo-Saxon England*, 14 (1985), 197–214.

Hooper, N., 'The Aberlemno Stone and Cavalry in Anglo-Saxon England', *Northern History*, 29 (1993), 188–96.

Howarth, D., *1066: the year of the Conquest* (New York, 1978).

Huard, G., 'Quelques Lettres de Bénédictins Normands à Dom Bernard de Montfaucon pour la documentation des *Monumens de la Monarchie Françoise*', *Bulletin de la Société des Antiquaires de Normandie*, xxxviii (1913), 343–75.

Hudson, J., 'The Abbey of Abingdon, its *Chronicle* and the Norman Conquest', *ANS*, XIX (1996), 181–202.

James, E.R., 'The Battle of Hastings, 14th October, 1066', *The Royal Engineers Journal*, v (1907), 18–34, and map opposite 60.

Janssen, A.L., 'La redécouverte de la Tapisserie de Bayeux', *Annales de Normandie*, 11 (1961), 179–95.

John, E., 'Edward the Confessor and the Norman Succession', *EHR*, xciv (1979), 241–67.

Keats-Rohan, K.S.B., 'William I and the Breton Contingent in the non-Norman Conquest 1060–87', *ANS*, XIII (1990), 157–72.

Ker, N.R., *Catalogue of Manuscripts containing Anglo-Saxon* (Oxford, 1957).

Keynes, S.D., 'The Æthelings in Normandy', *ANS*, XIII (1990), 173–205.

Kiff, J., 'Images of War: Illustrations of Warfare in Early Eleventh-Century England', *ANS*, VII (1984), 177–94.

Körner, S., *The Battle of Hastings, England, and Europe 1035–1066* (Lund, 1964).

Lake, R.D. and Shephard-Thorn, E.R., *Geology of the country around Hastings and Dungeness: Memoir for 1:50:000 geological sheets 320 and 321 (England and Wales)* (London, 1987).

Lancelot, A., see Bayeux Tapestry under Primary Sources.

Lappenberg, J.M., *A History of England under the Anglo-Saxon Kings*, trans. B. Thorpe (London, 1845).

Larson, L.M., *The King's Household in England before the Norman Conquest* (Madison, 1904).

Lawson, M.K., *Cnut: the Danes in England in the Early Eleventh Century* (Harlow, 1993).

Lawson, M.K., 'Observations upon a Scene in the Bayeux Tapestry, the Battle of Hastings and the Military System of the Late Anglo-Saxon State', in *The Medieval State*, ed. Maddicott and Palliser, pp.73–91.

Lemmon, C.H., 'The Campaign of 1066', in D. Whitelock *et al.*, *The Norman Conquest: its setting and impact* (London, 1966), pp.77–122.

Lemmon, C.H., *The Field of Hastings* (4th edn, St Leonards-on-Sea, 1970).

Lewis, C.P., 'The Earldom of Surrey and the date of Domesday Book', *Historical Research*, lxiii (1990), 329–36.

Lewis, C.P., 'The French in England before the Norman Conquest', *ANS*, XVII (1994), 123–39.

Lewis, S., *The Rhetoric of Power in the Bayeux Tapestry* (Cambridge, 1999).

Leyser, K.J., 'Early Medieval Warfare', *Communications and Power in Medieval Europe: The Carolingian and Ottonian Centuries*, ed. T. Reuter (London, 1994), pp. 29–71.

Lingard, J., *The History of England from the First Invasion of the Romans to the Accession of William and Mary in 1688* (6th edn, London, 1854).

Lot, F., *L'Art Militaire et les Armées au Moyen Age en Europe et dans le Proche Orient* (2 vols, Paris, 1946).

Loud, G.A., *The Age of Robert Guiscard: Southern Italy and the Norman Conquest* (Harlow, 2000).

Lower, M.A., 'On the Battle of Hastings', *Sussex Archæological Collections*, vi (1853), 15–40.

Maitland, F.W., *Domesday Book and Beyond* (Cambridge, 1897).

Mann, J., 'Arms and Armour', *The Bayeux Tapestry*, ed. Stenton, pp. 56–69.

Maund, K.L., 'The Welsh Alliances of Earl Aelfgar of Mercia and his Family in the mid-Eleventh Century', *ANS*, XI (1988), 181–90.

Mawer, A. and Stenton, F.M., *The Place-Names of Sussex* (English Place-Name Society, vols vi–vii, Cambridge, 1930).

The Medieval State: Essays presented to James Campbell, ed. J.R. Maddicott and D.M. Palliser (London, 2000).

Montfaucon, B. de, see the Bayeux Tapestry under Primary Sources.

Morillo, S., 'Hastings: An Unusual Battle', *The Haskins Society Journal*, 2 (1990), 95–104; reprinted *The Battle of Hastings*, ed. Morillo, pp. 220–27. References here are to the reprint.

Morillo, S., *Warfare under the Anglo-Norman Kings 1066–1135* (Woodbridge, 1994).

Morillo, S., '*Milites*, Knights and Samurai: Military Technology, Comparative History, and the Problem of Translation', *The Normans and Their Adversaries at War*, ed. Abels and Bachrach, pp. 167–84.

Morton, C., 'Pope Alexander II and the Norman Conquest', *Latomus*, 34 (1975), 362–82.

Muntz, H., *The Golden Warrior: the story of Harold and William* (London, 1948). A novel.

Neumann, J., 'Hydrographic and Ship-Hydrodynamic Aspects of the Norman Invasion, AD 1066', *ANS*, XI (1988), 221–43.

Nip, R., 'The Political Relations between England and Flanders (1066–1128)', *ANS*, XXX (1998), 145–67.

Norgate, K., 'The Battle of Hastings. Part II', *EHR*, ix (1894), 41–76, 608–11.

The Normans and Their Adversaries at War: Essays in Memory of C. Warren Hollister, ed. R.P. Abels and B.S. Bachrach (Woodbridge, 2001).

Oleson, T.J., 'Edward the Confessor's Promise of the Throne to Duke William of Normandy', *EHR*, lxxii (1957), 221–28.

Oman, C.W.C., *The Art of War in the Middle Ages: A.D. 378–1515* (Oxford, 1885).

Oman, C.W.C., *A History of the Art of War: The Middle Ages from the Fourth to the Fourteenth Century* (London, 1898).

Oman, C.W.C., *A History of the Art of War in the Middle Ages* (2nd edn, 2 vols, London, 1924).

Ordnance Survey, Pathfinder Series, Sheet 1290 (TQ61/71), at 2½ inches to 1 mile, *Battle & Herstmonceux*.

Ordnance Survey, Explorer Series, Sheet 124, at 2½ inches to 1 mile, *Hastings & Bexhill*.

Ordnance Survey, see also British Geological Survey.

Orlandi, G., 'Some Afterthoughts on the *Carmen de Hastingae Proelio*', in *Media Latinitas: A Collection of Essays to Mark the Occasion of the Retirement of L.J. Engels*, ed. R.I.A. Nip *et al.*, (Turnhout, 1996), pp. 117–27.

Palmer, J.J.N., 'The Conqueror's Footprints in Domesday Book', *The Medieval Military Revolution*, ed. A. Ayton and J.L. Price (London, 1995), pp. 23–44.

Palmer, J.J.N., 'War and Domesday Waste', *Armies, Chivalry and Warfare*, ed. Strickland, pp. 256–75.

Partner, N.F., *Serious Entertainments: the Writing of History in Twelfth-Century England* (Chicago, 1977).

Peirce, I., 'Arms, Armour and Warfare in the Eleventh Century', *ANS*, X (1987), 237–57.

Pryce, T.D., 'A Note on the Bayeux Tapestry', *The Antiquary*, xliii (1907), 346–47.

Ramsay, J.H., *The Foundations of England* (Oxford, 1898).

Ratkowitsch, C., *Descriptio Picturae: Die literarische Funktion der Beschreibung von Kunstwerken in der lateinischen Großdichtung des 12. Jahrhunderts* (Vienna, 1991).

Renn, D., 'Burhgeat and gonfanon: two sidelights from the Bayeux Tapestry', *ANS*, XVI (1993), 177–98.

Rodger, N.A.M., 'Cnut's Geld and the Size of Danish Ships', *EHR*, cx (1995), 392–403.

Rodger, N.A.M., *The Safeguard of the Sea: A Naval History of Britain. Volume One 660–1649* (London, 1997).

Round, J.H., Anonymous article in the *Quarterly Review* (Vol. 175, No. 349), July 1892, 1–37, reviewing E.A. Freeman, *The History of the Norman Conquest of England* and *The History of William Rufus*.

Round, J.H., Anonymous article in the *Quarterly Review* (Vol. 177, No. 353), July 1893, 73–104, reviewing *Poème adressé à Adèle, fille de Guillaume le Conquérant, par Baudri, Abbé de Bourgeuil*, ed. L. Delisle.

Round, J.H., 'Wace and his Authorities', *EHR*, viii (1893), 677–83.

Round, J.H., 'Mr Freeman and the Battle of Hastings', *EHR*, ix (1894), 209–60.

Round, J.H., *Feudal England* (London, 1895).

Round, J.H., 'La bataille de Hastings', *Revue Historique*, 65 (1897), 61–77.

Round, J.H., 'The Battle of Hastings', *Sussex Archæological Collections*, xlii (1899), 54–63.

Sansonetti, V., see the Bayeux Tapestry under Primary Sources.

Sauvage, R.N., *L'abbaye de Saint-Martin de Troarn* (Caen, 1911).

Searle, E., *Lordship and Community: Battle Abbey and its Banlieu 1066–1538* (Toronto, 1974).

Smail, R.C., *Crusading Warfare 1097–1193* (2nd edn, Cambridge, 1995).

Spatz, W., *Die Schlacht von Hastings* (Berlin, 1896).

Stenton, F.M., *William the Conqueror* (New York & London, 1908).

Stenton, F.M., Article on J.H. Round in *Dictionary of National Biography 1922–1930*, ed. J.R. Weaver (Oxford, 1937).

Stenton, F.M., 'The Historical Background', *The Bayeux Tapestry*, ed. Stenton, pp.9–24.

Stenton, F.M., *Anglo-Saxon England* (3rd edn, Oxford, 1971).

Stephens, W.R.W., *The Life and Letters of Edward A. Freeman* (2 vols, London, 1895).

Stevenson, W.H., 'Senlac and the Malfossé', *EHR*, xxviii (1913), 292–303.

Stewart, I., 'Coinage and recoinage after Edgar's reform', *Studies in Late Anglo-Saxon Coinage*, ed. K. Jonsson (Stockholm, 1990), pp.455–85.

Stothard, C.A., see the Bayeux Tapestry under Primary sources.

Stothard, C.A., 'Some Observations on the Bayeux Tapestry', *Archaeologia*, xix (1821), 184–91; reprinted *The Study of the Bayeux Tapestry*, ed. Gameson, pp.1–6. References here are to the original.

Stothard, Mrs Charles, *Letters written during a Tour through Normandy, Brittany, and other parts of France, in 1818…* (London, 1820).

Strickland, M., 'Military Technology and Conquest: the Anomaly of Anglo-Saxon England', *ANS*, XIX (1996), 353–82.

Strickland, M., *War and Chivalry. The Conduct and Perception of War in England and Normandy, 1066–1217* (Cambridge, 1996).

Studies in Medieval History presented to R. Allen Brown, ed. C. Harper-Bill *et al.* (Woodbridge, 1989).

The Study of the Bayeux Tapestry, ed. R. Gameson (Woodbridge, 1997).

Swanton, M.J., 'King Alfred's ships: text and context', *Anglo-Saxon England*, 28 (1999), 1–22.

La tapisserie de Bayeux: oeuvre d'art et document historique, ed. L. Musset (1989).

Tetlow, E., *The Enigma of Hastings* (London, 1974).

Thierry, A., *Histoire de la Conquête de L'Angleterre par les Normands* (5th edn, Paris, 1838).

Thomson, R.M., *William of Malmesbury* (Woodbridge, 1987).

Tilliette, J.-Y., 'La chambre de la comtesse Adèle: savoir scientifique et technique littéraire dans le c. CXCVI de Baudri de Bourgeuil', *Romania*, 102 (1981), 145–71.

Tilliette, J.-Y., 'Culture classique et humanisme monastique: les poèmes de Baudri de Bourgeuil', *La Litterature Angevine Médiévale: actes du colloque du samedi 22 mars 1980* (Centre de Recherche de Littérature et de Linguistique de l'Anjou et des Bocages, Université d'Angers, 1981), pp. 77–88.

Turner, D., *Account of a Tour in Normandy* (2 vols, London, 1820).

Van Houts, E.M.C., 'The adaptation of the *Gesta Normannorum Ducum* by Wace and Benoît', *Non Nova, Sed Nove: Mélanges de civilisation médiévale dédiées à Willem Noomen*, ed. M. Gosman and J. van Os (Groningen, 1984), pp. 115–24.

Van Houts, E.M.C., 'The Ship List of William the Conqueror', *ANS*, X (1987), 159–83.

Van Houts, E.M.C., 'Latin poetry and the Anglo-Norman court 1066–1135: The *Carmen de Hastingae Proelio*', *Journal of Medieval History*, 15 (1989), 39–62.

Van Houts, E.M.C., 'The Norman Conquest through European Eyes', *EHR*, cx (1995), 832–53.

Van Houts, E.M.C., 'The Memory of 1066 in Written and Oral Traditions', *ANS*, XIX (1996), 167–79.

Van Houts, E.M.C., 'Wace as Historian', *Family Trees and the Roots of Politics: The prosopography of Britain and France from the tenth to the twelfth century*, ed. K.S.B. Keats-Rohan (Woodbridge, 1997), pp. 103–32.

Verbruggen, J.F., *The Art of Warfare in Western Europe during the Middle Ages from the Eighth Century to 1340*, trans. Col. S. Willard and Mrs R. W. Southern (Woodbridge, 1997).

Vidler, J. (published anonymously), *Gleanings Respecting Battel and its Abbey* (Battel, n.d.).

Walker, I. W., *Harold: The Last Anglo-Saxon King* (Stroud, 1997).

Walker, S., 'A Context for *Brunanburh*?', *Warriors and Churchmen in the High Middle Ages: Essays presented to Karl Leyser*, ed. T. Reuter (London, 1992), pp. 21–39.

Wenham, P., 'Seven Archæological Discoveries in Yorkshire: 3. Human skeletons, Riccall Landing', *The Yorkshire Archæological Journal*, xl (1959–62), 301–7.

White, G.H., 'The Battle of Hastings and the Death of Harold', *The Complete Peerage*, vol. XII, part I (London, 1953), Appendix L.

Whitelock, D., *et al.*, *The Norman Conquest* (London, 1966).

Williams, A., *The English and the Norman Conquest* (Woodbridge, 1995).

Wolf, K.B., *Making History: the Normans and Their Historians in Eleventh-Century Italy* (Philadelphia, 1995).

Wormald, F., 'Style and Design', *The Bayeux Tapestry*, ed. Stenton, pp. 25–36.

Wormald, P., 'James Campbell as Historian', *The Medieval State*, ed. Maddicott and Palliser, pp. xiii–xxii.

ILLUSTRATION LIST

PICTURE SECTIONS

305

ILLUSTRATIONS IN THE TEXT

INDEX

Page numbers in **_bold italics_** refer to illustration numbers; _LP_ to the numbers of the Lancelot plates, pp.272-83; _GT_ to the numbers of the Genealogical Tables, pp.276-70. Abbreviations: abb = abbot, abp = archbishop, bp = bishop, br = brother, ct = count, d = daughter, dk = duke, k = king, q = queen s = son. The characters Æ and æ have been indexed as AE and ae.